JEFFREY B. RUSSELL (1934–2023) was
at the University of California, San
various works on medieval Europe and the

BROOKS ALEXANDER is the author of *Witchcraft Goes Mainstream*
(2004) and has written numerous articles on witchcraft,
neopaganism and other new religious movements.

JEFFREY B. RUSSELL
BROOKS ALEXANDER

A HISTORY OF WITCHCRAFT

Sorcerers, Heretics & Pagans

With 21 illustrations

For Ky Russell and Michael Thomas
and for Anastasia

COVER: Cover illustration based on a fifteenth-century
woodcut showing witches making rain.
FRONTISPIECE: Francisco de Goya, *The Sabbat, c.* 1794–5.
Lazaro Galdeano Museum, Madrid.

First published in the United Kingdom in 1980 by
Thames & Hudson Ltd, 181A High Holborn, London WC1V 7QX

First published in the United States of America in 1980 by
Thames & Hudson Inc., 500 Fifth Avenue, New York, New York 10110

Second edition published under the title *A New History of Witchcraft* in 2007
This revised paperback edition published in 2024

A History of Witchcraft © 1980 and 2024 Thames & Hudson Ltd, London
A New History of Witchcraft © 2007 Thames & Hudson Ltd, London

Text © 1980 Jeffrey B. Russell
Text © 2007 and 2024 Jeffrey B. Russell and Brooks Alexander

Designed by Karolina Prymaka
Cover designed by Jo Walker

British Library Cataloguing-in-Publication Data
A catalogue record for this book is available from the British Library

Library of Congress Control Number 2023944854

ISBN 978-0-500-29728-5

Printed and bound in the UK by CPI (UK) Ltd

MIX
Paper | Supporting
responsible forestry
FSC® C171272

Be the first to know about our new releases,
exclusive content and author events by visiting
thamesandhudson.com
thamesandhudsonusa.com
thamesandhudson.com.au

Contents

Preface 6

Introduction: What is a Witch? 8

PART I
SORCERY AND HISTORICAL
WITCHCRAFT

1 Sorcery 20

2 The Roots of European Witchcraft 38

3 Witchcraft, Heresy, and Inquisition 55

4 The Witch-craze on the Continent of Europe 69

5 Witchcraft in Britain and America 89

6 Witchcraft and Society 105

7 The Decline of Witchcraft 120

PART II
MODERN WITCHCRAFT

8 Survivals and Revivals 134

9 Neopagan Witchcraft: the Sources 140

10 Neopagan Witchcraft: the Movement 165

11 The Role of Witchcraft 191

12 Witchcraft Today 197

Appendix 204
Notes on the Text 205 | Bibliography 209
Illustration Credits 215
Index 216

Preface

In Galicia, Spain, a popular phrase is *Yo no creo en meigas – pero hayas*: 'I don't believe in witches – but they exist!' Whether or not one believes in the powers of witchcraft, one must believe in the existence of witches: I have known quite a few personally. This book is a revised edition of *A History of Witchcraft: Sorcerers, Heretics and Pagans*, published by Thames & Hudson in 1980. It includes a new preface; a new introduction; two completely new chapters (written by my collaborator Brooks Alexander) that bring the history of modern witchcraft up to date; a revised conclusion; and a completely updated bibliography. It is, in many respects, a new book. I also refer readers to my article on 'Witchcraft' in the 2002 *Encyclopaedia Britannica*.

I would like to thank all those who worked with me on the original book, especially my late wife Diana M. Russell. I gladly offer special thanks to our editor Jamie Camplin, whose continued interest in the book sparked the new edition, to my wife Pamela C. Russell, who has worked on historical witchcraft with me now for several years, and of course to Brooks Alexander, whose knowledge of contemporary witchcraft makes this new book possible.

JEFFREY B. RUSSELL

Like modern witchcraft itself, this presentation is an assemblage dependent on the contributions of many people – not least of which is that of the witches themselves. I have known, interviewed, visited, and spoken to a number of witches over the years and their generous advice, insiders' insight, and patient explanations have been indispensable in the creation of this manuscript. I am particularly indebted to Wiccan Elder Don Frew, whose tireless accessibility has foreshortened my research in innumerable ways. I am also grateful to the ecumenically minded witches of CoG (Covenant of the Goddess), who have consistently struggled (sometimes against resistance from within their own community) to make their religion more widely known and understood by the public at large; among them, my special thanks go to Anna Korn, Alison Harlow, Jennifer Gibbons, Gus DiZerega, and Diana Paxson – witches whose personal friendship and cooperation have opened avenues of research and comprehension that would otherwise have remained obscure to me.

My wife Victoria and my daughters Leslie and Anastasia have been a profound source of support and encouragement during this project, offering strength in the face of difficulty and a defence against despair. And finally, I want to thank the man whose breadth of vision and depth of knowledge created this remarkable work to begin with: Jeffrey Russell has left us all with a legacy of understanding that will endure, and I am honoured to participate in the revised edition of his book.

BROOKS ALEXANDER

Introduction:
What is a Witch?

If you ask your acquaintances what a witch is, they are likely to tell you that witches do not exist. Witches, they will say, are imaginary old hags with warts on their noses, conical hats, broomsticks, black cats, and evil, cackling laughs. Walt Disney's wicked queen in *Snow White*, Margaret Hamilton's performance as the wicked witch in *The Wizard of Oz*, and behind them a long tradition of art stretching back through Goya to the thirteenth century have fixed such an image in our minds. Probably no one ever fitted this stereotype.

Yet witches do exist. In fact, witchcraft is considered by a number of institutions, including the US military and the US legal system, to be a recognized religion. Of the witches the authors have known, none have ever looked (except perhaps at costume parties) like the stereotype.

Other of your acquaintances may say that a witch is a person who has psychic powers. It is true that many witches claim psychic powers, but that does not prove whether or not they actually *have* them, and possession of such powers would not make such a person a witch. There is much more to witchcraft than that. A few may vaguely imagine that witches practise something like Voodoo, which is a misunderstanding of both witchcraft and Voodoo. Voodoo is a religion combining Christianity and African paganism, and its rites are designed to protect *against* witchcraft.

More accurate and helpful answers are: (1) a witch is a sorcerer: this is the anthropological approach; (2) a witch worships the Devil: this is the historical approach to European witchcraft; (3) a witch worships gods and goddesses and practises magic for good ends: this is the approach favoured by most modern witches. Each approach can be justified.

Someone hoping to delve deeper into the question will be helped little by most of the popular books in the occult sections of bookshops. Recent books abound with claims for the tarot, astrology, Satanism, channelling, mediums, crystals, Ouija, palmistry, extraterrestrials, and psychedelic drugs – as well as witches. Witchcraft is not the same as the occult, and many witches take pains to dissociate themselves from the occult. A number of recent books do, however, make serious efforts to understand the subject (see the Bibliography).

The most common misconception about witchcraft is that 'there is no such thing as a witch'. Stephen Jay Gould, the great palaeontologist and essayist, continually deplored the human tendency to dichotomize – to insist on a simple yes or no, and thus to block the route to deeper answers. Witches exist – or don't exist – depending on one's definition of a witch. And this is the main point of this book.

A whole catalogue of errors must be addressed before proceeding. 'A witch-doctor is a witch.' On the contrary, a witch-doctor practises magic, but his function is to *combat* the threats or effects of witchcraft. 'Witchcraft is the same the world over.' In fact great differences exist in the witchcraft of various cultures. Further, as will be shown, there is a great historical difference between European witchcraft and that of other cultures. 'Possession is related to witchcraft.' Possession is an internal attack upon an individual by evil spirits, an invasion of the psyche; obsession is an external, physical attack by such spirits. In neither does the victim make a voluntary agreement with the evil spirit. In the alleged diabolical witchcraft of the Renaissance and Reformation eras in Europe, on the other hand, the alleged witch voluntarily invited the evil spirit through invocation or other means. Almost all modern witches eschew such invocations entirely. Another misconception is that 'witches practise the black mass'. The black mass is unknown in historical European witchcraft and is certainly not in the repertory of modern witches. The only time that the black mass was historically performed (and even then as a sort of camp satire of Catholicism) was at the court of Louis XIV. Some modern Satanists perform the black mass for much the same reasons, but again Satanism has nothing to do with modern witchcraft. 'Witchcraft was characteristic of the Middle Ages.' Quite the contrary, charges of diabolical witchcraft emerged only towards the very end of the Middle Ages. The great witch-hunts occurred during the Renaissance, the Reformation, and the seventeenth century. 'Witches are old women.' This is a heedless exaggeration and a distortion of the truth. Both in the past and in the present many men have practised witchcraft, and many female witches have been quite young – sometimes even children.

'The Inquisition was responsible for the witch-hunts.' This is a half-truth at most. Most witch prosecutions were conducted locally and by members of both civil and ecclesiastical authorities who were usually in low-level positions. As the Inquisitions (there was never one, united Inquisition) gradually became more formalized from the sixteenth century onwards, they drew up strict rules of procedure and evidence for witch-accusations; these rules often led to the overturning of local convictions and the freeing of the accused. The case is similar on the secular side. The more formal and centralized secular, legal procedure became (as with the Parlement de Paris, the supreme court of northern France), the more convictions were overturned. To a very large extent, the witch-hunts sprang up locally rather than being imposed by religious or secular elites.

'Witchcraft is a silly and trivial subject.' Not so, on several counts. During the witch-hunts between 1450 and 1750 about 110,000 people were tortured as alleged witches and between 40,000 and 60,000 were executed. This cruel fact is certainly not trivial. Also, the number of modern witches has grown enormously since the 1960s, and witchcraft must now be treated as an important religious phenomenon. Further, witch beliefs have had great psychological and sociological effects, affecting a significant number of cultures over long periods of time. Anthropologists, psychologists, and historians now treat witchcraft as a serious subject, as can be seen by the huge increase in literature on the subject since the first edition of this book was published in 1980.

But then what *is* a witch? One answer lies in the roots and development of words. The word 'witch' derives from the Old English *wicca* (pronounced 'witcha' and meaning 'male witch') and *wicce* (pronounced 'witcheh' and meaning 'female witch'). Both nouns derive from the verb *wiccian* (pronounced 'witchan', 'to cast a spell'). Contrary to the beliefs of some modern witches, the word is definitely not Celtic in origin and it has nothing to do with the Old English *witan*, 'to know', or any other word relating to 'wisdom'. The explanation that witchcraft means 'craft of the wise' is entirely false.

The term 'warlock', seldom used today, is still falsely thought to mean 'male witch'. 'Warlock' derives from the Old English *waer*, 'truth', and *leogan*, 'to lie', and originally meant any traitor or oath-breaker. It applied to women as well as men. The term 'warlock' was revived in Scotland in the sixteenth and seventeenth centuries and at that time was associated with diabolical witchcraft. It is not a helpful term. The word 'witch' applies to both sexes alike.

'Wizard', unlike 'witch', really does derive from the Middle English *wis*, 'wise'. In about 1425 the word 'wizard' appeared, denoting a wise man or woman thought to possess certain extranormal knowledge and power. In the sixteenth and seventeenth centuries it designated a 'high magician', and only after 1825, and then seldomly, was it used to mean a 'witch'.

'Sorcerer' derives from the French *sorcier*, from Late Latin *sortiarius*, 'diviner'. But in French, *sorcier* means both a sorcerer and a witch. The English word was introduced from the French in the fourteenth and fifteenth centuries and became common in the sixteenth. As in French, the English word has always been ambivalent: sometimes it refers to simple sorcery, sometimes to diabolical witchcraft. 'Magician derives from the Latin *magia* and from the Greek *mageia*. The Greek word *magos* originally designated the Iranian astrologer-priests who accompanied the army of Xerxes into Greece (it is probable that the 'wise men' who journeyed to the baby Jesus were such Iranian astrologers). In English, 'magic' has often implied a sophisticated intellectual system as opposed to the crude practices of 'sorcery'; it was often called 'high magic'.

The concepts behind the words also need to be clarified. One concept is 'superstition'. Witchcraft is not necessarily a superstition. Commonly people think of a superstition as something not consonant with the prevalent worldview in their society at that time. This usage is unfortunate, because it helps rigidify and confine thought. The creed of one age is the superstition of another; many of our cherished twenty-first-century beliefs will one day merit being called superstitions. It is more helpful to define superstition as *a belief not founded in any coherent worldview*. Indeed, this comes closest to the original meaning of the thirteenth-century word, which meant a false or irrational belief or practice. Medieval Catholics, ancient Egyptians, twentieth-century Dayaks, and modern witches are not necessarily more superstitious than twenty-first-century secular Westerners. If you hold a belief that you have thought through and placed in a coherent worldview, then that belief is not a superstition for you, although it would be if held by someone with a different worldview. But caution is needful, for if you hold a belief loosely or uncritically and fail to set it properly in a coherent worldview, then that belief *is* a superstition for you. On the whole, the number of scientific, religious, and political superstitions are no fewer than in the past. Some people are superstitious all of the time, and all people are superstitious some of the time. When witchcraft fits into a coherent worldview, it is not a superstition.

The supernatural is another concept that needs clarification. Witchcraft is often thought to involve supernatural powers. But the boundary between the natural and the supernatural is always being adjusted. In this process scientists have sometimes curbed the quest for knowledge by declaring certain subjects unfit for scientific investigation. In reality, everything that exists must be natural, whether science is able to demonstrate its existence or not. If, for example, angels – or extraterrestrials – exist, they are part of the natural order of the universe. Except in the context of a special technical sense in Christian theology, the term 'supernatural' is too vague to allow definition.

'Unscientific' is a slightly more helpful term, though the lines are still blurred, because what is unscientific in one field at one time may be scientific in another field at another time. Most importantly, we do not want to fall into the current dominant superstition that only things demonstrable by 'science' are true. There are many roads to reality. Magic need not be thought of as an inferior brand of science. The eighteenth-century theory that humanity progresses naturally upwards from sorcery through religion to science, though still popular among politicians (as well as scientists), is no longer regarded favourably by most scholars. Lynn Thorndike's monumental twentieth-century eight-volume *History of Magic and Experimental Science*[1] was not idly named: Thorndike knew that the origins of science lie in magic (as well as in religion) and that most of the great scientists of the sixteenth and seventeenth centuries were also magicians, a point reinforced later in the twentieth century by Frances Yates's *Giordano Bruno and the Hermetic Tradition.*[2]

This is where the concept of high magic as opposed to simple sorcery comes in. The basis of high magic is the belief in *kosmos*, an ordered and coherent universe where the various elements are all interrelated – one who plucks a flower disturbs the furthest star. There is scientific evidence for this being so, an example being the famous 'Butterfly Effect', where the change in the air caused by a single butterfly beating its wings in France could set off a train of events that would eventually cause a tornado in Kansas. In a universe in which all parts are related and affect one another, however remotely, there is a relationship between each individual human being and the stars, plants, minerals, and other natural phenomena. This is the magical belief in correspondence, a doctrine that was carefully worked out in early modern Europe in a coherent and sophisticated pattern. This sophisticated high magic, intellectually fashionable in the seventeenth century, for a while seriously competed with the physicalist science derived from John Locke and David Hume. Over the succeeding centuries the physicalist approach triumphed owing to the many practical successes it had as opposed to the few produced by the high magicians. Now, in the twenty-first century, only the feeblest traces of the high magical system exist, such as truly superstitious fashions for astrology.

Though their origins were common, a fundamental difference between high magic and science does exist. Magic is not submitted to the tests of empirical investigation and coherent theory and it therefore has a validation problem. There are many paths to truth other than the scientific, but on every path the rules of critical thought must be used to test every assertion. The sophisticated high magicians of the seventeenth century sincerely attempted to found coherent systems but were unsuccessful, and an unfortunate characteristic of many modern books espousing magic is that they make little if any such attempt. Their validation problem is much more acute than that in the seventeenth century. If someone tells you that he has made an astral voyage to Vega or that he has seen an intergalactic spacecraft, or that extraterrestrials built the great pyramids, or that she is channelling an ancient warrior sage, your belief should be suspended until the evidence is absolutely overwhelming. And usually in fact there is no evidence. Modern magic, like science, seeks knowledge, but its means of obtaining knowledge is usually incoherent.

The high, intellectual magic of the early modern astrologers and diviners is not an integral part of the history of witchcraft. During the great witch-hunts in Europe very few people indeed were accused of both high magic and witchcraft. The two traditions are, and were then, distinct. Nonetheless, witchcraft does depend in part upon the magical worldview that there are hidden relationships between all elements of the cosmos. The power that the witch or sorcerer exerts is presumed to be a natural power gained through the witch's understanding of, and ability to control, these hidden relationships.

Quite different from the sophisticated systems of high magic is magic applied almost technologically to obtain practical ends. This is low magic or simple sorcery. Simple sorcery is automatic magic: one performs a certain action and one gets results accordingly. One man practises sorcery, another technology: one man fertilizes a field by slitting a hen's throat over it at midnight, another by spreading steer manure over it at twilight.

Some anthropologists make no distinction between sorcery and witchcraft. Others use an African distinction between maleficent magicians who use material objects such as herbs and blood in their evil spells and those who injure others by means of an inherent and invisible quality they possess (for example, waving a wand and chanting in order to kill someone). These anthropologists assign the English word 'sorcerer' to the former and 'witch' to the latter. The distinction is valid, but the choice of English words arbitrary.

Most historians distinguish between European alleged witchcraft, which was a form of diabolism – that is, the worship of evil spirits – and worldwide sorcery, which involves not worshipping spirits but exploiting them. The English word *wicca*, which appears in a ninth-century manuscript, originally meant 'sorcerer', but during the witch-hunts it was used as the equivalent of the Latin *maleficus*, a Devil-worshipping witch. Modern witches have a different view from either anthropologists or historians. For some of them, witchcraft is the survival of ancient paganism long suppressed by Christians. Others, more accurately, argue that they have created a new religion that can be described as Neopagan.

One important way that modern witches differ from historical witches is that they reject belief in both the Christian God and the Christian Devil. They differ from sorcerers in their worship of goddesses and gods – or of nature, or of *kosmos* – rather than practising low magic.

None of these usages is exclusively correct, so this book needs to clarify its own set of usages. 'Sorcery' is the sorcery (or low magic) practised around the world, whether beneficent or maleficent and whether mechanical or invoking spirits. 'Witchcraft' means *either* the alleged diabolical witchcraft of the witch-hunts or modern Neopagan witchcraft. It must be emphasized again that there are no traditions or connections of any kind between the alleged Devil-worshippers of the Renaissance and Reformation and modern Neopagans. Some parallels do exist between these alleged diabolical witches and beliefs in other societies; in some cultures it is believed that witches cause plagues, have sexual intercourse with the dead, practise cannibalism, and abduct children. But the idea of continuity in Western society between ancient sorcerers, medieval witches, and modern witches is unsupported by any valid evidence.

Sorcery is widespread in many societies. It must therefore perform useful functions, or else it would wither away. One function of sorcery is to relieve social tensions. Simple sorcery, at least when beneficent, is frequently part of the generally accepted fabric of a society. Belief in sorcery helps define and sustain social values. It provides explanations of frightening events and terrifying phenomena. It gives the individual a sense of power in a mystifying and frightening world. Sorcery may also serve as a strange system of justice, a way of righting wrongs, or getting even: curses are usually employed by the weak against the strong, whom otherwise they cannot hurt, but this easily backfires, for the alleged victim may become the centre of attention and sympathy.

Even belief in malevolent sorcery has a function. It helps affirm the boundaries of a community and enhances solidarity against hostile outsiders. When a sorcerer is identified as the agent of a hostile power, driving him or her out of the community or otherwise persecuting him or her gives the orthodox a sense of comradeship and self-justification. Once such a person is identified as a scapegoat, society can project upon him every kind of evil that it has repressed in itself. Just as individuals can (and do) commit the error of negative projection – assigning to others the hostile feelings we have within ourselves – so societies can demonize their opponents. Most ethnic, political, and religious hatred and genocide comes from demonizing opponents. The negative projection is reinforced by guilt, for the scapegoat *must* be guilty; otherwise the guilt of scapegoating him must be our own, which is unbearable for us to imagine.

In times of dislocation and dissolution of values, sorcery and witchcraft may have the additional function of providing a focus and a name for diffuse anxieties. In such conditions, scapegoating becomes widespread and intense, as it did during the European witch-hunts, when the insecurities and terrors of society were projected upon certain individuals who could then be tortured or killed. A similar approach is to investigate where witchcraft fits into the overall structure of a society. Anthropologists have identified in the sorcery of diverse societies characteristic patterns of accusation deriving from the tensions in particular social relationships. Rather than relieving social tensions, sorcery beliefs may prolong and exacerbate them; such beliefs may arise from family divisions or feuds or from contests for authority within families or groups. Anthropologists observe that 'witchcraft accusations are not random' but rather follow observable social lines.[3]

Many modern historians have adapted anthropological and sociological methodologies to the study of sorcery and witchcraft and are thereby opening up different perceptions of the question. Their works are listed in the Bibliography, but at least a few of the most influential can be mentioned here: Wolfgang Behringer, Paul Boyer and Stephen Nissenbaum, Robin Briggs,

Stuart Clark, Valerie Flint, Ronald Hutton, Richard Kieckhefer, Arthur C. Lehmann, Brian P. Levack, H. C. Erik Midelfort, E. William Monter, Edward Peters, and Rodney Stark; for modern witchcraft Margot Adler, James A. Herrick, and Aidan Kelly. As Boyer and Nissenbaum commented, 'Historians ... have begun more fully to realize how much information the study of "ordinary" people living in "ordinary" communities can bring to the most fundamental historical questions.' They used 'the interaction of [this] "ordinary" history and the extraordinary moment [the Salem witch trials of 1692] to understand the epoch which produced them both.'[4] Whatever the approach, the essential thing is to keep our minds open to evidence that may change our viewpoint, and to maintain understanding of our fellow human beings even when we do not agree with them.

The resurgence over the past four decades of interest in the history of witchcraft has been extraordinary. Many approaches have considerable value. To attempt to follow them all would be to blur the central point that the idea of witchcraft develops through time, and its development is discernible as a historical pattern.

This development begins in worldwide sorcery.

PART I

SORCERY AND HISTORICAL WITCHCRAFT

CHAPTER 1

Sorcery

Sorcery occurs in almost every society in the world. It is also the oldest and deepest element in the historical concept of European witchcraft, which was formed out of pagan religion, folklore, Christian heresy, and theology.

As with all magic, sorcery is based on the assumption that the cosmos is a whole and that hidden connections therefore exist among all natural phenomena. The sorcerer attempts through his knowledge and power to control or at least influence these connections in order to effect the practical results he desires. Closely related to sorcery is divination, the determination of facts or prediction of future events on the basis of the secret links between human beings on the one hand and herbs, stones, stars, the liver of a sheep, or the tracks of a jackal on the other. Though divination is close to sorcery, I distinguish between them for the purpose of tracing the origins of European witchcraft. In Europe, diviners entered a tradition that brought them close to high magic, while witchcraft took a different path.

The simplest sorcery is the mechanical performance of one physical action in order to produce another: tying a knot in a cord and placing it under a bed to cause impotence; performing sexual intercourse in a sown field to increase the harvest; thrusting pins into an image in order to cause pain or injury (see plate II). The meaning of a given action varies among societies: thrusting pins into an image of a deity, for example, may be designed to release the deity's power rather than to cause anyone harm.

More complex sorcery goes beyond mechanical means and invokes the aid of spirits. If a member of the Lugbara tribe in Uganda was injured, he went to the shrines of his dead ancestors and invoked their aid; the ghosts would issue forth and punish the culprit. The distinction between this invocational sorcery and religion is sometimes fuzzy, but in the main the sorcerer tries to compel, rather than to implore, the powers that be to do his bidding.

The thought processes of sorcery are intuitive rather than analytical. They may derive, for example, from the individual's observations of single critical incidents. A critical incident is an emotionally charged experience. In a state of rage, you wish your father dead and strike a pillow in imitation of a blow aimed against him. The next day you learn that he has suddenly died. Even in a materialistic society, you will probably feel guilt, and when you assume a universe of hidden connections, the guilt is likely to be intense, for you may believe that your action really did cause the death. Critical events that an empirical methodology ignores because they cannot be replicated and empirically verified may be assumed to be significant in a magical worldview. Sorcery beliefs may also arise from unconscious thoughts expressed in dreams and visions. In dreams one being or person shifts and merges into another, and many other strange events occur. In societies where dreams are taken seriously and distinctions between dream and physical reality are blurred, dreams and visions have great power to persuade. In most societies, detailed sets of beliefs regarding sorcery are handed down by tradition and become part of the social and psychological systems of individuals. Those individuals will then all the more readily accept critical incidents and dreams as confirmation of the traditions. Linkages hidden from the empirical or analytical observer may appear obvious to the intuitive thinker.

Often sorcery has an integral function in society. In some societies it is closely related to religion. A priest or priestess of a public religion may perform ritual acts to make rain, ripen the harvest, procure peace, or secure success in the hunt or victory in war. So long as these acts are public and social in intent, sorcery may be a handmaid of religion. But when the sorcerer's acts are performed privately for the benefit of individuals rather than of society they are antisocial and do not form part of religion. In some cults, Voodoo for example, or Macumba in Brazil, the distinctions are not clear, but usually societies distinguish legally between public, religious sorcery and private sorcery, approving the one and outlawing the other.

The effects of sorcery can be real for those who believe in it. Volunteers from technologically advanced countries seeking to serve in societies where sorcery is taken seriously are often asked the question: a man in your village is suddenly seized by severe cramps; whom do you call, the physician or the witch-doctor? The proper answer is that you call both. The cause of the pain may be purely physical, but if the man believes himself to be bewitched, his fear may produce or sharpen the pain.

Sorcery worldwide

Such are the general characteristics of sorcery. Its particulars vary from society to society. One of the first thorough anthropological investigations of sorcery was made by E.E. Evans-Pritchard, who studied the Zande of southern Sudan. The Zande distinguished three varieties of magic. The first was good, benevolent magic, which included the consultation of oracles and diviners, the use of amulets for protection against charms, rites to procure the fertility of crops, and even *bagbuduma*, homicidal magic, so long as it was limited to revenge upon those who had slain one's kin. Good magic was used to procure justice as understood by Zande society, and *bagbuduma* was rendered ineffective when employed to unjust purpose. Sorcery, on the other hand, was unjust. Sorcery was the use of magic, especially magic using material objects, in order to harm those whom one hated for no just reason. Sorcery was a form of unjust aggression springing from jealousy, envy, greed, or other base human desires. Sorcery worked magic in an antisocial fashion and was condemned by Zande society. Evans-Pritchard called the third variety of magic 'witchcraft'. This 'witchcraft' was an internal power inherited by a man from his father or by a woman from her mother. The source of this power, or *mangu*, existed physically inside the 'witch's' stomach or attached to his liver, as an oval, blackish swelling in which various small objects might be found, or as a round, hairy ball with teeth.

Zande witches had meetings at which they feasted and practised evil magic together. They made a special ointment that they rubbed on their skins in order to render themselves invisible. They rode out at night either in spirit or in their bodies. Often the witch was supposed to lie in bed at night with his spouse while sending out his spirit to join the other witches in eating the souls of the victims. Sometimes the witches attacked the victim physically, tearing off pieces of his flesh to devour in their secret meetings. Anyone having a slow, wasting disease was likely to be the victim of the witch. Witch cats had sexual relations with women. The powers of the Zande witches were enormous:

> If blight seizes the groundnut crop it is witchcraft; if the bush is vainly scoured for game it is witchcraft; if a wife is sulky and unresponsive to her husband it is witchcraft; if a prince is cold and distant with his subject it is witchcraft; if, in fact, any failure or misfortune falls upon anyone at any time and in relation to any of the manifold activities of his life it may be due to witchcraft.[1]

The Zande employed diviners and medicine men to protect them from witches and cure them of the effects of witchcraft.

The Bechuana of Botswana distinguish between day-sorcerers, who practise sorcery only irregularly on specific occasions and usually for pay, and the more terrifying night-witches, who are accompanied by familiars in the form of animals (usually owls). The night-witches are universally malicious and cast their spells over one and all. They are generally thought of as elderly women. The Basuto, a Bantu tribe in South Africa, also distinguish between two groups of sorcerers, one of which consists mainly of women who fly out at night, ride 'on sticks or on fleas, meet in assemblies, and dance stark naked'.[2] In other societies, sorcerers are variously accused of cannibalism, incest, nymphomania, and other activities offensive to society.

The variation in sorcery among different societies is natural. What is surprising is the degree of similarity. The similarity between many African witch beliefs and those of historical Europe is pronounced. Both African and European 'witchcraft' include the following characteristics: the witch is generally female and often elderly. The witches meet in assemblies at night, leaving their bodies or changing their shapes in order to fly to the meeting-place. The witch sucks the blood of victims or devours their organs, causing them to waste away. Witches eat children or otherwise cause their deaths, sometimes bringing their flesh to the assembly. They ride out on brooms or other objects, fly naked through the air, use ointments to change their shapes, perform circular dances, possess familiar spirits, and practise orgy. Of course, no one group of sorcerers is supposed to do all these things, but all these beliefs may be found in Europe as well as in Africa. In all, at least fifty different motifs of European witchcraft can be found in other societies.[3]

The worldwide similarity of sorcery beliefs constitutes the most curious and important dilemma in the study of witchcraft. When we find, centuries and continents apart, the idea of a night-hag seducing men and murdering children or a sorceress riding a broomstick, we are not entitled to dismiss the question of how these similarities arise.

Possible explanations of the similarities include (1) coincidence; (2) cultural diffusion; (3) archetypal/structural inheritance;

(4) the existence of an ancient and coherent world religion of witchcraft. The volume of the evidence over such a wide variety of cultures and geographies through millennia renders coincidence virtually impossible. On the other hand, postulating a world religion of witchcraft ignores the enormous dissimilarities that also exist among societies and the fact that no evidence of any explicit connections exists. The explanation of archetypal or structural inheritance is an open option. It is certain that the structure of the human brain is determined by genetic patterns and probable that the structures of the mind are therefore also genetically inherent. Worldwide similarities of mental structure derived from the common human gene pool may then exist. It is possible (though far from demonstrated) that such similar mental structures produce archetypes, or similar responses to similar ideas. Jungians argue, for example, that everyone responds to the notion of 'the wise old man', the kindly and benevolent older person there to guide us. The image of such a wise old man varies from culture to culture (Tolkien's Gandalf presumably would strike no deep chords in Botswana), but the underlying archetype is universal. Yet the worldwide similarities in sorcery beliefs exceed those that these theories would predict. Cultural diffusion, the exchange of ideas among societies, is doubtless part of the answer. But the number and detail of the similarities across wide gulfs of time and geography is astounding. The puzzle remains.

The problem has several direct implications for the interpretation of European witchcraft. Many recent historians have explained witchcraft solely as a variety of Christian heresy or as an invention of scholastics and inquisitors, dismissing as unimportant its similarities to the sorcery of other cultures. This has led to an overstatement of the Christian elements and an improper isolation of the phenomenon. The anthropologists, on the other hand, have tended to understate the Christian elements. The truth lies somewhere in between: sorcery, similar to that existing worldwide, is the oldest and most basic element in historical European witchcraft, but other elements gradually transformed European sorcery into diabolical witchcraft.

Anthropologists and historians have done much to illuminate the social history of sorcery. In Africa, sorcery is more commonly practised by women than by men, but witch-doctors or curers are more frequently men. Accusations of sorcery generally appear in situations of tension within families or groups, particularly in turbulent and unsettled periods. Accusations pass frequently among wives in polygamous households, and between mothers-in-law and daughters-in-law. Accusations are lodged against old and young alike, but older persons are more likely to be singled out, perhaps because age and infirmity have rendered them unsociable, perhaps simply because they are weak. A common charge is that an old person has prolonged his life by devouring the bodies or souls of children. Anyone who is notably strange or unsociable is prone to accusation. Boyer and Nissenbaum's careful study of Salem witchcraft emphasized the importance of local geography and local religious politics in influencing the pattern of sorcery charges.

Cultural differences in determining patterns of witch accusations have been observed by anthropologists. Among the Nyakyusa of southern Tanzania sorcerers may be of either sex. They are chiefly accused of eating the internal organs of sleeping neighbours and of drying up the milk of cattle. On the other hand Pondo sorcerers, in the Cape province of South Africa, are women; their most common crime is having sexual intercourse with familiar spirits. The apparent reason for the difference is that the Nyakyusa are sexually secure but nutritionally insecure, so that they envy their neighbours' food and attribute their nourishment to illicit eating, while the Pondo, who are sexually more insecure, express their fears more in terms of sex than of food.

Just as the expression of witchcraft may change from society to society depending on its function, so its function may change over time in one society. The Bakweri of the western Cameroon, for example, were deeply afraid of sorcery in the period preceding the 1950s. Racked by ambivalence about riches and poverty, by a sense of collective guilt about the decline of their power and status, and by the fear that their low fertility rate would cause them to die out, they were dominated by jealousies that translated into fear of sorcery. In the 1950s their economic status improved remarkably owing to a boom in their major crop, bananas, and the period of prosperity brought first a purge of suspected sorcerers and then, the catharsis over, a decline in accusations and in belief in sorcery generally. During the 1960s, when the Bakweri suffered an economic setback, a resurgence of fear and accusations occurred.

Witch-doctors, medicine men, and *curanderos* ('witch-doctors' of Mexico and south-west USA), whose job it is to control and thwart sorcery, form part of the pattern of sorcery beliefs. The tribal chief, village headman, or other authorities are invested with the responsibility of protecting their people from the effects of sorcery. Witch detectors (called 'oracles' by anthropologists) are consulted in order to identify and foil evil sorcerers. 'The Nyoro, in the west of Uganda, consult men who they believe are possessed by spirits (called *mbandwa*) and reveal secret matters as their mouthpieces.'[4] A diviner may also be consulted: he does not speak with the voice of a spirit but 'interprets the answer that is supposed to be given by the behaviour of the mechanical objects he uses.'[5] A message may be read in the paths of the planets or in the tracks of beasts. Dances or other rituals, such as those of the *ndakó-gboyá* dancers of the Nupe, may serve to detect and drive off evil spirits and evil sorcerers. The *ndakó-gboyá* dancers wore tall, cylindrical disguises and identified sorcerers by nodding these weird shapes at them. In other cults, the witch-doctors identify the sorcerers from a line of villagers by looking at them in a mirror and then use their enormous social powers to extract confessions from those they have selected. Such witch-cleansing activities spread in times of stress when whole communities feel the need of protection against sorcery. Whole cults, such as that of the *ndakó-gboyá*, may arise in such a time. These cults, practising a relatively simple ritual intended to detect and neutralize the power of evil sorcerers, lack formal structure, organization, and doctrine, and easily cross ethnic boundaries and adapt themselves to the traditions of different peoples.

In Central Africa and Central America, anthropologists have found that communities that are small and in which the social structure is tightly knit are particularly prone to sorcery beliefs, because they feel surrounded and threatened (see plate III). Their fears increase whenever internal relations are confused or when the society is under unusually strong external pressure. This is why in some societies sorcery accusations increased at least temporarily during the period of European colonialism. In larger communities, or where social associations are freer and escape from unwanted ties easier, as in nomadic societies, sorcery beliefs are less common. The beliefs vary in intensity, kind, and function as social patterns vary, but anthropologists have not been able to correlate specific kinds of belief with particular kinds of social patterns. Much work remains to be done in this field. With all its variations, sorcery is widely believed in and widely practised. It speaks to human needs for justice, protection, and revenge in a world that too often seems out of our control.

Some similarities between European witchcraft and non-European sorcery result from the exportation of European ideas through colonialism. Voodoo is an example. Voodoo began as a religion brought to Haiti by slaves imported from West Africa (the name means 'spirit' in Ewe, Gun and Fon languages). Under the influence of Christianity and other European ideas it became

> a syncretistic religion that has blended together not only different African cults but also certain beliefs from European folklore. ... In short, this is a sort of conglomeration of elements of all kinds, dominated by African traditions. This religion

is practised by ninety percent of the Haitian people. ... At the same time these people consider themselves Catholic.[6]

The basis of the religion is the worship of *loa* (gods or spirits). The Catholic Church has diligently attacked Voodoo, equating the *loa* with demons, but the people have resisted such identifications. As a Haitian peasant told an inquiring anthropologist, 'To serve the *loa* you have to be a Catholic.'[7]

Voodooists distinguish between worship of the *loa*, which is a religion, and the practice of magic. All magic is considered black. It may be worked mechanically or with the help of the *loa*. The *loa* may thus be bent to evil ends, but it is to the *loa* that one must also turn for protection against evil magic. Prayers to the *loa* and magical invocations of the *loa* are difficult to distinguish. Voodoo sorcery, a mélange of European and African ideas, includes incantations, spells, the use of images, rain-making, and a cult of the dead. One of its more peculiar beliefs is the concept of zombies, 'the living dead', corpses who are exhumed and made by sorcerers to walk and do their bidding. Voodoo sorcery also contains a number of elements probably derived from Europe. Sorcerers may slay children at their ritual meetings or else catch them at night in their homes and suck their blood. Sorcerers rub their bodies with an ointment that removes their skin so that they may fly in the air. Shooting stars are really sorcerers in flight. Sorcerers change their shape into wolves, pigs, horses, or black cats.

This mixture of European and African elements is an advanced example of the syncretism found in other societies colonized by Europeans. It is difficult to distinguish native from imported elements. For example, belief in shape-shifting is common world-wide as well as in Europe, though the emphasis in Haiti on wolves and black cats suggests strong European influence. Anthropologists have described how actual experiences during cult practices may have reinforced belief in shape-shifting. 'At night huge fires were lit in [the] camp; naked women carried out hideous dances round the fires … twisting their bodies into frightening shapes.'[8] Another European observer saw a Voodoo priest possessed by the spirit of the Haitian 'emperor' Desselines: 'It was the man himself. ... I saw the ferocious face, the fanatic cast of countenance, and the whole body moulded in a vengeful attitude.'[9] Such powers of unconscious imitation account for the strength of the world-wide belief in shape-shifting.

Sorcery in ancient times

Though European witchcraft influenced sorcery in modern non-European societies, non-European societies had little demonstrated influence on the development of European witchcraft. But the ancient Near East, Greece, and Rome also had similar beliefs, and from these civilizations came many of the ideas on which European witchcraft was based. Throughout there was a blurring of sorcery with demonology. Characteristics assigned to a demon might also be assigned to a witch. For example, the devouring hag Lilitu (see below) was a spirit, but her characteristics were transferred in the Middle Ages to the diabolical witch.

The Sumerians and Babylonians invented an elaborate demonology. They believed that the world was full of spirits and that most of them were hostile. Each person had a tutelary spirit to protect them from demonic enemies. Among the most terrible Sumerian demons was Ardat Lili or Lilitu, a cousin of the Greco-Roman Lamia and the prototype of the Hebrew Lilith. Lilitu was a frigid, barren female spirit with wings and taloned hands and feet; accompanied by owls and lions she swept shriek-ing through the night, seducing sleeping men or drinking their blood. Another female demon, Labartu, went out with a serpent in each hand and attacked children and their mothers or nurses. Against such powers every kind of magic was needed, including amulets, incantations, and exorcisms, but especially the protec-tion of the tutelary deity, for 'the man who hath not a god as he walketh in the street, the demon covers him as a garment'.[10]

The worldview of ancient Egypt was less terrifying. Gods and spirits were all part of the one, living cosmos, and no distinction was made between natural and supernatural. The sorcerer used their wisdom and knowledge of amulets, spells, formulas, and figures to bend the cosmic powers to their purpose or that of their clients. As all spirits were part of the cosmic whole, none were evil, but the sorcerer could turn spiritual powers in ways that could harm their adversaries as well as benefiting themself.

The two most influential sources of European thought in general were the classical Greco-Roman and the Hebrew. The Greeks created both philosophy and a sophisticated system of magic. The highest form of magic in Greece was *theourgia*, literally 'working things pertaining to the gods'. A high, benevolent magic, theurgy was close to religion. A lower grade of magic, *mageia*, was much closer to sorcery. Originally a *magos* was an astrologer from Iran, or else a Greek following the high magical tradition of the Iranians. But by the end of the fifth century BC the *magoi* had already gained a reputation for harmful sorcery and even fraud: Plato viewed them as a menace to society. The *magoi* were private individuals claiming the technical knowledge and powers to help their clients and harm their clients' enemies by performing certain rites or supplying certain formulas. Lower than the *magoi* were the *goētes*, practitioners of a crude, lowbrow variety of magic. 'Howlers' of incantations, mixers of potions, and weavers of spells, the practitioners of *goēteia* had a wide reputation for charlatanism.

The Roman authorities were generally intolerant of all varieties of sorcery. The practice of sorcery, as opposed to the approved public rites connected with religion, was viewed as a threat to society. The emperors, always terrified of plots against their lives, feared sorcery as the least detectable and therefore most dangerous threat. Repression was indiscriminately harsh. A young man seen in the public baths touching first the marble tiles and then his chest while repeating the seven Greek vowels, a spell prescribed against stomach trouble, was arrested, tortured and executed. The harsh tradition of Roman law was one of the foundations upon which the medieval prosecution of witchcraft was based.

The image of the sorcerer in classical literature is almost uniformly dark: Circe the seductress, Medea the murderess, Ovid's Dipsias, Apuleius' Oenothea, and especially the Canidia and Sagana of Horace, who with pale and hideous faces, naked feet, dishevelled hair, and clothed in rotting shrouds, meet at night in a lonely place to claw the soil with their taloned fingers, rip apart a black lamb, eat its flesh, and invoke the gods of the underworld. This literary tradition of the evil sorceress readily supported the later Christian image of the witch.

Greco-Roman thought also began the close linking of sorcery with demonology that became the dominant characteristic of European witchcraft. The Greeks believed that all varieties of sorcerer worked their trade by consulting *daimones.* The Greek *daimōn*, from which our word 'demon' is derived, was used by Homer almost as a synonym for *theos*, 'god'. After Homer, the word came to mean a spiritual being inferior to a god. At the time of Socrates, a *daimōn* could be either good or evil, and Socrates himself claimed to have a *daimōn* that whispered good advice into his ear. But when Plato's pupil Xenocrates divided the spiritual world into gods and demons, he shifted the dark qualities of the gods on to the demons, who henceforth were considered evil. The sorcerers' consultation of demons then linked them firmly with the powers of darkness.

Other elements of Greco-Roman religion also contributed to the formation of the image of the witch. Lamias, spirits who like Lilitu roamed the world seducing men and killing infants, and Harpies, winged women who swept the world on the wind perpetrating gross indignities, bequeathed their characteristics to the human witch. The festivals of Dionysos became a blueprint for the rites allegedly practised by the medieval witches (see plate IV). The

Dionysian rites took place at night, often in a cave or grotto, locations connected with fertility and the powers of the underworld. The worshippers were usually women led by a male priest. The procession bore torches and a phallic image, and led a dark goat or its image. The goat, symbol of fertility, represented Dionysos, who was usually portrayed as shaggy and horned. The rite concluded in wine-drinking, ecstatic dancing, and animal sacrifice.

Human sacrifice, made much of in literature, probably did not actually extend into historical times. Accusations of orgy against the Dionysiacs are also exaggerated, but in the Hellenistic period orgiastic practices seem to have spread, and the rites of Cybele and the Magna Mater were characterized by ecstatic dancing and sexual frenzy. The Roman version of the rites of Dionysos, the Bacchanalia, became so notorious for licence that it was outlawed by the Senate in 186 BC. The historian Livy's description of the Bacchanalia became an important part of the literary tradition of European witchcraft: men and women were said to meet at night and to celebrate by torchlight rites including orgiastic feasting, drinking, and sex. It is difficult to say how much of this is true. Similar accusations were lodged against any group perceived as a secret society. Not only religious groups, such as the Dionysiacs, but also clandestine political groups, such as Catiline and his conspirators, were frequently accused of orgy and cannibalism.

Hebrew sorcery, largely derived from that of the Canaanites and Babylonians, had a great though indirect influence on European witchcraft. When the Hebrew Bible was translated into Greek, Latin, and modern tongues, the meaning of the Hebrew words underwent transformation. Sometimes the translations promoted persecutions. The most important case in point is Exodus 22:18, which in the original Hebrew ordains that a *kashaph* be put to death. A *kashaph* was a magician, diviner, or sorcerer, but nothing resembling a diabolist. In the Latin Vulgate, the Hebrew was translated as *Maleficos non patieris vivere*, 'You shall not permit *maleficos* to live'. At the time the Vulgate translation was made, the term *maleficus* itself was still vague: it could mean any kind of criminal, though it was frequently applied to malevolent sorcerers. As the European witch-craze developed, *maleficus* came specifically to denote a diabolical witch, and the text was used as proof and justification for the execution of witches. And that was not the end of the transformation. The translators of the King James Bible (1611) rendered most references to Hebrew sorcerers by the English word 'wizard', connoting a magician or sorcerer. But James I, who authorized the new translation, had expressed violent hatred of witches in his book *Demonolatry*. For the king, a witch was a member of a diabolical cult who had made a pact with Satan. He wanted witches exterminated, and his translators deliberately translated *kashaph* as 'witch' in order to provide clear biblical sanctions for their execution. The 'witch' of Endor whom King Solomon consulted was originally a *ba'alath ob*, 'mistress of a talisman'; in the Latin she was a *mulierem habentem pythonem*, 'a woman possessing an oracular spirit'; but in the King James version she too appears as a sinister 'witch'. Thus Hebrew sorcery was transformed to fit the prejudices of Christian demonology.

Sorcery and religion

Hebrew sorcery was far from diabolism, but Hebrew religion was influential in creating the concept of the Devil. Most world religions were and are monist, postulating one divine principle that is both good and evil. The gods were manifestations of this one principle, so they too were morally ambivalent. Perhaps the best illustration of this ambivalence is the figure of the Mexican god Quetzalcoatl, who is life and death, love and destruction. The first major break with monism occurred about 600 BC with the teachings of Zarathushtra in Iran. Zarathushtra's revelation was that evil is not a manifestation of the divine at all; rather it proceeds from a wholly different source. This religious dualism posits the existence of two principles, one goodness and light, the other darkness and evil. Mazdaism, the religion derived from

Zarathushtra's thought, had enormous influence on both Greek and Hebrew thought, and through them on Christianity.

Eastern religions such as Hinduism and Buddhism continue to profess one or another form of monism, but Western religions are monotheistic religions modified by dualism. A spectrum of Western religions goes from the extreme dualism of Mazdaism through Gnosticism, Manicheism, Christianity, Judaism, and Islam (where dualism is very attenuated). All these religions, however different from one another, posit a God who is wholly good and omnipotent yet who paradoxically tolerates evil, which is a force or at least a void in opposition to or limitation of the good God.

The problem of evil has always been the most difficult problem of Judaeo-Christian theology. How is it that God can be all-powerful and all-good yet create a world in which cancer, famine, and torture are abundant? One answer is that evil is at least in part caused by an evil spirit of great power. The Hebrews named this spirit the *satan*, 'the obstructor'. *Satan* was translated into Greek as *diabolos*, from which came the Latin *diabolus* and the English 'devil'. Contrary to a widespread belief among modern witches, the word 'devil' is not related to 'divinity' and does not mean 'little god'. The Indo-European roots of the two words are completely different: gwel for 'devil' and deiw for 'divine'. The figure of Satan emerged only gradually and unclearly in the Old Testament, but later, in the period of Apocalyptic and Apocryphal literature (200 BC to AD 150), it received sharp definition. Judaism remained monotheistic, so that Satan could never become a fully independent principle as his counterpart had in Mazdaism, but the power that Apocalyptic Judaism assigned to him was considerable. The Lord and the Devil were perceived as being in ethical and cosmic opposition. Each has his own kingdom: that of the Lord is light, while that of Satan is darkness. The Devil's plan is to lure Israel away from Yahweh, and he enjoys some successes, but at the end of the world Israel will repent, and the Messiah will bring the kingdom of the Devil to an end. Meanwhile, the

Devil heads a host of fallen angels and evil spirits who roam the world seeking the ruin and destruction of souls.

This concept of the world transforms the concept of sorcery. At its simplest, sorcery was purely mechanical. Then it was linked to the invocation of spirits. Then the spirits were defined as hostile to humanity. Now they were defined as hostile to God. Apocalyptic Judaism perceived the spirits as evil demons in league with one another under the generalship of the Devil, the principle of evil. It followed from this belief that a sorcerer who invokes spirits is calling upon the servants of Satan. Christianity made the argument air-tight. Good spirits such as angels and saints could not be compelled, Christians argued, but only supplicated. The only spirits that could be compelled were evil spirits. A sorcerer compelled spirits; therefore, the spirits he called upon were evil. Further, the power of the Devil is so overwhelming that anyone foolishly attempting to control his servants will find himself instead controlled by them. The sorcerer becomes the servant of the demons and a subject of Satan. The grounds for the transformation of sorcery into witchcraft had been fully prepared.

After the Apocalyptic period, Satan's role in Judaism dwindled, since the Rabbis, who dominated Judaism from the first century onwards, gave him little attention. But Christianity was founded in the midst of the Apocalyptic period, and in consequence the New Testament and subsequent Christian thought have given Satan a considerable role. The function of the Devil in the New Testament is as counterprinciple to Christ. The central message of the New Testament is that Christ saves us. What he saves us from is the power of the Devil. The opposition between the Lord and the Devil is fierce and profound, and any who stand in the Saviour's way or attempt to frustrate his plan of salvation are either explicitly or implicitly servants of Satan. The Devil has under his supreme command all opposition to the Lord both natural and supernatural, including demons, infidels, heretics, and sorcerers. The early Christians had a particular distaste for sorcerers. Claiming that the wonders worked by Christ were evidence of his divine mission, the Christians were obliged to attack claims of similar wonders performed by sorcerers as spurious. Their own enemies, such as the pagan Celsus, dismissed Christianity by claiming that Christ was merely another sorcerer. Thus the Christians perceived sorcery as both an insult and a threat.

The Christian attitude towards sorcerers was clear from the Books of Acts onwards. When Paul and Barnabas visited Paphos they found there 'a certain sorcerer, a false prophet' named Barjesus or Elymas. Elymas sought to turn the apostles away from the faith, and Paul, filled with the Holy Spirit, cursed him: 'O full of all subtlety and mischief, thou child of the Devil, thou enemy of all righteousness ... the hand of the Lord is upon thee, and thou shalt be blind, not seeing the sun for a season' (Acts 13:6–12). Simon the *magos*, whose conversion and baptism are recorded in Acts 8:9–13, became in later Christian tradition one of the prototypes of the diabolical sorcerer. The stance of Christianity was clear. On the one hand there were the followers of goodness and light, on the other, the minions of evil and darkness, among whom the sorcerers were prominent. Sorcery had come a long way from its origins in simple, mechanical magic.

The Roots of
European Witchcraft

A strange picture of witchcraft was drawn by writers of the fifteenth and sixteenth centuries during the witch-craze.

The sun has gone down, and honest people are asleep. The witches, including some men but mostly women, creep silently out of their beds, making sure that they do not disturb their husbands or wives. They are preparing for the sabbat. Those who live near the meeting ground will go on foot; those who live farther away will go to a private place, rub their bodies with an ointment that enables them to levitate, and fly off on animals, fence-rails, brooms, or stools. At the meeting, which takes place in a cellar, cave, or deserted heath, they meet ten to twenty of their fellow witches. If a neophyte is there, an initiation ceremony precedes the ordinary business of the meeting. The novice will be bound to the cult in such a way that he or she will find it difficult to withdraw. Accordingly, she is obliged to swear to keep the secrets of the cult, and she further seals herself to the group by promising to kill a young child and bring its body to a subsequent meeting. She orally renounces the Christian faith and seals her apostasy by stamping on, or excreting on, a crucifix or a consecrated host. Next she adores the male master of the cult, the Devil or his representative, by offering him the obscene kiss on the buttocks.

When the initiation has been completed, the assembly takes part in feasting and drinking. The witches enact a parody of the eucharistic feast, bringing in the bodies of children whom they have previously murdered. The infants may be stolen from Christian families, or they may be the offspring conceived by the witches at previous orgies. The children are offered up in sacrifice to the Devil. The witches may boil the children's bodies, mix them with loathsome substances, and render them into the levitating ointment. Or they may consume the children's body and blood in ritual parody of the Lord's Supper.

After the feast the torches are extinguished, or the candelabras are over-turned by a black dog or cat. The orgy commences. Cries of 'Mix it up' are heard, and each person takes the one next to him in lascivious embrace. The encounters are indiscriminate: men with men, women with women, mothers with sons, brothers with sisters. When the orgy is concluded, the witches take ritual leave of their master and return home replete to join their sleeping spouses.

Such a scene never occurred, but this is what was almost universally believed to happen at a witch's sabbat (see plate XVII). What people believe to be true influences their actions more than what is objectively true, and the conviction that this picture was accurate brought about the execution of nearly a hundred thousand people. The charges on which these people were put to death were at best distorted and exaggerated; at worst they were an invention and an imposture.

What are the origins of these beliefs and how did they come to be assembled? What social and psychological patterns produced and maintained these beliefs and their consequences? What is the significance of such behaviour for our understanding of human nature today? These are some of the questions that will be addressed in the following chapters.

What are the origins of these beliefs? The picture of witchcraft drawn above did not fully emerge before the fifteenth century. In the beginning, European sorcery was similar to that elsewhere in the world. The transformation was largely the result of the action of Christian thought upon pagan sorcery and religion.

But Christianity did not conquer Europe overnight. Within the Roman Empire, conversion required four centuries from the birth of Christ to the establishment of Christianity by Theodosius. Beyond the northern boundaries of the Empire the process was not completed until the seventh century (England), ninth century (Germany), or even twelfth century (Scandinavia).

During this long period Christian theology gradually moved the transformation of sorcery along. Augustine, the most influential Christian theologian, argued that pagan magic, religion, and sorcery were all invented by the Devil for the purpose of luring humanity away from Christian truth. Some of the effects of sorcery are illusions, Augustine said; others are real. Both reality and illusion are works of the Devil. Sorcerers summoning up spirits are calling up demons. And now Christian theologians made another important identification: the demons that the sorcerers were calling up were the pagan gods. Jupiter, Diana, and the other deities of the Roman pantheon were really demons, servants of Satan. As Christianity pressed northward, it made the same assertion about Wotan, Freya, and the other gods of the Celts and Teutons. Those who worshipped the gods worshipped demons whether they knew it or not. With this stroke, all pagans, as well as sorcerers, could be viewed as part of the monstrous plan of Satan to frustrate the salvation of the world. This was the posture of most theologians and church councils. Yet at the same time popular religion often treated the pagan deities quite differently, transferring the characteristics of the gods to the personalities of the saints. In modern Greece, or in modern Ireland, one can still find traces of the old gods in saints who bring storms, protect holy wells, or bellow out the thunder. In fact considerable differences existed between the religions of the Mediterranean and those of the north, but Christianity lumped them all together as 'pagan'. The term 'pagan', meaning 'hick' or 'bumpkin', was an opprobrious one that the Christians applied uncritically and without distinction to all the monist/polytheist religions they encountered.

The encounter between Christianity and Celtic and Teutonic religions was one of the most important steps in the formation of historical witchcraft. It is also a crucial point in the interpretation of witchcraft today.

Interpretations of European witchcraft

At least four major interpretations of European witchcraft are current. The first is the old liberal view that witchcraft never existed at all but was a monstrous invention by the ecclesiastical authorities in order to enhance their powers and enlarge their purses. For this school, the history of witchcraft is a chapter in the history of repression and inhumanity.

The second tradition is the folklorist or Murrayite tradition. Margaret Murray published her *Witch-Cult in Western Europe* in 1921, at a time when Sir James Frazer's *Golden Bough* and his ideas about fertility cults were dominating a whole generation of writers. Influenced by Frazer and by her own background as an Egyptologist, Murray argued that European witchcraft was an ancient fertility religion based on the worship of the horned god Dianus. This ancient religion, Murray claimed, had survived into the Middle Ages and at least into the early modern period. Murray was enshrined in fiction as Rose Lorimer in Angus Wilson's *Anglo-Saxon Attitudes*; the *Encyclopaedia Britannica* used her article on 'witchcraft' for decades; and a number of historians and folklorists followed her lead. In Germany, Anton Meyer argued a variant that was to become popular with modern witches: Meyer's view was that the ancient fertility religion emphasized the earth goddess more than the horned god.

Modern historical scholarship rejects the Murray thesis with all its variants. Scholars have gone too far in their retreat from Murray, since many fragments of pagan religion do certainly appear in medieval witchcraft. But the fact remains that the Murray thesis on the whole is untenable. The argument for the survival of any coherent fertility cult from antiquity through the Middle Ages into the present is riddled with fallacies:

1. The original religion from which Murray asserted witchcraft derived was the religion of Dianus. This religion never existed; it is a composite artificially created by Murray out of the characteristics of discrete and divergent religions from Asia Minor to Wales. Murray's argument verged on accepting the Christian polemic that all pagan religions are alike.

2. Even if such a composite fertility religion had existed, evidence for its survival is wholly inadequate. Certainly paganism did not die out at the first trumpet of Christianity, and it lingered longer in some areas – such as Scandinavia and Russia – than others. But by the twelfth century virtually all of Europe had been converted. In every area, bits and pieces of pagan beliefs and practices survived the conversion and persisted through the Middle Ages. But no evidence exists that any organized pagan cult or theology existed in the Middle Ages. As Elliot Rose observed, 'Of course, many popular festivals ... were survivals *from* paganism; this is not the same as a survival *of* paganism.' And 'in no single instance of all those [explanations] put forward by Miss Murray is there not an alternative and a better explanation of the facts.'[1]

3. Not until about 1300, a thousand years after the conversion of Constantine, does a substantial body of evidence about witchcraft appear, and this evidence shows witchcraft not as a fertility religion but as a Christian heresy based upon diabolism. Whether this diabolical witchcraft actually existed or whether it was invented by the Christians, the Murrayite thesis fails. If witches *did* exist in the 1300–1700 period, all the evidence shows them as heretical diabolists, not pagans. If on the other hand witchcraft was an invention, then it did not exist

at all. In either case the survival of an 'old religion' is out of the question.

4. Two huge time gaps in the evidence exist. The first is the one from the conversion to the beginning of the witch-craze; the second extends from the end of the witch-craze to the time of Leland's *Aradia* at the end of the nineteenth century (see p. 146). In the late eighteenth and nineteenth centuries there is no evidence for the existence of witchcraft at all. Some isolated pagan practices, yes. Sorcery, yes. But neither witchcraft as diabolism nor witchcraft as 'the old religion'. That this 'old religion' persisted secretly, without leaving any evidence, is of course possible, just as it is possible that below the surface of the moon lie extensive deposits of Stilton cheese. Anything is possible. But it is nonsense to assert the existence of something for which no evidence exists. The Murrayites ask us to swallow a most peculiar sandwich: a large piece of the wrong evidence between two thick slices of no evidence at all.

A third school, currently the most influential, emphasizes the social history of witchcraft, especially the social pattern of witch accusations. These historians generally assume that witchcraft (as opposed to sorcery) never really existed, their difference with the old-fashioned liberals being that they blame belief in witchcraft on widespread general superstition rather than on the impostures of an evil Church. A fourth group of historians emphasizes the history of ideas and argues that witchcraft is a composite of concepts gradually assembled over the centuries. Of these, Christian heresy and theology are more important than paganism. Both these groups have ignored or dismissed modern witchcraft. This book takes both historical witchcraft and modern witchcraft into account but treats them as separate phenomena with no historical connection between them.

Sorcery, folklore, and religion in pagan Europe

The roots of historical European witchcraft lie partly in Greco-Roman and Hebrew thought and partly in the sorcery, folklore and religion of northern Europe. The Bronze Age sorcery of northern Europe was of a piece with sorcery all over the world: a burial site reveals a Bronze Age woman, possibly a sorceress, buried with the claw-joint of a lynx, the bones of a weasel, spinal joints of snakes, horses' teeth, a rowan twig, a broken knife blade, and two pieces of iron pyrites, all of which were apparently believed to possess magical qualities. The almost total lack of sources prohibits any investigation of the course of sorcery from the Bronze Age to the time of conversion, and the vast cultural shifts and differences rule out the likelihood of any coherent tradition. Yet the folk-sorcery of the early Christian period in the north is still, like that of the Bronze Age, common sorcery.

The Norsemen raised evil spirits and destroyed the spiritual protection of an enemy by placing a horse's head with its mouth open on a pole in front of his house. Teutonic sorcerers used herbs, sieves, and figures of wax, dough, or lime in their work. In hostile magic, they took the figure and hung it up in the air, plunged it in water, heated it at the fire, or stabbed it with needles. Charms were used to hurt or heal. A simple charm that persisted into the nineteenth century was: *Sprach jungfrau Hille/blut stand stille*, 'The maiden Hille has spoken/the flow of blood is checked'. The charm illustrates the survival of pagan elements long after the extinction of paganism. The maid Hille is the ancient Valkyr Hilda, but the modern peasant mumbling the charm was no more a pagan than the modern Italian who a generation ago used the exclamation *perbacco*, 'by Bacchus'. Many individuals today shout 'Jesus Christ' or 'God damn it' without either hope of salvation or fear of damnation.

To destroy an enemy, the Anglo-Saxons recited a spell reducing him to nothing by associating him with tiny and perishable things in nature:

May you be consumed as coal upon the hearth,
May you shrink as dung upon a wall,
and may you dry up as water in a pail.
May you become as small as a linseed grain,
and much smaller than the hipbone of an itchmite,
and may you become so small that you become nothing.

Some Anglo-Saxon magic was simple and mechanical:

> Against warts. Take the water of a dog and the blood of a mouse, mix together, smear the warts with this; they will soon disappear.

Sometimes the curse mingled mechanical with religious elements:

> If a man is troubled by tumours near the heart, let a girl go to a spring that runs due east, and let her draw a cupful of water moving with the current, and let her sing on it the Creed and an Our Father.

Or:

> A pleasant drink against insanity. Put in ale hassock, lupine, carrot, fennel, radish, betony, water-agrimony, marche, rue, wormwood, cat's mint, elecampane, enchanter's nightshade, wild teazle. Sing twelve Masses over the drink, and let the patient drink it. He will soon be better.[2]

Christian penitentials, guides for priests in the early Middle Ages for use in hearing confessions and assigning penances, condemn customs derived from ancient sorcery. These customs, whatever their original rationales, had become superstitions, since they now lacked any integrating or coherent worldview. 'If any woman', prescribed the penitential of Theodore about AD 600,

puts her daughter upon a roof or into an oven for the cure of
a fever, she shall do penance for seven years.

The unconscious symbolism of this particular spell is universal, at least as regards the oven. An oven, like a cave, represents the womb: passing a child into an oven and bringing it out again symbolizes rebirth. In sorcery, the symbol becomes a part of the occult system of interconnections and produces a physical cure. The Christian authorities viewed all such work as being effected by the intervention of demons and sought to repress it. The Confessional of Egbert (about 750) decrees:

If a woman works [sorcery] (*drycraeft*) and enchantment (*galdor*) and [uses] magical philters, she shall fast for twelve months. ... If she kills anyone by her philters, she shall fast for seven years.[3]

The Norse *Edda* says that *seithr* (sorcery) was performed at night, when men are asleep, by *völvas* (sorceresses) who rode out at night on boars, wolves, or fence-rails to meet their fellow-sorcerers at the *trolla-thing* or spirit meeting. 'Ketill was roused at night', the *Edda* relates,

by a great uproar in the wood; he ran out and saw a sorcer-ess with streaming hair; being questioned, she begged him not to balk her, [for] she was bound for a magic [meeting], to which were coming Skelking king of spirits from Dumbshaf [and other spirits].

Christians of course interpreted such a meeting as a diabolical 'sabbat'.

Peasants often practised sorcery in order to improve their own position at the expense of their neighbours, or simply to exercise their spite. Sometimes the threat of a hex could be lucrative.

Visigothic laws of the sixth century prescribed whipping as punishment for self-advertised 'storm-makers' who made farmers pay them to spare their fields. Many of the charges of evil magic common during the witch-craze were of such ancient origin: making storms, causing death or disease in animals or humans, and producing impotence.

Folk-tales about witchcraft and sorcery generally reflect both a fear of sorcerers and a sense of their power. The 'witch' of the folk-tale is basically a sorcerer (rarely do charges derived from the witch-craze enter into folk-tales). She is closely associated with the powers of nature and has many of the aspects of a nature spirit herself. She is close to the 'woodwives' or 'wild women' of folklore who represent the wildness of nature as opposed to the world of civilized humanity. Here is a common motif:

A girl becomes the servant of a black witch in the woods. There is a forbidden chamber ... into which she may not go. She has to clean the house for many years.... She eventually opens the door of the secret forbidden chamber and finds in it the black witch who, through her cleaning, has already turned nearly white. The girl shuts up the room again but is then persecuted by the witch for having transgressed the taboo. [The witch] persecutes the girl, takes away her children and brings every kind of misery over her, [compelling her to lie and say that she has not seen her in the chamber].[4]

Folk-tales, like dreams, express the concerns of the unconscious in symbols; the meaning of the figure of the witch, like the meaning of any symbol, varies with the story. Usually, however, she represents an elemental natural force possessing enormous and unexpected powers against which a natural person is unable to prepare or defend themself, a force not necessarily evil, but so alien and remote from the world of mankind as to constitute a threat to the social, ethical, and even physical order of the cosmos. This manner of portraying the witch is very ancient and probably archetypal. This witch is neither a simple sorceress, nor a demonolater, nor a pagan. She is a hostile presence from another world. The gut terror inspired by this archetypal witch helps to explain the excesses of hatred and fear that welled up during the witch-craze.

Sometimes Celtic and Teutonic traditions (see plate IX) merged with those of Greece and Rome. The Roman goddess Diana, for example, blended with the Teutonic fertility goddesses in the early Middle Ages. Diana was goddess of the moon, virgin huntress, and heavenly sister of the sun-god Apollo. But Diana was not always light and airy. Her association with animals made her a feral protectress of animals as well as a huntress, and her function of assuring plenitude of game connected her with fertility in general. Her power over the moon associated her with the monthly cycles of women; and the horns of the crescent moon, symbolizing growth, reinforced the element of fertility.

Since the underworld both pushes up the new crops to the light and swallows them up when they die and rot, fertility deities are also associated with death, and Diana was identified with three-faced Hecate, dread pale goddess of death, patroness of evil sorcery, and mother of lamias. In this dark form, Diana appeared in early medieval belief as a leader of witch processions and rites. But the origins of these Dianic processions, unknown in Rome, are more Teutonic than Mediterranean and have their roots in the Wild Hunt. The Wild Hunt was a procession of spirits or ghosts who roamed through the countryside revelling and destroying. The leader of this ghastly rout was sometimes female, sometimes male. The female leader was in northern Germany called Holda, Holle, or Holt, 'the friendly one', wife of Wotan, goddess of marriage and fecundity; in the south she was called Perchta, Berhta, or Berta, 'the bright one'. This goddess was associated through the hunt, the moon, and the night, with Diana. The association was probably made in the minds of scholars and

1 Goya, *Conjuro, c.* 1794–5. Goya, himself a sceptic, painted grotesque scenes of witchcraft for satirical purposes. Here the stereotyped witches are accompanied by familiars, stick pins in images and carry a basket of dead babies for use in their cannibalistic orgy.

II TOP A wooden Congolese image stuck with pins. The dividing line between magic and religion is sometimes weak. Pins may be thrust into an image to cause pain or, as here, to release the power of the deity.

III ABOVE A witch-mask from the Sankuru River area representing a spiritual power who is invoked in the periodic witch-hunting drives of the Songe, southern Zaire.

IV Festival of Dionysos: satyrs and maenads with Dionysos and Ariadne. Amphora dating from the last quarter of the sixth century BC. The orgiastic rites of Dionysos, which appeared in Rome as the Bacchanalia, were a prototype of the witches' sabbat.

v Fourteenth-century French manuscript of St Augustine's *City of God* illustrating the fall of the rebel angels. The angels in heaven have beautiful, bird-like wings, but these are transformed into the bat-wings of the evil angels.

vi OPPOSITE The execution of two Cathars: *Auto-da-fé*, by Pedro Berruguete. Catharism strongly emphasized the power of the Devil in the world. It paved the way for the assimilation of heresy to witchcraft in the popular imagination.

VII *The Nightmare*, by Henry Fuseli, 1791. A modern conception of the incubus, a demon who sexually abuses sleeping women. In witchcraft, the incubus had a slightly different function, as the witches voluntarily submitted to its embraces.

VIII OPPOSITE ABOVE *Herne the Hunter*, by George Cruikshank, 1843. Herne was one form of the mysterious and deadly leader of the Wild Hunt; he was often associated with the Devil.

IX OPPOSITE BELOW An antler-headed Celtic god, a detail from the Gundestrup cauldron deposited as a votive offering in a Danish bog during the second or first century BC. Horns are a worldwide symbol of power, fertility and plenitude of game.

X ABOVE Swimming a witch. One of the common tests of witchcraft was to throw the witch into deep water. If the water, God's creature, rejected her and she floated, she was guilty. If she sank, she was innocent. Two men hold her with ropes so as to draw her up again if she sinks.

XI LEFT In the strappado, the prisoner's 'arms were tied behind his back with a rope attached to a pulley and he was then hoisted in the air'.

XII OPPOSITE ABOVE Frontispiece to Matthew Hopkins' *Discoverie of Witches*, 1647. The 'Witchfinder-General of England' is shown looking at two witches surrounded by their familiars.

XIII OPPOSITE BELOW The witch-house at Bamberg. Constructed by Bishop Johann Georg II, it contained prison cells and notorious torture chambers.

churchmen who applied a familiar classical name, Diana, to the unfamiliar goddess of the Teutons. An even more curious connection was made between Berta/Holda and Herodias, the murderous wife of Herod: the dark reputation of Herodias and the *Her*-element in her name seem to have caused the association. When the leader of the Wild Hunt was male, his name too began with *Ber*- or *Her*- (Berthold, Herlechin, or Herne), relating him to brightness and the cult of the moon (see plate VIII).

The members of the Wild Hunt roamed the wilderness, the heaths, and the forests. They were akin to the 'wild men and women' who, part human, part animal, and part spirit, were believed to roam the medieval forests. Elements of the wild woman, often perceived as a murderess, child-eater, and bloodsucker, lingered in the folk-tales of the lonely witch who dwelt in the forest: gradually in the early Middle Ages the characteristics of the wild huntresses and wild women were transferred to the witches.

Nothing persists in the mind more than the memory of a holiday, and traces of ancient pagan festivals can be clearly found in the Middle Ages and down to the present. Some of the pagan festivals are still (though by the turn of the millennium self-consciously) practised in small towns and villages in the British Isles, Germany, and elsewhere in Europe. Some of the more important festivals acquired a sinister reputation and came to be associated during the witch-craze with the meetings or 'sabbats' of witches. Contemporary witches, drawing proudly on both the ancient festivals themselves and their association with medieval and early modern witches, have made these ancient feasts the foundation of their own major 'sabbats'.

During the witch-craze, five festivals most frequently appear in the sources. The first was 31 October. The purpose of the original pagan rite on this day was to restore the power of the waning sun. Among the Anglo-Saxons this rite was called the 'need-fire', because great bonfires were kindled to lend strength to the sun through imitative magic. When the Christians established 1 November as

All Saints' Day or All Hallows' Day, the need-fire festival fell on All Hallows' Eve and was transformed into Hallowe'en. In England, this religious displacement of the holiday was followed in the seventeenth century by a political displacement. After the arrest of Guy Fawkes for plotting to blow up Parliament, the date of his apprehension, 5 November, became a national holiday. On that day bonfires are still lit and rockets set off. In America, Hallowe'en became a kind of Saturnalia for children, a night when the rules were suspended for a while and children ventured out, like elves, to demand treats and threaten reprisals against the stingy. It has since become commercialized, but still the memory of strange spirits and weird fires lingers.

Another festival designed to bring back the sun and ensure fertility was practised about the time of the winter solstice, and in the early Middle Ages some people were still dressing as stags and bulls on 1 January and performing a ritual dance to ensure the plenitude of game. Another fire festival, later associated with the Christian feast of Candlemas, was celebrated about 1 February. Another occurred on 30 April, the eve of May Day, which has always been a common date for the celebration of the return of spring. 30 April happened by chance to become the Christian feast of an obscure Anglo-Saxon missionary named St Walpurga, and from this coincidence derives the name Walpurgisnacht or Walpurgisnight. Then, on 30 June, Midsummer's Eve, the return of the sun and the bounty of summer were celebrated. *A Midsummer Night's Dream* preserves the magical atmosphere of this festival.

The familiars of later witches originated with the dwarves, fairies, trolls, kobolds, or other small spirits of northern folklore. They could be friendly, mischievous, or malignant. In origin they were nature spirits, but Christianity could admit the existence of no spiritual entities other than God, angels, and demons. The Church equated these spirits with minor demons and took the association of the sorcerer with the familiar spirit as another sign of his relationship with the Devil. Yet the origin of the familiars in folklore rather than in demonology appears in the names assigned them, names such as Robin Goodfellow, Haussibut, Federwisch, or Rumpelstiltskin. Such spirits are to be found in cabbage rows or behind larch boughs rather than in the serried ranks of Satan's hell.

The legal status of sorcery

All survivals of pagan belief, worship, and practice were condemned as demonic and gradually suppressed by Christian theology and law. Roman law had been stern in dealing with sorcery. Teutonic law was much milder. But in the course of the eighth and ninth centuries the growing influence of theology upon civil law produced a legal association of sorcerers with demons. The word *maleficium*, originally 'wrongdoing' in general, now came to mean malevolent sorcery in particular, and the *maleficus* or *malefica* was presumed to be closely associated with the Devil. Sorcery could now be prosecuted not simply as a crime against society but as a heresy and a crime against God.

The law fixed the identification of paganism with demonolatry. A 'List of Superstitions' drawn up at the Council of Leptinnes in 744 prohibited sacrifice to saints, evidence of the lingering confusion in the popular mind between new saint and old deity. The same council approved a baptismal formula that asked the catechumen to 'renounce all the works of the demon, and all his words, and Thor, and Odin, and Saxnot, and all evil beings that are like them.' Charlemagne ordered death for anyone sacrificing 'a human being to the Devil and [offering] sacrifice to demons as is the custom of the pagans.'[5]

The law helped transfer the characteristics of evil spirits to human witches. The pagans had set out offerings of food and drink for minor spirits. The Synod of Rome in 743 assumed that these spirits were demons and outlawed the offerings. The demonic spirits were then transformed into *bonae mulieres*, the ghostly 'good women' who wandered out at night going into houses and stealing food. Finally, the *bonae mulieres* were transformed into witches. Likewise, the term *striga* or *stria*, originally a blood-drinking night spirit, became a common word for a witch.

The early Middle Ages were tolerant of sorcery and heresy in comparison with the tortures and executions of the Roman Empire and with the hangings and burnings of the later Middle Ages and Renaissance. Two or three years' penance was normal for *maleficium*, incantation, and idolatry. But the law gradually became both more comprehensive and more severe. The Synod of Paris on 6 June 829 issued a decree with sinister implications for the future, citing the stern passages of Leviticus 20:6 and Exodus 22:18. The synod argued that since the Bible decreed that a *maleficus* should not be permitted to live, the king had a right to punish sorcerers severely. In England Alfred the Great threatened *wiccan* with the death penalty, and Ethelstan ordered execution for *wiccecraeft* if it resulted in death.

Such measures were bound to reduce and eventually eradicate pagan practices, and condemnations of pagan rites gradually became perfunctory repetitions of earlier condemnations issued when the problem was more serious. Once in a while the sources report something fresh, such as the struggle of St Barbato against the residual paganism of the Lombards in the ninth century. At Benevento these pagans adored a snake and a sacred tree, around which they danced in a circle. The Synod of Rome in 826 complained that 'many people, mostly women, come to Church on Sundays and holy days not to attend the Mass but to dance, sing broad songs, and do other such pagan things.'[6]

The most important legal document of the early Middle Ages relating to witchcraft is the Canon Episcopi, issued about AD 900. The canon says:

> Some wicked women are perverted by the Devil and led astray by illusions and fantasies induced by demons, so that they believe that they ride out at night on beasts with Diana, the

pagan goddess, and a horde of women. They believe that in the silence of the night they cross huge distances. They say that they obey Diana's commands and on certain nights are called out in her service.... Many other people also believe this to be true, although it is a pagan error to believe that any other divinity exists than the one God. ... Such fantasies are thrust into the minds of faithless people, not by God, but by the Devil. For Satan has the power to transform himself into the figure of an angel of light. In this form he captures and enslaves the mind of a miserable woman and transforms himself into the shapes of various different people. He shows her deluded mind strange things and unknown people, and leads it on weird journeys. It is only the mind that does this, but faithless people believe that these things happen to the body as well.[7]

The Canon Episcopi had enormous influence. It was widely and incorrectly believed to date back to the fourth century and, thus possessing the authority of great antiquity, entered into the major medieval collections of canon law. Since the canon dismissed the physical reality of witchcraft and condemned those who believed in it as weak in faith, it helped to forestall the witch-craze. Later, when canon lawyers and theologians accepted the reality of witchcraft, they had to twist and bend their way around the canon. Yet the Canon Episcopi is far from a monument to early medieval scepticism, for it indicates that belief in these strange phenomena was widespread, and its influence helped to spread them. The Canon Episcopi itself helped establish the historical concept of the sabbat. As the chief of a demon horde, Diana was equated with Satan. The women who followed her must then be worshippers of the Devil. Though they did not really follow her out in their physical bodies, they did ride with her in spirit, so that their spirits were servants of Satan. They obeyed the Lady goddess (*domina*) rather than the Lord Christ (*dominus*), and they met secretly on specified nights to worship her. A century later, the canon lawyer Burchard of Worms equated the Diana of the Canon with Holda, whom he called 'the witch Holda'. The Classical goddess Diana had been identified with the Teutonic mother-goddess Holda, and both had been judged to be manifestations of Satan. The ambivalent identification of Holda as a witch, together with the image of the women who followed her out at night, created a picture on which the witch-craze would later draw extensively.

Witchcraft, Heresy, and Inquisition

Sorcery, pagan religion, and folklore were the first three elements in the formation of European witchcraft. Christian heresy was the fourth. When the witch-craze began at the end of the Middle Ages, its most important beliefs were: (1) the ride by night, (2) the pact with the Devil, (3) the formal repudiation of Christianity, (4) the secret, nocturnal meeting, (5) the desecration of the eucharist and the crucifix, (6) the orgy, (7) sacrificial infanticide, and (8) cannibalism. Every one of these elements was either introduced into the tradition of witchcraft by heresy or at least heavily modified by it.

The idea of pact was crucial, because it put the cap on the demonization of the sorcerer. A *maleficus* was now by definition one who makes a pact with Satan. Pact helped distinguish witchcraft from possession. The Devil may possess a person against their will, but pact is always voluntary. The witch, then, serves the Devil of their own free will. The idea of pact began to gain currency in the eighth century, when Paul the Deacon, one of Charlemagne's advisers, translated a sixth-century Greek story about a priest named Theophilus who obtained promotion to the episcopate by solemnly promising the Devil to renounce Christ. The motif of pact in medieval legend culminated in the story of Faust, the fictional high magician of the Renaissance who made a pact with the Devil to obtain both wisdom and sensual delight. The legend mingled the traditions of high and low magic and remained popular for centuries; witness Marlowe's *Dr Faustus* of the sixteenth century and Goethe's *Faust* of the nineteenth.

A typical story was told by Archbishop Hincmar of Reims in 860. A young man went to a sorcerer in order to procure the favours of a young girl. The sorcerer agreed to help him but on the condition that he renounce Christ in writing. The boy agreed, and the sorcerer wrote the Devil a letter expressing his hope that the dark lord would be pleased with his new recruit. The sorcerer handed the letter to the young man and told him to go out at night and hold the letter up in the air. That very night the boy went out, lifted up the letter, and called upon Satan for help. The Prince of Power of the Shadows appeared and led him into the presence of Satan, who examined the boy in a parody of the rite of baptism. 'Do you believe in me?' the Devil asked. 'I believe,' the boy replied. 'Do you renounce Christ?' 'I do renounce him.' 'You Christians always come to me when you need help and then try to repent afterwards, relying upon the mercy of Christ. I want you to promise yourself to me in writing so that there will be no possibility of escape.'

The boy agreed, and the Devil in return caused the girl to fall in love with him. She asked her father to give her to the boy in marriage, but her father refused, as he wished her to enter a convent. The girl realized that she was under the power of demons but was unable to resist; she told her father that she would die unless she married the young man. But the boy could continue the imposture no longer and confessed. By the intervention of St Basil the girl was released from Satan's grip and went demurely into the nunnery; the boy turned to a good Christian life. The story is a typical *exemplum*, a moral tale designed for use in sermons.

Pact did not remain in the world of story. It was the basis of the transformation of the sorcerer into the heretic. If you worshipped Satan, it followed that you believed that Satan could save you from the justice of God, which is heresy; if you renounced Christ as your lord and put Satanism in his place, this was the most despicable and dangerous of all heresies.

The earliest heresies of the Middle Ages were far from diabolical; most of them were characterized instead by a zealous desire for the moral reform of the Church. But as early as the eighth century some elements of witchcraft began to appear in heresy, or at least in what people believed about heresy. Then, in 1022, one event linked heresy and witchcraft decisively.

The dualist heresies

In 1022 King Robert of France presided over the first execution for heresy in the Middle Ages. During the trial a vast mob assembled outside the episcopal palace at Orleans and was barely restrained from lynching the heretics before they could be formally condemned and burnt. The events of 1022 at Orleans are noteworthy. First, after several centuries in which reports of heresy were sparse, a sizable group of heretics appeared in northern France without any antecedents. Second, their trial attracted the attention of the king and queen. Third, a vast crowd of ordinary people were so incensed by the heresy that they tried to murder the defendants. Fourth, the heretics were alleged to believe doctrines tinged with dualism to a degree unheard of in Western Europe for four hundred years – the ancient cosmic conflict between light and darkness, spirit and flesh, good and evil, had reappeared. Finally the heretics were accused of beliefs and practices that for the first time closely resembled those alleged of the witches at the height of the witch-craze. Whether any of the charges were valid, the core ideas of historical witchcraft were now assembled for the first time at a trial for heresy.

The Orleans heretics were accused of holding sex orgies at night in a secret place, either underground or in an abandoned building. The members of the group appeared bearing torches. Holding the torches, they chanted the names of demons until an evil spirit appeared. Now the lights were extinguished, and everyone seized the person closest to them in sexual embrace, whether mother, sister, or nun. The children conceived at the orgies were burned eight days after birth (a grotesque echo of Christian baptismal practice), and their ashes were confected in a substance that was then used in a blasphemous parody of holy communion.

The heretics were accused of believing that when filled with the Holy Spirit they had angelic visions and were transported without lapse of time from place to place. They adored the Devil and paid him homage; he appeared to them in the form of a beast, an angel of light, or a black man. They recited a litany of demons. They formally renounced Christ and desecrated the crucifix.

Of these witch charges the most significant are the sexual orgies, the sacrifice of human beings, specifically children, and cannibalism. These charges are all ancient. The Syrians brought them against the Jews, the Romans against the Christians, and the Christians against the Gnostics. Now they were being brought against the medieval heretics. A long succession of heresy trials drew upon the Orleans charges, and by the fourteenth and fifteenth centuries licentious and orgiastic excesses were so frequently alleged against the heretics that the transition from the prosecution of heresy to the witch-craze was made almost without difficulty. The reason that these ancient charges came to light again at Orleans in 1022 is that the Orleans heretics were accused of holding doctrines tinged with dualism. Not all the early heretics had been accused by the Christians of orgy and other ritual crimes. Only the Gnostics, the inheritors of religious dualism, were so stigmatized. When Gnosticism died out, the charges disappeared. Now the return of dualism to European heresy revived and developed the charges until they became a central part of heresy and witchcraft.

Extreme dualism had begun in ancient Iran, as we have seen (see p. 35), passed on to the Gnostics and Manicheans, and entered the Balkans, where it became the basis of the religion of the Bulgarian Bogomils. But Christianity itself was a semi-dualist religion, and in their zeal for reform and spiritual purity the heresies of the eleventh and twelfth centuries exaggerated the dualism inherent in Christianity to the point that their views appeared Gnostic to the orthodox. Thus when the orthodox condemned the heretics of Orleans they applied to them terms similar to those the Church fathers had used against the Gnostics.

Then, more than a century after Orleans, the Bogomils sent missionaries to Western Europe. Beginning in the 1140s, Bogomil ideas united with the dualism inherent in already existing heresy to produce a new heresy called Catharism, 'the religion of the pure' (see plate VI). Catharism was a strongly dualist religion, in that it emphasized the power of the Devil in the world. The Catharists taught that the Spirit of Evil, the Devil, created the material world for the purpose of entrapping spirit in matter. He imprisoned the human soul in a cage of flesh. Since the God of the Old Testament created the material world, he is the Spirit of Evil. The true God, the God of goodness and light, is hidden and remote from this world. All the personages of the Old Testament are demon followers of the Spirit of Evil and darkness who rules the world. Christ was a pure spirit sent down by the good, hidden God in order to teach humanity how to escape from the matter that confined them. Since matter is evil, Christ was pure spirit, his body an illusion; he was not truly a man. Being pure spirit, he did not truly suffer on the cross, and the cross is to be despised as a symbol of a lie. The worst sin is procreation, since conception imprisons another individual spirit in the flesh. The Catholic Church was established by the Devil in order to delude people, but an individual may free himself from the bondage of matter by following the teachings of Catharism.

The Catharist emphasis upon the Devil influenced orthodox theology, so that the Devil came to play a much larger role in late medieval thought than he had earlier. Fear of the Devil's powers was one of the chief ingredients of the witch-craze. But the Catharist Devil had a curious influence of another kind as well. The Catharists emphasized the power of the Devil, not to serve him, but to fight him. Yet their insistence upon his power as Lord of this World contained the seed of a curious misinterpretation. If the Devil really has powers nearly equal to the Lord's, and if the true God of light is distant and hidden, and if the Devil presides over wealth, fame, sex, and other earthly delights, some might prefer to worship the deity that gave them access to such pleasures. This kind of thinking, twisted from a Catharist as well as from a Catholic point of view, may have emerged from a zealous but faulty grasp of Catharist doctrine. Evidence that this occurred comes from fourteenth-century Italy, where heretics believed that the Devil created the material world. Since the Devil was the creator of the world, he was more powerful than God, and should be worshipped in his place.[1]

The pronounced dualism of the Catharists also left them open to the same charges of cannibalism, infanticide, and orgy that had already been brought against the much less dualist heretics of Orleans. Though on the whole the Catharists were innocent of such charges, it is possible that some may have been guilty. It is clear that some of the Gnostics of the second and third centuries AD (the Barbelognostics for example) did engage in such practices. The union of the ascetic with the licentious, of disgust for matter with indulgence of matter, is a strong theme in dualistic Gnosticism, which developed at least five doctrinal reasons for negating sexual and other morality: (1) the flesh must do service to the flesh before it can be overcome; (2) the body, being evil, should be degraded by obscene practices; (3) once we are filled with the Holy Spirit we can do no wrong, and the laws of this world do not apply to us; (4) those who are not filled with the Spirit may as well sin, since nothing can save them anyway; (5) true freedom and life in the Spirit requires the destruction of law. These Gnostic arguments were all available to the medieval Catharists.

If some Gnostics practised libertinism, most did not, and the evidence that Catharists practised it is all biased and suspect. Catharist doctrines and practices were open to such antinomian interpretations, but it is not clear that libertinism really was a serious problem with the Catharists. What is clear, however, is that the orthodox thought that it was and assumed that such practices took place on a large scale. Again, what people believed to happen was more important than what really happened, and the widespread belief in the libertinism of the heretics helped to shape the witch-craze. Alan of Lille, writing towards the turn of the thirteenth century, reported that the heretics argued that a person must practise promiscuity in order to free himself from attachment to all things earthly and diabolical. Alan's contemporary, Walter Map, said that the heretics engaged in obscene rites. Map's description of 1182 uses the word 'synagogue' to describe the meeting for the first time. This usage, obviously designed to spite the Jews, was common throughout the Middle Ages, being replaced only towards the end of the fifteenth century by the equally anti-Jewish term 'sabbat'. Here is what Map thought happened at the assembly:

> About the first watch of the night, when gates, doors, and windows have been closed, the groups sit waiting in silence in their respective synagogues, and a black cat of marvelous size climbs down a rope which hangs in their midst. On seeing it, they put out the lights. They do not sing hymns or repeat them distinctly, but hum through clenched teeth and pantingly feel their way toward the place where they see their lord. When they have found him they kiss him, each the more humbly as he is the more inflamed by frenzy – some the feet, more under the tail, most the private parts.[2]

More than a hundred years before the witch-craze began, the paradigm of the witch's 'sabbat' was already clear in the accusations brought against the heretics. Such a description is inherently unlikely to be an accurate account of what the heretics did, or of what the witches would do. The history of European witchcraft is essentially the history of a concept whose relationship to physical reality was tenuous. And the concept took the lives of about sixty thousand people.

Another contribution of heresy to witchcraft is the idea that the witches met in groups. Sorcerers almost always practised magic singly, but heretics worked in communities. The Alpine Italian heretics of the fourteenth century met in assemblies of seven to forty-seven, with an average meeting of about twenty.[3] Once sorcery was transformed into heresy, the inquisitors assumed that the sorcerer-heretics, or witches, also practised in groups.

From sorcery to witchcraft

The gradual transformation from sorcery to witchcraft can be seen in popular beliefs as expressed in some stories of the twelfth and thirteenth centuries. William of Newburgh tells a tale about the reign of Henry I (1100–35). A country fellow was walking alone at night past an ancient burial mound. Looking around, he found a door hidden in the side of the mound and entered. Inside was a cave, brightly lit with lamps, where men and women were seated at a solemn banquet. One of them rose, invited the peasant in, and offered him a cup. The farmer pretended to drink but instead secretly poured out the liquid and then hid the cup under his clothing. Returning home, he found the cup to be of rich material and beautiful design, so he took it to King Henry, who gave him a reward. The feeling of this story is still very much the feeling of folklore: these are still fairy folk, not witches. Yet the feasting attributed to the fairies is close enough to the feasting attributed to the heretics to encourage assimilation.

William of Malmesbury tells the story of 'the witch of Berkeley' about 1142. In spite of her traditional name, the woman of Berkeley was still more a sorceress than a witch.

> A woman living at Berkeley was a practitioner of sorcery and ancient divinations. She was a glutton and engaged

in unbounded debaucheries, for she was not as yet an old woman. One day when she was feasting, a jackdaw, one of her favourites, set up a great commotion. When she heard his chattering, she dropped the knife from her hand, turned pale, and groaned: 'Today my plough has come to the end of its row; today I shall hear dreadful news.' [She later heard of the death of her son and his family. Discouraged, she turned her face to the wall to die. Calling her other children to her, she told them that she had lost her soul by practising diabolical arts and pleaded with them for help.] 'Although you cannot lift the sentence that has been passed on my soul, you may be able to save my body. Sew up my corpse in the skin of a stag, lay it on its back in a stone coffin; fasten the lid with lead and iron and lay upon it a stone bound round three times with a heavy chain; and let psalms be sung and masses said for fifty days.' [The children endeavoured to fulfil their dead mother's last wish, but] so heavy was the woman's guilt and so terrible the Devil's violence that their work and their prayers were in vain. For on the first two nights, while the choir of priests was singing psalms around the body, a band of demons smashed the bolt and forced their way through the door of the church. On the third night, towards dawn, the whole monastery was shaken to its foundations by the noise of the approaching enemy. One demon, who was taller and more terrible than the others, broke the gate to pieces. [He called the woman up from the coffin and dragged her out of the church, bearing her off screaming on a black horse.][4]

In the thirteenth century the tales bring the sorcerers ever closer to the Devil. Writing about 1214, Gervaise of Tilbury tells stories that he claims to have garnered from eye-witnesses. Men and women ride out at night over long distances. Certain people have seen their flight as they passed over land and sea. They are able to fly all over the globe, so long as none of them makes the mistake of uttering the name of Christ while in flight, for this will make them immediately fall and plunge to the ground. At Arles, Gervaise himself saw a woman who had thus been plunged into the Rhone and soaked as far as her navel. The witches enter people's houses in the course of these nocturnal journeys. They disturb sleepers by sitting on their chests and causing nightmares of suffocation and falling. They have sexual relations with sleeping men. They suck blood, steal infants from their beds, and rummage through baskets and bins for food. They take the form of cats, wolves, or other animals at will. Caesarius of Heisterbach; writing about 1220, tells of a knight of Liège who lost his money and was persuaded by one of his peasants to call up the Devil for financial assistance. The knight formally renounced God and rendered feudal homage to the Devil in exchange for the improvement of his fortunes. However, when the Devil went so far as to ask him to deny the Blessed Virgin, his chivalry rebelled, and he was saved by our grateful Lady's intervention.

To what extent are such tales popular legend and to what extent learned embroidery? Peasants did not write, so the stories we have are in the language of scholars. The change in emphasis from folklore and sorcery to diabolical witchcraft results in part from the influence of ancient literary tradition going back through the trials at Orleans to the early Church Fathers. The scholars' stories, widely circulated and preached as *exempla* from the pulpit, soon entered into popular culture, so that by the end of the thirteenth century both scholars and ordinary people were prepared to believe in the existence of a widespread witch-cult. This development was speeded by the growth of scholastic theology.

Theology was the fifth major element in the witch concept. Theological concern with the problem of the Devil had been increasing from the mid-twelfth century onwards, largely in response to the introduction of Catharism in the 1140s. Though rejecting the extreme dualism of the Catharists, Christian writers began to place greater emphasis upon the Devil's power as the chief of an army of demons who roamed the world actively attempting to undermine the saving mission of Christ and tempting people to sin. Renunciation of Christ and adoration of the Devil constituted the worst possible sin. The scholastic philosophy and theology that dominated Europe from the twelfth century onwards, though it brought few new elements to the concept of witchcraft, refined details, established rationales, and provided a coherent and authoritative intellectual structure that the witch-hunters could draw upon for support for their ideas.

Scholasticism emphasized the idea of pact. It also firmly established the idea of ritual intercourse between the witches and Satan. The ancient notion of orgy had the worshippers mingling sexually with one another. But the scholastics added to this tradition the notion of the incubus (see plate VII), the demonic spirit that has sexual intercourse with women, and so established the idea that at the sabbat witches submitted sexually to their master Satan.

The scholastics firmly established the tradition that witches were more likely to be women than men. The master of the witch assembly was supposed to be not an inferior demon but the Devil himself, the prince and principle of evil. As an angel, the Devil was sexless, but also as an angel, he could take on either male or female form as he chose. But in theology, literature, and art, he almost invariably appeared as masculine. This is the result of an odd sexual bias. As the principle of evil and age-old adversary of the Lord, the Devil was a figure of great power, almost divinity. The Judaeo-Christian tradition was unable to attach such divinity to a female figure. Like God himself, then, the Devil was almost universally perceived as male. From this it followed that the Devil's sexual activity at the sabbat was that of a male, and though homosexuality was not precluded, he almost invariably cohabited with women. Hence the belief in the preponderance of women at the sabbat. Other suggestions as to the predominance of women have been made (see Chapter 6), but sexist religious assumptions are the most important reason. In the notorious *Malleus Maleficarum* of the late fifteenth century (see p. 77), sexism was explicit. Women, the *Malleus* claimed to demonstrate at length, were more likely than men to be witches because they were weaker, as well as more stupid, superstitious and sensual.

Ideas introduced by the inquisitorial and other courts constitute the last major element in the concept of European witchcraft. In prosecuting the witches with the laws against heresy rather than with the laws against sorcery, the courts finalized the separation of witchcraft from sorcery. English law was an important exception, and witchcraft in England was always associated more with sorcery and less with heresy than on the continent. For this reason, English witches were hanged while their counterparts on the continent were burned: in England the crime of witchcraft was a civil crime, while on the continent it was a crime of religion.

From the twelfth century onwards both civil and canon law became gradually more severe in dealing with heresy. The authorities tightened their control over the courts, aided by the revival of Roman law with its centralized and systematic approach. Under Roman law, men and women were part of the corporation of the state and bound to conform to its principles. In the late Roman Empire, the codes of Theodosius and of Justinian had declared heresy lèse-majesté against God and hence at least as worthy of death as lèse-majesté against the emperor. The revival of such Roman concepts encouraged the imposition of much harsher penalties. Under their influence, German law codes of the thirteenth and fourteenth centuries commonly decreed death both for sorcerers and for relapsed heretics. As the laws tightened, they encouraged active searches for witches. Before the thirteenth century, individual personal accusation had been the only way of bringing a sorcerer to trial. But the bishops had initiated inquisitions – formal investigations – of their dioceses for heresy by the late twelfth century, and under the influence of Roman law the secular courts began to search out malefactors actively. When the authorities began actively seeking for culprits rather than passively waiting for accusations, the witch-craze had started.

Canon law was becoming stricter, partly under the influence of Roman law, partly because of the influence of the scholastic method in law, which called for careful organization and thoroughness. St Augustine had taught that error had no rights (see plate v). St Thomas Aquinas insisted on the rights of the individual conscience but then went on to argue that heresy was a sin because such ignorance must be the result of criminal negligence. All pacts with demons, whether explicit or implicit, were tantamount to apostasy from the Christian faith, Aquinas argued, and this doctrine of 'implicit' pact became a favourite of the witch-hunters. In explicit pact, the individual would literally call up the Devil or a demon and enter into an agreement with him. In implicit pact, such an agreement was not necessary. Anyone who tenaciously professed heresy was assumed to have subjected themself to the Devil whether or not they had called him up, or intended to do so, or indeed even thought it was possible to do so. Under this doctrine all heretics, whatever their doctrines or intentions, were considered implicitly in league with Satan.

From the beginning of the eleventh century, burning was imposed on relapsed heretics with increasing frequency. In 1198 Pope Innocent III called for the execution of those who persisted in heresy after they had been punished by excommunication. As witchcraft was associated with heresy, the punishment of burning was extended to witches as well, and from the fifteenth century onwards, witches were treated even more severely than heretics, being burned on first conviction instead of upon relapse. As fear of heresy and witchcraft grew, torture, a feature of Roman rather than Germanic law, became common practice in Europe.

The inquisition was the most powerful agent in the enforcement of legal sanctions against heretics and witches. So long as heresy was only a minor threat, the Church left responsibility for the correction of dissent in the hands of the bishops. With the growth both of heresy and of ecclesiastical efficiency, the popes began to press for firmer measures. First the bishops were encouraged to expand their own 'inquisitions', and then, in the years between 1227 and 1235, the papal inquisition was established. The power of the inquisition was repeatedly corroborated by papal actions such as the bull *Ad extirpanda* issued by Innocent IV in 1252, which authorized the seizure of heretics' goods and their imprisonment, torture and execution, all on minimal evidence.

The inquisition moved decisively to assimilate sorcery to heresy. The manuals for inquisitors that began to appear about 1230 often included questions on witchcraft as well as on conventional heresy. In 1233 Pope Gregory IX accused the Waldensian heretics – really evangelical moralists – of attending assemblies where the Devil incarnate presided over orgies. Pope Alexander IV (1254–61) refused the request of the inquisition to give it jurisdiction over all sorcery, but he turned over to it all cases of sorcery that 'clearly involved heresy'. The inquisitors rapidly learned to use this loophole and to introduce charges of heresy into sorcery trials. The identification of sorcery with witchcraft had become a bureaucratic and legal convenience. Furthermore, conviction rates rose rapidly, because inquisitorial procedures were constructed in such a way as to make guilt easy to prove and innocence difficult to defend. The inquisitors were taught what to look for, and through examination, threats, and torture usually were able to find witchcraft wherever it existed, and wherever it did not. Each conviction crystallized the image of the witch more concretely in popular consciousness and established yet another precedent for generations of future inquisitors. The stage was now fully furnished for the opening of the great witch-craze.

The Witch-craze on
the Continent of Europe

By 1300 all the elements of European witchcraft had been assembled. For the next century and a half fear of witches spread gradually throughout Europe. Then, about 1450, at the end of the Middle Ages, the fear became a craze that lasted more than two hundred years. The popular idea that the craze was medieval is the result of a false prejudice that links everything bad to the clericalism of the so-called 'Dark Ages'. Rather, the witch-craze was a product of the Renaissance and Reformation. Many of the intellectuals of the Renaissance and leaders of the Reformation were among the most forceful advocates of belief in diabolical witchcraft.

Some historians have attempted to treat the witch-craze in Europe as the anthropologists treat sorcery in Africa, and have looked for the function of witch beliefs in European society. But this approach has limitations. For one thing, European witchcraft is quite different from African sorcery; for another, the social and intellectual conditions of European witchcraft varied widely from area to area and period to period. It is possible to argue that witchcraft was a product of social anxiety and then link its beginnings with the social unrest of the fourteenth century and its plagues, famines, and wars. But that is too simple. Plagues, famines, and wars were endemic in the Middle Ages and early modern period. Every period in human history is troubled, but every period has not produced a witch-craze. Social explanations based more narrowly on local considerations help more, but then it remains difficult to explain why local outbreaks should have melded into a madness that engulfed almost the entire culture.

Historians have long debated the geographical origins of witchcraft. Josef Hansen, followed by Hugh Trevor-Roper, argued that witchcraft began in the mountains, where the thin air was conducive to hallucinations, severe natural phenomena such as storms and avalanches encouraged belief in demonic powers, and ancient sorceries lingered in benighted minds. The view is not wholly fair to mountain dwellers. In fact, witchcraft descended from heresy more than from sorcery and first appeared in the lowland cities where heresy was strong, only later spreading into the mountains where it gained strength from the lingering practices of ancient sorcery. Linked to the mountain theory is the idea that the Dominican inquisitors who led the attack on witchcraft in the fifteenth century generated witch beliefs by bringing into the mountains the unfamiliar social assumptions of the settled, feudal society of the lowlands. The generalization is too broad, but often the local church authorities did resist the inquisitors, and the intrusion of the Dominicans did generate tensions that promoted witch beliefs.

Psychology helps explain the craze. People projected evil desires and passions most easily upon isolated and lonely outsiders such as old widows and crones. Some of the accused, driven by fear and guilt, came to believe in their own guilt. The crazed nuns of Louviers and Loudun (see p. 86) apparently believed that they made love with the Devil. The witch-craze is an important study in human evil, comparable to Nazism and Stalinism in the twentieth century.

Legal sanctions against witchcraft grew steadily harsher as the notion grew that all sorcery involved pact with the Devil. The increasing harshness of legal theory was matched by the rising cruelty of legal practice. Each new conviction justified harsher measures, including torture; torture produced more confessions,

confessions produced more convictions, and belief and repression fed one another.

A new intellectual ideology helped turn this vicious wheel. Many of the great Renaissance humanists were magicians. The Neoplatonism of these learned high magicians was quite different from the Aristotelianism that in scholastic circles encouraged the growth of witch beliefs. Neoplatonism held that magic could be worked by natural means, Aristotelianism that all magic had to be done with the aid of spirits. Yet the rise of the witch-craze was concurrent with the rise of Renaissance magic. The humanists' belief in magic entailed belief in witchcraft, however much they took pains to insist that the wise and benevolent magic they practised was quite different from the evil magic of the witches. And this distinction was generally lost on public opinion, with the result that humanistic magic itself abetted the rise of the witch-craze.

Theologians and jurists agreed that witchcraft was the worst of heresies. In the early fifteenth century tracts dealing specifically with diabolical witchcraft began to appear. The scepticism and moderation that had characterized the medieval Canon Episcopi yielded more and more to belief that witchcraft was a sinister plot against the Church conceived and promoted by Satan himself. A learned debate on the reality of witchcraft continued between sceptics and believers, but after the publication of the *Malleus Maleficarum* in 1486 (see plate xv), the believers dominated for two centuries. 'It is rating our conjectures too highly to roast people alive for them,' the sceptic Montaigne exclaimed, but his was a minority voice. Ironically, the invention of the printing press in the 1450s at just the time that treatises on witchcraft were becoming common propagated the craze more rapidly. The invention of printing, like that of television later, did not necessarily promote wisdom or virtue.

At the beginning of the fourteenth century the old elements of folklore and heresy were still shaping witchcraft. In Austria a group of heretics were accused of worshipping Lucifer and believing that he would one day be restored to heaven while St Michael was cast into hell. On meeting, the heretics hailed one another with the words, 'May the injured Lucifer greet you'. They were supposed to have underground orgies, and one young woman was said to argue that she was a virgin above ground though sexually experienced under the earth. These Luciferans also preached doctrines similar to those of the Catharists and Waldensians. The Waldensians (*vaudois* in French) were actually reform-minded heretics, but so closely did the orthodox perceive the connection between witches and Waldensians that the witches were often called *vaudois*, and *aller en vauderie* came to mean 'to go to the witches' meeting'. The most common term for the meeting continued to be 'synagogue', though 'sabbat', equally insulting to Jews, became common in the next century.

Carlo Ginzburg carefully investigated the only reliable evidence for the existence of a fertility cult in the period of the craze.[1] In Friuli, northern Italy, the *benandanti* were members of a group that practised rites to insure the fertility of the fields and a good harvest. But the inquisitors associated these rites with the Canon Episcopi and the nocturnal gatherings to worship Diana/Holda, and thus translated the meetings of the *benandanti* into diabolical sabbats.

From the beginning of the fourteenth century onwards the concept of witchcraft underwent little further development, remaining almost static for the next three hundred years. Some geographical variations persisted. In England, for example, as we have seen, the *maleficia* – evil sorceries – of the witches were emphasized much more than the linkage of witchcraft with heresy (of which there was relatively little in England). In Scotland, the term coven, a variant of convent, from Latin *conventus*, 'assembly', was introduced about 1500 as a name for the witches' meeting and then, by extension, as a name for the local group of practising witches. The term was seldom used until the modern witchcraft revival. In Spain, the relatively scrupulous fairness of the Spanish inquisition generally limited the manifestations of witchcraft in that country to simple sorcery. Diabolical witchcraft developed primarily in France, Germany, Switzerland, the Low Countries, and northern Italy – areas where heresy had been strong – and then spread into Scandinavia in the sixteenth and seventeenth centuries.

The growth of the witch-craze

The early fourteenth century produced the first vicious use of witch accusations for political purposes. Often in this early stage of the craze the accused were clergymen or other learned people who were capable of reading and writing magic. (By the end of the fourteenth century, accusations had spread more widely to ordinary people.) Pope Boniface VIII (d. 1303) was tried posthumously by his enemies for apostasy, murder, and sodomy. He allegedly entered into a pact with the Devil for the purpose of encompassing the ruin of the Christian people. Popes had been deposed before and accused of crimes, but the charge of demonolatry was new. Philip IV of France accused Bishop Guichard of Troyes of doing homage to the Devil. Under Edward I of England (1272–1307) accusations of *maleficia* were brought against Walter, bishop of Lichfield and Coventry. In 1317–19, Pope John XXII, obsessed with the fear of witchcraft, accused a doctor, a barber, and a clergyman of plotting against his life through magic. Pope John went on to issue the bull *Super illius specula*, specifically authorizing the inquisition to proceed against all sorcerers, since they adored demons and had made 'a pact with hell'. The inquisitor Bernard Gui affirmed that witchcraft implied pact, pact implied heresy, and since the inquisition had the duty to proceed against heretics it also had the duty to proceed against witches. But politicians, not inquisitors, engineered the infamous trial of the Templars in 1305–14.

Originally the Order of the Temple had been founded to liberate the Holy Land from the Muslims, but the Templars had become rich and corrupt and now presented a tempting target to rulers whose governmental costs were rapidly rising. Pope Clement V, King Philip IV of France, and King Edward II of England succeeded in having the Templars condemned as heretics, claiming that they invoked the Devil, rendered him homage, veneration, and service, and made a pact with him. The fame and eminence of the case spread the belief that an organized religion rejecting Christ and worshipping Satan existed.

The middle years of the fourteenth century saw a lull in the craze. The evidence for substantial witch trials at Toulouse and Carcassonne in the period 1330–50 has been proven a forgery. Then, towards the end of the century, the number of accusations increased. Many secular courts adopted inquisitorial procedures, doing away with judicial penalties for accusers failing to prove their cases. Secular, episcopal, and inquisitorial courts shared the burden, and the profit, of the witch prosecutions down through the fifteenth century. In 1398 the University of Paris declared the working of *maleficia* a heresy if it was accomplished through pact with the Devil. The pact might be explicit or implicit. No document needed to be signed or official promise given: the mere act of summoning demons constituted an implied pact and rendered the accused subject to prosecution for heresy. In such an atmosphere witch trials began to take on a standard form. Inquisitors' manuals listed the questions that were to be put to the accused, and torture or fear of torture readily elicited confessions such as those of 1387–8 in Lombardy. A small group was arrested for heresy. In the course of the interrogation they were tortured and compelled to implicate most of the town in the crime. Though their basic doctrines seem to have been a mixture of Waldensianism and Catharism, they confessed that both men and women in 'synagogue' once or twice a month formally renounced the Catholic faith and adored Satan as their God. Satan, they claimed, would one day defeat

Christ. They feasted and drank loathsome potions; then, with lights extinguished, they fell to an orgy where each seized the one next to him. These clichés were derived from the inquisitorial model, and each trial reinforced the model.

As belief and confessions reinforced one another, the number of trials increased radically, especially in France, Germany, and the Alps. In a book about the trials Richard Kieckhefer argues that the prime responsibility falls on the intellectuals.[2] Accusations commonly began, he says, with charges of simple sorcery. The courts, whether secular, ecclesiastical, or inquisitorial, then presented the accused with a list of the crimes the courts expected, and the original charge of sorcery was transformed into witchcraft.

The standardization of witch accusations produced a dramatic change in the powers assigned to the Devil. Hitherto, the witch making a pact with Satan enjoyed almost a contractual equality with the dark lord; further, she was frequently rescued from the effects of her folly by the intervention of the Virgin or another saint. Now, the Devil's power over her once she had made the pact was complete, and her soul was damned. Her only hope of salvation was to be arrested and to recant before her execution. By such reasoning the torment and killing of witches was for their own good as well as that of God and of society.

Joan of Arc and Gilles de Rais both frequently appear in histories of witchcraft, but neither is relevant. Witch charges were very much in the background in both trials. Joan was condemned – for political reasons of course – on charges of heresy, not of witchcraft. Gilles was a sexual pervert and murderer whose alleged activities bear no resemblance to those alleged against the witches.

The trial of an old man in southern France in 1438 is typical of the period. Pierre Vallin was charged with witchcraft and seized by the inquisition. Allowed no defence, he was repeatedly tortured. The record of the trial states that he made his confession 'voluntarily', which simply means that he was tortured, removed from the place of torture, and then given the choice of confessing voluntarily or of being returned for more torture. Pierre confessed to invoking Beelzebub, to whom he used habitually to kneel and pay tribute. He had served the Devil for sixty-three years, during which time he had denied God, trampled and spat on the cross, and sacrificed his own baby daughter. He went regularly to the 'synagogue', where he copulated with Beelzebub, who had taken the form of a girl – only this is unusual – and where he and the other witches ate the flesh of innocent children. The judges condemned him as a heretic, idolater, apostate, and invoker of demons. All his worldly possessions were confiscated and, after the expenses of the trial were deducted, a third of what remained was reserved for the archbishop and the inquisition. But that was not enough. Pierre was required to name his accomplices. He was tortured again and again for a week, until he had named a number of people. His ultimate fate and theirs is not known, but it is probable that they were burned to death. The inquisitors' repeated efforts to persuade Pierre to name not only poor men but 'priests, clergymen, nobles and rich men' indicate that thoughts of confiscation were not absent from their minds.

Tens of thousands of such trials continued throughout Europe generation after generation, while Leonardo painted, Palestrina composed, and Shakespeare wrote. The witches in *Macbeth* may be difficult to take seriously today, but *Macbeth* was written in the reign of James I, who hanged more witches than any other English monarch.

The craze, far from declining at the end of the fifteenth century, took on new strength. In large part this was owing to the efforts of the German inquisitor Heinrich Institoris. Institoris, born near Strasbourg about 1430, entered the Dominican Order. A clever politician, he acquired influential friends in Rome and was appointed inquisitor in southern Germany in 1474. At first he investigated heresy but in 1476 began to devote himself almost exclusively to witchcraft. Helped at first by his Dominican colleague Jakob Sprenger, who later repented and condemned him, Institoris compiled a record of great severity and corruption. He was condemned by his own Order in 1490 for embezzlement and other crimes, but he was still active as a witch-hunter at the turn of the century. Through his influence at the papal court, he persuaded Innocent VIII to issue the bull *Summis desiderantes affectibus*, 'Wishing with the greatest concern' (1484), which confirmed full papal support for the work of the inquisition against witches.

In 1486, Institoris published the *Malleus Maleficarum*, 'the Hammer against the Witches', with the pope's approval and with the bull of 1484 as preface. The *Malleus* was reprinted in fourteen editions by 1520. Well-organized, impassioned, and enjoying papal approval, the *Malleus* became one of the most influential of all early printed books. Its influence overwhelmed the moderate tradition within the Catholic Church. The *Malleus* declared that the four essential points of witchcraft were: renunciation of the Catholic faith, devotion of body and soul to the service of evil, offering up unbaptized children to the Devil, and engaging in orgies that included intercourse with the Devil. In addition, witches typically shifted their shapes, flew through the air, abused the Christian sacraments, and confected magical ointments. The great majority of witches were women, and the reason for this is, Institoris declared, that women are more stupid, fickle, lighter-headed, weaker, and more carnal than men. All witches, men and women, must be accused, arrested, convicted, and executed.

With the *Malleus*, witchcraft theory caught up with and surpassed the practice of the courts. In his description of the witch trials in Lorraine, Etienne Delcambre argues that most judges were honest, sincere, and idealistic men who believed that they were performing a necessary service for society, God, and even the accused, whose soul they hoped to save by extracting confession.[3] If a person were innocent of the accusations, they believed that God would intervene to save them from torment. Delcambre suggests that often the accused may have shared this belief, for in Lorraine only 10 per cent persisted in denying their guilt to the moment of death, the rest confessing in the hope of obtaining a gentler execution or of sparing their families further persecution. Some of the accused even took the opportunity to bring personal enemies down with them in death. One defendant in the region of Bar accused all the officers of the court from the judges down to the court clerk of being witches. On the whole, the use of torture is sufficient explanation for most of the confessions.

Some torments were designed to test the guilt or innocence of the witch, such as 'swimming' (see plate x). A survival of the ancient ordeal by water, 'swimming the witch' involved tying the accused hand and foot and throwing her into deep water. If she sank, it was a sign that God's creature water accepted her, and she was deemed innocent and hauled ashore. If she floated, the water rejected her, and she was judged guilty. Another test was weighing. The witch was placed on one side of the scale and the Bible on the other. If the witch weighed lighter than the Bible, she was guilty. Another was pricking. Witches were thought to have insensitive spots on their bodies where the Devil had marked them. Sometimes these Devil's marks were visible as a scar or mole, but sometimes they were invisible and could be detected only by pricking the accused all over with a sharp instrument until such an area of insensitivity were found. Another was the search for the witch's mark. The witch's mark, quite distinct from the Devil's mark, was any unusual protuberance on the body that could conceivably be considered a supernumerary teat that the demons might suck in the form of familiars. Witches were stripped and searched minutely for any such sign of their traffic with evil.

Other tortures were devised to elicit confessions and the implication of accomplices. The infamous witch-house of Bamberg contained thumbscrews, leg vices, whipping stocks furnished with iron spikes, scalding lime baths, prayer stools furnished with sharp pegs, racks, the strappado (see plate xi) and other devices. In the strappado, the prisoner's arms were tied behind his back with a rope attached to a pulley, and he was then hoisted in the air. Frequently, weights were attached to his feet to pull his shoulders from their sockets without leaving visible marks of rough treatment. Sometimes toescrews and thumbscrews were applied while the victim was suspended.[4]

The tortured were confronted by standard lists of questions and in their agony usually confessed to most of what was put to them. Each confession convinced the authorities of the validity of the lists and reinforced their use at the next trial. The list prepared for the judges at Colmar in Alsace is typical:

How long have you been a witch? Why did you become a witch? How did you become a witch, and what happened on the occasion? [What demon did you choose to be your lover?] What was his name? What was the name of your master among the evil demons? What was the oath you were forced to render him? How did you make this oath, and what were its conditions? ... Where did you consummate your union with your incubus? What demons and what other humans participated [at the sabbat]? ... How was the sabbat banquet arranged? ... What devil's mark did your incubus make on your body? What injury have you done to such and such a person, and how did you do it? ... Who are the children on whom you have cast a spell? ... Who are your accomplices in evil? ... What is the ointment with which you rub your broomstick made of? How are you able to fly through the air?[5]

The question was not whether you had done it, but when and how you had done it.

The Protestant Reformation of the sixteenth century aimed at eradicating the accretions of doctrine in the Middle Ages and insisted upon a return to the apostolic age. But one accretion of doctrine they did not choose to jettison was belief in witchcraft. The Protestants pursued witches with comparable cruelty and in comparable numbers to the Catholics. Luther argued with his typical violence that all witches should be burned as heretics for having made a pact with the Devil, even if there was no evidence that they had done anyone any overt harm. The witches, he said, were an important battalion in the vast legion of enemies that the Devil was assembling against the true Church. Calvin, whose doctrines emphasized the omnipotence of God, found less room for witchcraft in his theology than Lutherans or Catholics, but he accepted the reality of witchcraft and its danger to Christian society. Persecutions in Calvinist territories were (except at Geneva itself) comparable to those in other regions.

In Germany the Protestants were more severe in the sixteenth century and the Catholics in the seventeenth. In France, the Catholics were worse, but in countries won to the Protestant cause, such as England, Scotland, and Scandinavia, the persecutions were nearly as bad. In some Catholic countries, such as Spain and Portugal, very few witch trials occurred. Variations in time and region were great, but in general the Protestants do not seem to have taken advantage of the fact that they were not bound by the views of the *Malleus* and of the bull of Innocent VIII. These documents were based upon a long tradition of witch beliefs that the Protestants accepted as fully as did the Catholics.

Prosecution of witches by Christians of all persuasions increased enormously in the sixteenth century, as the religious conflicts, popular movements, and wars engendered by the Reformation exacerbated the social tensions that produced witchcraft. The 'Caroline Code' or *Constitutio Criminalis Carolina*, the basic law code of the Holy Roman Empire issued in 1532, imposed heavy penalties on witchcraft. Witch fears were also fuelled by the increasing number of tracts and books on popular theology issued for an increasingly literate population, books that emphasized the power of the Devil and portrayed him as responsible for most human sins and vices.

The climax of the witch-craze

The height of the witch-craze occurred between 1560 and 1660. Increasing tensions between Protestant and Catholic, worsening into war, were the most important cause. The craze was most severe in areas where religious strife was linked with strong social antagonisms, where misfortunes such as storms, plagues, and famines heightened social tensions, and wherever, as in France, a long tradition of heresy trials had laid the basis for judicial repression of witchcraft. Both ecclesiastical and secular prosecution of witchcraft increased greatly in scope and severity during these years, particularly in the Catholic areas of Europe. After 1580, the more thorough Jesuits replaced the Dominicans as the chief Catholic witch-hunters, and the Catholic Rudolf II (1576–1612) presided over a long and cruel persecution in Austria. Geographical variations in the trials continued to occur. William Monter has shown that witch panics were not so severe in the Jura Mountains as in southern Germany and that in the Jura many arrested suspects were not convicted. In the Jura, Monter explains, torture was imposed only within the precise limits of the Caroline Code of 1532, little attention was paid to the accusations and confessions of children, and specific *maleficia* had to be charged openly and publicly against a suspect before he could be arrested.[6] Such legal limitations could contain the mania; in areas where they were ignored, anyone and everyone could be accused.

Rossell Hope Robbins charged that the chief motive behind the prosecutions was the desire to appropriate the property of the condemned. If this were so, we would expect to find a relatively high percentage of rich and powerful people condemned and a large over-all number of decrees of confiscation. In fact we find neither. The number of confiscations was relatively small, and a disproportionately great number of people convicted were of small means. It was generally only in areas where the craze was completely out of hand that people of substantial means were convicted. One of the exceptions was Dietrich Flade, burned at Trier for witchcraft in 1589.

Flade was a secular judge at Trier, a man of prominent family and connections who became rector of the University of Trier. For a while he was himself in charge of the prosecution of witches. In that capacity he was judicious and restrained, demanding careful presentation of evidence. His moderation was fiercely opposed by the suffragan bishop Peter Binsfeld and the governor, Johann Zandt, who had had experience as a witch-hunter in the countryside around Trier. The efforts of Binsfeld and Zandt to obtain fiercer prosecution of witches gathered popular support after 1580 when bad climatic conditions, plagues of mice and locusts, and ravaging freebooters of both religious persuasions rendered people fearful and anxious. Times were bad: the witches must be responsible. Flade's continued efforts to keep the mania under control led his enemies to devise a plan to remove him. They caused a boy to accuse Flade of plotting to poison the archbishop; they persuaded an old woman who was about to be executed to name Flade as a witch in order to obtain the mercy of strangulation before burning; other accusations followed, until on 15 April 1588 a woman swore that she had seen Flade at a sabbat, that he had caused the destruction of crops by hail, slugs, and snails, and that he had persuaded the other witches present to eat a child's heart. Flade was arrested and tortured. His pain was intense, and he finally confessed that he had attended sabbats, had intercourse with the Devil, and magically formed mud into living slugs to destroy the crops. Flade was strangled and burnt, but not before he had been forced under torture to name accomplices, thus widening the circle of accusations, assuring Binsfeld and Zandt of more victims, and providing the peasants more scapegoats for their troubles.

Simple people were much more frequently accused than prominent men such as Flade. In 1587 Walpurga Hausmannin, a midwife, was tried and burnt at Dillingen. Arrested and tortured, she admitted to having intercourse with the Devil and making a pact with him, riding out at night on a pitchfork, trampling on the consecrated host, keeping a familiar named Federlin as a lover, manufacturing hailstorms, and committing a long list of *maleficia* relating to her duties as midwife. She rubbed Anna Hämännin during childbirth with a salve that caused both mother and child to die. She crushed the brain of Dorothea Wachter's baby while delivering it. She poisoned the child of Anna Kromt. She rubbed a salve on the son of the Chancellor, giving the boy a hobby horse to ride until he lost his senses and died. She sucked the blood out of one of the twin children of the publican Kuntz. Forty-three of these charges of *maleficia* were combined with the accusations of demon worship.[7] The process is simple. A number of children die. The midwife is a lonely and unpopular widow. Blame for the deaths is fixed on her and expressed in supernatural terms. She must therefore be a witch. But it is well known that all witches fly out at night, make pacts with the Devil, and practise other kinds of demonolatry. Questions about all this are put to her under torture, and in her agony and fear she confesses. The confession again reinforces the accepted image of the witch. Misfortunes are interpreted as evil deeds, evil deeds are seen as sorcery, sorcery is perceived as witchcraft, and another human being is tortured and killed.

Some contemporaries recognized the injustice. In 1563, Johann Weyer wrote a treatise *On Magic*, which argued that witches were really harmless old women suffering from mental disorders and that most alleged cases of witchcraft were really susceptible of natural explanations. But Jean Bodin and other intellectual leaders hastened to refute this voice of moderation, accusing Weyer himself of being a witch, and arguing that the similarity of the confessions proved the fact that the sabbat was always and everywhere identical. A little later, in 1602, Henri Boguet wrote in his *Discours des sorciers* that he wished that all witches should be 'united in one single body, so that they might all be burned at once in a single fire.' This mania, this eagerness to torture and kill human beings, persisted for centuries. Perhaps we put the wrong question when we ask how this could be. The past hundred years have witnessed the Holocaust, the Gulag Archipelago, the Cambodian and Rwandan genocides, and secret tortures and executions beyond number. The real question is why periods of relative sanity, such as those from 700 to 1000 and from 1700 to 1900, occur.

For the seventeenth century was as bloody as the sixteenth. A century of religious strife culminated in the Thirty Years War of 1618–48 that ravaged Germany and involved most of Europe. In such a time the persecutions increased, notably at Cologne in 1625–36 and in Bamberg, where from 1623 to 1633 Bishop Johann Georg II burnt at least 600 witches, trying them in the notorious 'witch-house' (see plate XIII), mentioned above, where he had constructed a torture chamber whose walls were adorned by biblical texts. It was at Bamberg that one of the most infamous prosecutions occurred, that of Johannes Junius.

Junius was examined on 28 June 1628. Maintaining his innocence, he demanded to be confronted with a single human being who had seen him at a sabbat. One Doctor Georg Haan, probably hoping to buy mercy for himself by accusing others, was brought in and swore on his own life that he had seen Junius a year and a half earlier at a sabbat. Next a servant woman swore that she had seen him at a sabbat where the Eucharist was desecrated. Junius denied both accusations, but he was warned that other accomplices had confessed against him and that he had best admit his crimes. On 30 June he was examined again, though the threatened witnesses did not appear, and he again refused to confess. He was then tortured, first with thumbscrews and then with legscrews. He was stripped and examined, and a bluish mark was found on his right side. This Devil's mark was pricked. He was then put to the strappado. On 5 July, 'without torture, but with urgent persuasions' – i.e., threat of torture – Junius at last confessed to worshipping the Devil, attending the sabbats, performing *maleficia*, and other clichés of witchcraft.

What makes Junius unusually interesting is that he was able to bribe the jailer before his execution to smuggle out a letter. It is dated 24 July 1628 and is addressed to his daughter:

Many hundred thousand good-nights, dearly beloved daughter Veronica. Innocent have I come into prison, innocent have I been tortured, innocent must I die. For whoever comes into the witch prison must…be tortured until he invents something out of his head…. When I was the first time put to the torture, Dr Braun, Dr Kötzendörffer, and two strange doctors were there. Then Dr Braun asks me, 'Kinsman, how come you here?' I answer, 'Through falsehood, though misfortune.' 'Hear, you,' he retorts, 'you are a witch; will you confess it voluntarily? If not, we'll bring in witnesses and the executioner for you.' I said, 'I am no witch, I have a pure conscience in the matter; if there are a thousand witnesses, I am not anxious.' [The witnesses were brought forward.] And then came also – God in highest heaven have mercy – the executioner, and put the thumbscrews on me, both hands bound together, so that the blood ran out at the nails and everywhere, so that for four weeks I could not use my hands, as you can see from the writing…. Thereafter they first stripped me, bound my hands behind me, and drew me up in the [strappado]. Then I thought heaven and earth were at an end; eight times did they draw me up and let me fall again, so that I suffered terrible agony…. And so I made my confession…, but it was all a lie. Now follows, dear child, what I confessed in order to escape the great anguish and bitter torture, which it was impossible for me longer to bear. [He reported his confession.] Then I had to tell what people I had seen [at the sabbat]. I said that I had not recognized them. 'You old rascal, I must set the executioner at you. Say – was not the Chancellor there?' So I said yes.

'Who besides?' I had not recognized anybody. So he said: 'Take one street after another; begin at the market, go out on one street and back on the next.' I had to name several persons there. Then came the long street. I knew nobody. Had to name eight persons there.... And thus continually they asked me on all the streets, though I could not and would not say more. So they gave me to the executioner, told him to strip me, shave me all over, and put me to the torture.... Then I had to tell what crimes I had committed. I said nothing.... 'Draw the rascal up!' So I said that I was to kill my children, but I had killed a horse instead. It did not help. I had also taken a sacred wafer, and had desecrated it. When I had said this, they left me in peace.... Dear child, keep this letter secret... else I shall be tortured most piteously and the jailers will be beheaded.... Good night, for your father Johannes Junius will never see you more.[8]

Witchcraft hysteria produced a number of bizarre by-products in the early seventeenth century, among them cases of diabolism in convents, notably at Aix-en-Provence in 1611, Loudun in 1630, and Louviers in 1647. Not typical of witchcraft, these cases nonetheless illustrate the obsession of society with witchcraft and diabolism, and how under certain conditions frightened and suggestible people readily believed themselves to be in communion with Satan.

The story of the nuns of Loudun, made infamous by the novel of Aldous Huxley and the film of Ken Russell, requires little embroidery. It began as a plot by the enemies of Father Urbain Grandier, confessor at the Ursuline convent of Loudun. The mother superior and several of the nuns pretended to be possessed and accused Father Grandier of bewitching them. They feigned convulsions, rolled and gibbered on the ground, and accused Grandier of numerous indecencies. Grandier was no exemplary priest, but the evidence that he was a witch was deliberately and cleverly faked, including a silly alleged pact written right to left in Latin and signed by Satan, Beelzebub, Lucifer, Leviathan, and other evil spirits, one of whom marked his name with a drawing of a pitchfork. In spite of such ridiculous subterfuges, and despite the fact that many of the nuns who had accused the priest publicly recanted, Grandier's enemies were not to be deterred. He was tortured lengthily and denied even the small grace of strangulation before being placed in the flames.

But now events took an odd turn. The original plot having succeeded, no reasons remained for the nuns to feign possession. Yet their symptoms only grew worse. One nun

> fell to the ground, blaspheming, in convulsions, lifting up her petticoats and chemise, displaying her privy parts without any shame, and uttering filthy words. Her gestures became so indecent that the audience averted its eyes. She cried out again and again, abusing herself with her hands, 'Come on, then, f— me!' [At other times the nuns] struck their chests and backs with their heads, as if they had their necks broken, and with inconceivable rapidity.... Their faces became so fright-ful one could not bear to look at them; their eyes remained open without winking. Their tongues issued suddenly from their mouths, horribly swollen, black, hard, and covered with pimples.... They threw themselves back till their heads touched their feet, and walked in this position with wonderful rapidity, and for a long time. They uttered cries so horrible and so loud that nothing like it was ever heard before. They made use of expressions so indecent as to shame the most debauched of men....[9]

From pretending to be possessed, the nuns had in fact come to believe themselves possessed. Delusion had bred psychosis. Such events indicate the degree to which the social mania of witchcraft produced insanity in individuals.

But the fever was already past its peak. In 1687 Louis XIV issued an edict against *sorcellerie*. It was refreshingly moderate; condemning sorcery, it ignored black cats, sex-crazed nuns, and other lurid fantasies of the witch-mania. The worst was over. After 1700, the number of witches accused, tried and condemned fell off rapidly. The decline of the witch-craze is as interesting as its rise, but before we lay it to rest we will want to look at its course in Britain and the American colonies.

Witchcraft in Britain and America

Witchcraft in the British Isles

Witchcraft in the British Isles differed substantially from continental witchcraft. On the continent, heresy, law, theology, and inquisition transformed the old traditions of sorcery into a cult of Satan. But in England there was no inquisition, no Roman law, and only a weak tradition of heresy. The most important medieval dissent in England, that of the Lollards, was a moderate heresy with few continental connections, and it was never associated with witchcraft. English witchcraft remained closer to sorcery, though with greatly increased emphasis upon the negative powers of the witch to hex and curse. Notorious political cases such as that of the Duchess of Gloucester, accused in 1441 of plotting to kill Henry VI by witchcraft, abetted the rise of the delusion, but during the Middle Ages the British Isles were almost free of the concept of witchcraft as devil-worship.

The one important medieval exception proving the rule is unusual in almost every respect. This is the case of Dame Alice Kyteler. Dame Alice lived in Kilkenny in Ireland, and the case shows signs of Irish folk-elements as well as the more usual aspects of witchcraft and sorcery. Alice was a wealthy woman who had had four husbands and who infuriated her elder children by bequeathing all her property to her youngest child. In 1324, the elder children accused their mother and her companions before the bishop, who condemned her as a heretic and magician. The introduction of the charge of heresy is incongruous in fourteenth-century Ireland, and the catalogue of charges brought against Dame Alice is a strange mélange of English, continental, and Irish ideas. The most probable explanation is that for venal and political motives the bishop, Richard Ledrede, who had lived in London and knew something about the continental tradition, put together a hodgepodge of charges in order to gratify Alice's sons.

According to the account of the trial, Dame Alice had renounced Christ and the Church in order to obtain magical powers. She had sacrificed animals to demons, notably to her familiar, a minor demon by the name of Robert or Robin Artisson. Robin, one of the first named familiars in witchcraft, was probably a version of an Irish folk spirit to whom the attributes of continental demons were attached by Bishop Ledrede. Robin appeared as a cat, a shaggy dog, or a black man; as a black man he was accompanied by two taller comrades, one of whom bore an iron rod in his hands. These demons taught Lady Alice the arts of witchcraft, and under their instruction she learned to make loathsome ointments and other concoctions. She gave everything she possessed to the demons (the not too subtle hand of Alice's elder sons is visible in this charge), and they straightaway returned it for her use during her lifetime. Robin was Alice's demon lover, and at night the lady would gather her associates by candlelight. Blowing out the candles and calling out 'Fi fi fi, amen', they would fall into a sexual orgy. Alice and her friends were a group of twelve, so that with Robin as their master they mocked the number of Christ and his apostles. The concept and name of the coven were as yet two hundred years in the future, but the notion that a heresiarch would take twelve followers in imitation of Christ and the apostles was longstanding in the history of continental heresy. Dame Alice escaped with a fine, but at least one of her less influential associates was burnt.

The Kyteler case had little if any influence on subsequent trials, and the wide gap separating English from continental witchcraft continued well into the sixteenth century. Though the *Malleus Maleficarum* enjoyed fourteen editions by 1520, it had no English translation until modern times. As late as the 1560s, Essex witches differed markedly from their continental colleagues: they did not fly, meet for orgies, dance and feast, or practise sexual perversions. Most significantly, they did not sign a pact with the Devil or worship him. Rather, English witches, like African sorcerers, caused disease and fits, harmed livestock, hurt infants and small children, and kept familiars. Familiars were found on the continent, especially in Germany, but they were most common in England, where they had curious names such as Vinegar Tom, Pyewacket, Tibb, Sack and Sugar, or Grizel Gree-diguts. Is it possible that the English and German predilection for familiars stemmed from their fondness for pets? But these beings were in their origins the little people of folklore, transformed by Christian theology into demons and hence acquiring sinister attributes: they had intercourse with the witches, or sucked the blood of their mistresses through 'witches' teats'. The search for the witch's teat, or supernumerary protuberance, was one of the most appalling aspects of prosecution for witchcraft in England. In Scotland, pricking was more in favour. Concern about witchcraft was still moderate in England through the reign of Elizabeth I. John Dee (1527–1608), a magician having considerable influence at court, had a large library on all aspects of magic, including continental witchcraft, but continental ideas were still far from English practice.

The first statute against witchcraft in England was passed by Parliament in 1542, towards the end of the reign of Henry VIII, and it was soon revoked in 1547. A new statute was issued under Elizabeth I in 1563, ordering the death penalty for witches, enchanters, and sorcerers. These individuals were to be prosecuted under civil, not ecclesiastical law, and for this reason witches in England were always hanged rather than burnt as on the continent.

The first major trial under the statute of 1563 was at Chelmsford in Essex in 1566, a trial setting an unhappy precedent for later cases.

Elizabeth Francis, Agnes Waterhouse, and Agnes' daughter Joan were charged with witchcraft. Elizabeth had supposedly bewitched a child and committed other evil deeds or *maleficia*. Such were the charges originally brought, but a confession she allegedly made expanded the scope of her crimes considerably. According to the confession, she had learned witchcraft from her grandmother when she was twelve years old. The grandmother taught her to renounce God and gave her a white spotted cat named Sathan, who was in fact the Devil in animal form. Elizabeth was to nourish it with her own blood as well as with more traditional bread and milk. Elizabeth learned to speak with the cat, who promised her (in a hollow voice) that she would have riches. Sathan brought her livestock and promised her one Andrew Byles as a husband; when Byles refused marriage after enjoying her favours, Sathan caused his death and taught her how to abort the child that she was carrying. She later married and had a daughter, but the infant annoyed her, and she caused Sathan to murder it. Finally, after enjoying the cat's help for sixteen years, she gave it to Agnes Waterhouse in exchange for a cake. Agnes, wishing to divert to other purposes the wool that lined the cat's box, changed his Satanic Majesty into a toad; with its help Agnes effected a number of *maleficia*, drowning cows, killing geese, and spoiling butter. Both Elizabeth and Agnes gave Sathan blood that they produced by pricking their bodies; the evidence was found in the shape of blemishes on the bodies of the accused. Agnes was hanged in 1566 (her daughter Joan was found not guilty); Elizabeth received a lighter sentence but was hanged after a second conviction thirteen years later. The Chelmsford trial was typical of English witchcraft in many ways: the absurdity of the charges, the emphasis upon the familiar, and the lack of the classic, continental insistence upon pact, orgy, and homage to the Devil.

At the Essex assizes of 1579 several women were arraigned for witchcraft. Ellen Smythe was one of them. Her daughter had had a quarrel with a child named Susan Webbe. Encountering Susan,

Ellen gave the child a blow on the head, so that two days later she died. Directly after her death, Susan's mother saw 'a thing like a black dog go out of her door'. Ellen was hanged. Margery Stanton used magic to kill chickens, and caused a woman to swell up as if pregnant and cattle to give blood instead of milk. She was released for lack of evidence against her. Joan or Jane Prentice, charged at the assize of 1589, first encountered the Devil while sitting in her chamber. He came to her in the form of a 'dunnish coloured ferret' and said, 'Jane Prentice, give me thy soul.' She replied: 'In the name of God, what art thou?' And the ferret returned: 'I am Satan; fear me not.' Jane Prentice was also hanged.[1]

This was fertile soil for the sowing of continental ideas. These eventually made their way to England by way of Scotland, whose King James VI was a learned proponent of the witch-craze. James was convinced of the reality of witchcraft by the trial of the North Berwick witches in 1590–92. A young girl named Gilly Duncan had the reputation of being able to aid and cure the sick. Her employer, convinced that she must have diabolical powers, took it upon himself to torture her until she confessed that she had received help from the Devil. Justified by her confession, he turned her over for prosecution, and under threat of further torture Gilly accused a large number of men and women in and around Edinburgh. One of these, Agnes Sampson, an elderly woman of good education and reputation, was examined by the king himself. Since she refused to confess, she was stripped, shaved, and searched until the devil's mark was found.

> She was fastened to the wall of her cell by a witch's bridle, an iron instrument with four sharp prongs forced into the mouth, so that two prongs pressed against the tongue, and the two others against the cheeks. She was kept without sleep.[2]

Not surprisingly, Agnes eventually confessed. A large company of men and women had sailed in sieves to North Berwick on

Hallowe'en, she said. They danced, entered a church illuminated by black candles, and did homage to the Devil in the form of a man, whose buttocks they kissed. The witches plotted to raise a storm to sink the king's ship as he sailed to Denmark; if this failed, Agnes planned to work magic against the king with toad's blood. The evidence given by Agnes and the other accused brought many of them to the stake, a punishment approved under Scottish law. This trial had great influence because of James' attention to it, and it set the pattern for many seventeenth-century trials in both Scotland and England.

The bulk of learned opinion in England remained moderate throughout the sixteenth century. Reginald Scot's *Discoverie of Witchcraft* (1584) offered a distinctively Protestant argument against belief in witchcraft. Protestants affirmed that the age of miracles had ended with the death of the last apostle. Since God no longer worked marvels himself, Scot argued, he clearly would no longer permit the Devil to do so. But the age of relative tolerance was brought to an end by the succession of James VI to the English throne in 1603 as James I. James, who had developed a deep terror of witches as a result of the North Berwick incident, was enough of a scholar to be familiar with the continental books and arguments. In 1597 he had published his *Daemonologie*, a direct attack upon Scot and upon the German sceptic Weyer. A good Calvinist, James based his chief argument for the existence of witches upon predestination. Man was made in God's image, but he had lost that image through original sin. God restored the image to the elect through grace, but all the rest of mankind are 'given over in the handes of the Devill that enemie, to beare his Image', and thus take pleasure in the 'grossest impietie'. The grossest impiety was the worship of God's greatest enemy, the Devil. Since those who were not elect were followers of the Devil, it was natural that some should openly follow their dark lord in the witch-cult. The king commanded his Christian subjects to be diligent in searching out these enemies of Christ.

When James became James I of England, he quickly introduced these continental ideas into his new kingdom. The version of the Bible that he authorized used the term 'witch' more liberally than earlier translations, and a new statute against witchcraft in 1604 established pact, devil-worship, and other continental ideas in English law. James eventually revised his own views after investigating some alleged cases of witchcraft in which fraud was obvious, but English law and beliefs had been altered.

Traditionally, Englishmen had dealt with sorcery through direct, or at least local, remedies. 'Cunning-folk', men and women comparable to the German *Hexenbanner* or African witch-doctors, offered their services for sale to those who believed that they had been hexed. The cunning-folk could provide preventative magic to ward off spells, or, once you were hexed, they could provide incantations, counter-spells, or other magical remedies. The cunning-folk could use divination, oracles, or mirrors and other reflecting surfaces to identify the witch so that you might have recourse against her. At worst, the cunning-person exposed the witch to harsh abuse and even death. Well into the nineteenth century, lynching of alleged witches occurred. The clerical and civil authorities took a dim view of the cunning-folk, as much for their usurpation of authority as for their terrorizing of the people, and it is clear that the cunning-folk and their continental counterparts have caused misery over a longer span of time than the authorities of church and state. Yet the work of the cunning-folk and the occasional direct confrontation between supposed victim and witch were the folkways that had evolved to deal with the problem. The statutes of 1563 and 1604 erected a system of official prosecution atop this folk system.

Memories of Berwick, together with the statute of 1604, helped produce the Lancashire trial of 1612, where twenty alleged witches were tried together. The witches supposedly met secretly to feast, did bodily injury through magic, and kept a familiar demon in the form of a brown dog.

The height of the witch-craze in England occurred in the 1640s, when the Civil War produced unusual anxieties and insecurities, and particularly in Essex, a county where war tensions and a strong previous tradition of witchcraft came together. Into this opportune situation stepped an unsuccessful lawyer named Matthew Hopkins (see plate XII), who was to cause more people to be hanged in two years than had been hanged in the previous century. Hopkins, a Puritan, was able to play on the war anxieties of the Puritan population of Essex and convince them that a legion of witches was active among them. At a distance it is difficult to judge Hopkins' motivation. A man who had failed, he seems to have welcomed a chance for fame and success no matter how achieved; he may have relished the power; and he obtained a good deal of money for his efforts. He may even have believed in what he was doing: he relied heavily throughout his career on King James' *Daemonologie*. Whatever Hopkins' own purposes, his ministrations were well received. Making a name for himself first in 1644–5 in Chelmsford, a target for witch accusations since 1566, he then moved throughout southeastern England, appointing searchers to help him in his work.

Hopkins' methods were thorough and merciless. He stripped suspects to search for witches' marks, and used starvation, sleep deprivation, swimming, and other tests and torments. The confessions he elicited show his acceptance of the continental tradition: the witches were members of a sect worshipping the Devil; they met at night; held initiations; had sexual relations with the Devil; and sacrificed to him. Nor did Hopkins neglect English tradition: his witches kept familiars in the shape of dogs, cats, mice, moles, and squirrels, with names such as Prick-ears, Flo, and Bess. Hopkins and his assistant swore in court that they had seen such imps themselves. The witches allegedly performed a variety of *maleficia*: an elderly pastor of Brandeston, John Lowes, was condemned for sinking a ship from Ipswich by magic. Rossell Hope Robbins observed that the judges were so credulous under the influence of Hopkins' persuasion that they made no effort even to 'check whether any ship had foundered that day'.[3] But Hopkins had gone too far too fast. By 1646 considerable opposition to him was already surfacing; later that year he was forced to retire, and the following year he died in some disgrace. In the short space of two years he had earned for himself the informal title of witchfinder-general of England and the contempt of future generations.

The number of witch trials declined rapidly after the excesses of Hopkins and in spite of the continued defence of witch beliefs by learned writers. It is possible that the act of 1604 and the introduction of continental ideas helped speed the end of witchcraft, since they undermined credibility: the common people on the whole did not believe these ideas, and the results of the prosecutions were becoming distasteful to the authorities. The end of the Civil War calmed tensions, and Cromwell's government was not especially interested in suppressing witchcraft.

Learned debate about witch beliefs continued after the Restoration. In 1666 Joseph Glanvill issued *Some Philosophical Considerations Touching Witches and Witchcraft*, a defence of belief in witches on the basis of Christian theology. Denial of witchcraft, he argued, proceeded from atheism. Those who reject witches reject the Devil, and those who reject the Devil reject the entire spirit world, including God himself. But Glanvill's was the last substantial volley from those whom Elliot Rose called the anti-Sadducees, the learned defenders of witchcraft. John Webster's *Displaying of Supposed Witchcraft* (1677) attacked Glanvill with the argument that belief in God and angels rested on a much firmer theological foundation than belief in witches and could not be compared. Glanvill's work was issued in a greatly expanded version in 1681 under the title *Sadducismus Triumphatus*, 'Sadducism Overcome', but Francis Hutchinson's *Historical Essay Concerning Witchcraft*, published in 1718, was the final devastating blow to witch beliefs. A few learned men may have continued to believe in witchcraft, but they no longer dared say so.

Trials continued into the Restoration. At Bury St Edmunds in 1662 women were accused and convicted on the testimony of hysterical children, scholars, and because of alleged witches' teats. In Scotland the same year, Isobel Gowdie confessed to a whole catalogue of witch crimes. Isobel confessed voluntarily and without threat of torture, and it is probable that she believed what she was saying; her case is one of the clearest indications that people of unstable mind could under the influence of prevailing beliefs come to believe themselves diabolical witches. It cannot be supposed that she was really the inheritor of an ancient native tradition, because her ideas are strongly continental in flavour and derive from the learned tradition of James I and Glanvill. She claimed that she had met the Devil in church in 1647 and there made a pact with him,

> denying Christian baptism, receiving the new name of Janet, the devil's mark on her shoulder, and rebaptism in her own blood which the devil sucked from her. She swore allegiance [to the Devil] by placing one hand on her head and the other on the sole of her foot.[4]

She rode about through the air, changed herself into a jackdaw, a cat, or other forms, and regularly attended a coven of thirteen. What became of Isobel is unknown, but the fame of her trial seems to have penetrated to Somerset, where in 1664 witches were charged with attending covens of thirteen led by a little man in black clothing; they signed a pact, met at night, feasted and danced, and flew through the air with the aid of magical ointments. In 1667 Ursula Clarke of Dunstable was charged with witchcraft in trying to kill William Metcalfe. After a quarrel, she said that he would

> waste like dew against the sun.... Some people had wronged her, she said, but they had as good have left her alone, for

> she ... had seen the end of Platt, and ... the end of Haddon,
> and she hoped she should see the end of Metcalfe, and that
> she had never wished nor cursed anything in her life but it
> came to pass.[5]

With Ursula Clarke we have come full circle: back from the catalogue of continental diabolism to plain English cursing and hexing, ever a ready remedy of those who have no power to help or hurt in a natural way.

By the beginning of the eighteenth century, witchcraft was out of fashion among intellectuals, seldom regarded seriously by government prosecutors, and beginning to fade in popular belief. It has been argued that the significant increase in charges of arson and other malicious injury in the period 1686–1712 is the result of a shift in accusations from supernatural to natural crimes. Witch trials practically ceased in the last decades of the seventeenth century, and the last trial for witchcraft in England, that of Jane Wenham in 1731, ended in acquittal. In 1736, the statute of 1604 was repealed. But meanwhile, English witchcraft put on one last important show, not in England itself, but in the American colonies.

Witchcraft in the American colonies

America was culturally behind the mother country. Witchcraft had become a serious problem in England by the 1560s, but it was not till the 1640s that New England began to suffer. The first hanging of a witch in New England occurred in Connecticut in 1647; a number of other cases came to court in the 1640s to 1680s, and there were hangings at Providence in 1662. The intellectual leaders of New England defended belief in witches. Cotton Mather's *Memorable Providences Relating to Witchcraft and Possessions* (1689) and *Wonders of the Invisible World* (1693) both upheld the tradition. The most memorable and well-documented trials for witchcraft in America occurred at Salem in 1692. Both intellectual and legal precedents had prepared New Englanders to believe in witchcraft, and a number of social and political tensions existed in Massachusetts and particularly in Salem that inclined people to lodge accusations and to believe in them. The immediate cause of the frenzy was the occult activity of some children in Salem Village.

Two small girls aged nine and eleven began experimenting with divination in a half-serious attempt to discover who their future husbands would be. As often happens with people who play with magic, the children became terrified and began to exhibit nervous symptoms, thrashing about and assuming odd postures. The father of one of the girls was Samuel Parris, the minister of Salem Village. Parris called in a physician, but the doctor, unable to discern any physical cause, suggested to Mr Parris that the children might be the victims of a witch's spell. The girls' behaviour became worse, and now a number of other girls and young women began to suffer (or enjoy) fits and convulsions. These others may have been overcome by the power of unconscious suggestion. Or they may have enjoyed the attention they received, or the excitement of it all, or the bizarre behaviour that they were permitted to display on the assumption that they were bewitched: one daughter of a strict and pious father hurled the family Bible across the room; another pulled brands from the hearth and ran about shouting gibberish at the top of her voice. For some the spell may have been a delusion, for others a malicious prank. In the end, it cost nineteen people their lives.

The girls were subjected to intense questioning by adults and under pressure accused three women, Sarah Goode, Sarah Osborne, and a West Indian slave named Tituba, of bewitching them. Osborne and Goode denied the charges, but Tituba confessed with great gusto, declaring that she had commerce with the Devil as a 'thing all over hairy, all the face hairy, and a long nose'.[6] Tituba's motives for confessing are unclear, but her confession lent terror and panic to an already tense situation.

The irony is that her confession may have saved her. None who confessed to witchcraft was hanged, for the girls always reported an amelioration of their symptoms after a confession, but many who denied the charges were hanged, often after the girls' symptoms had worsened at their trials (see plate XIV).

Under pressure, threat, and suggestion the accusations grew. They followed the English tradition rather than the continental: the Devil apparently modified his behaviour according to national preferences. The witches frequented a secret society where the Devil appeared as a black man and baptized them in his name. They partook of an evil, black communion bread; they harboured demons in the forms of animals and suckled them with blood through their witches' teats, and they performed *maleficia* against their enemies, causing illness, moving objects supernaturally and, of course, tormenting the afflicted girls with fits and convulsions.

The fits continued to increase in intensity as time went on. The girls screeched and howled, reported visions of ghosts and imps, and suffered mysterious teeth-marks on their arms. The fear of witchcraft spread from Salem Village to Salem Town; learned clergymen in Boston debated the events, and one accused witch was arrested as far away as Maine and brought back to stand trial. As fear swelled, adults began to experience some of the hysterical symptoms themselves. A fourth witch – Martha Cory – was named, and when she appeared for interrogation in the village meeting-house, the possessed girls became uncontrollably agitated.

> When she wrung her hands, they screamed that they were being pinched; when she bit her lips, they declared that they could feel teeth biting their own flesh.[7]

More witches were accused, but trials had to wait until the new governor of the colony, Sir William Phips, arrived with a new charter. Meanwhile, Cotton Mather and other Massachusetts ministers met in June to urge both vigorous prosecution of witches and caution in passing judgment. Mather warned that though witchcraft was a serious problem, it was difficult to determine who was a witch, and innocent people might be destroyed by hasty action.

Unfortunately the ministers took no action at all as the trials progressed. Phips arrived and authorized the commencement of the trials. The first hanging occurred on 10 June 1692. Five more witches were hanged on 19 July, including Sarah Goode, and six more on 5 August. Far from attempting to stop the killings, Cotton Mather appeared at the scaffold during George Burroughs' execution, and when Burroughs shook the confidence of the assembly by reciting the Lord's Prayer fervently and perfectly, Mather gave a spirited impromptu speech urging that the execution continue. By the time of the final execution for witchcraft on 22 September 1692, nineteen persons had been executed and more than a hundred jailed. It had been a summer of horror begun by hysterical or malicious girls and in one sense ended by them: the girls were present at that last execution in September to taunt the victims as they awaited their deaths on the scaffold.

But now, as in Europe, the terrible toll taken by the craze generated a backlash of public opinion. At last the ministers spoke out. Cotton Mather's father, Increase Mather, gave a sermon in colonial Cambridge, arguing that 'it were better that ten suspected witches should escape, than that one innocent person should be condemned.'[8] Mather severely criticized the use of evidence in the trials, arguing that much of it had been suspect. His chief concern was that 'the evil deeds on which the indictments rested were not physically perpetrated by the witches at all, but by intangible spirits who could at times assume their shape.'[9]

Paul Boyer and Stephen Nissenbaum describe in their book on the Salem witchcraft the three main types of evidence provided at the trials. The first was direct confession, which was often supported by corroborating detail. In continental courts, confessions were usually obtained through torture, but following English law torture was used in Salem only when the accused refused to enter any kind of plea. However, confessions were encouraged by terror, suggestion, and sometimes severe physical persuasions amounting almost to torture, such as enforced sleeplessness.

A second variety of evidence was empirical proof of the witch's use of supernatural power. The witch might demonstrate supernatural strength: George Burroughs allegedly could lift enormously heavy weights. Or the witch might be unable to recite his prayers correctly: one poor wretch met his doom by saying 'hollowed be thy name' while reciting the Lord's Prayer. Or, of course, the witches might on examination be found to possess a devil's mark or witch's teat on their bodies. Anger on the part of a witch followed by trouble on the part of her victim was another such empirical demonstration. John Willard, accused of witchcraft, went in his distress to ask old Bray Williams for his prayers. Bray refused, and when he next encountered John he thought that he received a piercing glance. Immediately afterwards he found that he was unable to pass water, and a few days afterwards a young kinsman met an unexpected death. Upon Willard's conviction and execution, Bray Williams happily regained full use of his bladder. On her way to trial, Bridget Bishop cast her gaze on a meeting-house, whereupon a roof-beam crashed to the floor. Increase Mather was unwilling to admit such evidence as convincing, but the courts were more generous.

Mather was particularly opposed to the use of 'spectral evidence', and here again the courts proved more credulous. Many of the witnesses claimed to have seen demons manifest themselves as spectres visible only to the witness and not to others present at the same time. A 'short, dark man' might appear, or a 'gray cat'. Typically the witness would see the spectre and call out to a companion; the companion would see nothing; he would strike at the place with a weapon, and the witness would see the spectre's coat torn or some other effect of the blow. Mather argued that there could be no corroboration of such evidence and that it should therefore not be admitted, but again the courts had been more tolerant. The faultiness of such evidence was obvious to most open-minded people, and its use by the courts one of the elements undermining public confidence in the trials.

Had there been any truth at all in the accusations? The sources for the trials are extraordinarily full, so that they constitute the test case for the existence of witchcraft in America. The most credulous modern historian of witchcraft, Montague Summers, argued that most of the accused were innocent but that a few seem really to have been members of a secret group. For this assertion there is no reliable evidence at all. It is possible that some of the accused may have mumbled curses at their enemies and conceivable that one or two may have done so with intent to work malicious magic. It is also possible that the slave Tituba, who confessed so readily and freely, practised some kind of magic and believed that she had communed with the Devil, but of all the interrogations and trials, Tituba's is the only one that suggests this. The rest of the evidence is drawn from the traditions of English witchcraft so fully elucidated by Cotton Mather and the other intellectual leaders of the colony. It cannot of course be demonstrated conclusively that no coven of witches existed at Salem, but the evidence all points in the other direction. The antics of a group of silly girls, in the right (or wrong) social circumstances, and with an intellectual tradition of witch beliefs to hand, plunged the colony of Massachusetts into a late, but severe, manifestation of the witch-craze.

Witchcraft and Society

The history of witchcraft is the investigation of a concept; it is also an attempt to understand the social conditions and interactions that encouraged the development of the concept. In the past generation, most historians emphasized the social history of witchcraft, an emphasis that has both virtues and limitations. The chief virtue is the recognition that ideas do not develop in a vacuum and that social relationships do much to shape perceptions of reality. The second virtue is thoroughness. Macfarlane, Midelfort, Monter, and Boyer and Nissenbaum have concentrated upon narrow segments of space and time and examined these microcosms in as sophisticated a manner as the data permit. The chief dangers of the approach are that it has tended to be dogmatic, blocking or dismissing other approaches, and that in its search for the social mechanisms of witchcraft it misses the broader ethical, intellectual, and spiritual meaning of witchcraft.

One kind of insight provided by social historians is that witchcraft or witch beliefs performed a social function. Sometimes the function was conscious and cynical, as when Henry VIII accused Anne Boleyn of practising witchcraft in order to seduce him, or when the inquisitors plotted to arrest rich men and confiscate their goods. Much more frequently, the function was the unconscious need to blame someone for the misfortunes of daily life. If you are impotent, it is less embarrassing and better for your self-image if you can place the blame on a sorcerer. If your cow dies, or you fall ill with dysentery, it is more prudent to blame a witch than to blame God. Witchcraft shifts blame for misfortune from an abstract and inscrutable force to an identifiable, punishable individual. If God, or fate, has caused your illness, you have no means of fighting back, but if a witch is responsible, you may be able to fend her off or break her power. If you can have her arrested, tried, and executed, her power over you will fail, and your good fortune will return. This belief helps explain the large number of executions; killing the witch is the only way to make sure that she cannot return to exact magical revenge. As in Africa a person may be genuinely helped by a witch-doctor, so the European evidence suggests that witch trials had a genuine therapeutic effect on the alleged victims.

Another important function of witchcraft was the same as that of heresy: to define the boundaries of Christianity and achieve the cohesion of the Christian community in the face of a terrifying and powerful army of foes under the generalship of Satan himself.

Social historians have investigated the correlations between witchcraft and other social phenomena. In spite of caricatures of the witch as an ugly old hag, physical appearance was not a common ground for accusations of witchcraft. The most decisive traits tending to draw witch charges were begging, grumbling, cursing, and quarrelling. Witches were of all ages, though in Essex the commonest age category was fifty to sixty years old, possibly because age was supposed to enhance magical wisdom. Though children were frequently possessed, they were seldom accused of witchcraft themselves. Much more frequently they were the alleged victims of witchcraft, becoming accusers or at least the catalysts for accusations. The cases of the Burton Boy (1596), the Bilson Boy (1620), the Throgmorton Girls (1688), the Goodwin Children (1688), and of course the Salem girls (1692) are examples of the many accusations growing out of the alleged bewitchment of children. This is not surprising. Children were more susceptible both to disease and to irrational fears; they caused mischief and antagonized neighbours; they were perceived as vulnerable to attack; and above all they were less sensitive than adults to the pain that accusations would bring to others.

Psychologists have investigated the state of mind in which a person might believe in his own powers as a witch, but historians have found no convincing correlation between witchcraft and mental illness on the part of either accusers or accused. The concept of individual psychopathology is not helpful when an entire society embraces a delusion. An educated American who today believed that Jews were engineering the troubles of the world would probably have an individual psychological problem; a German believing this in 1940 might well be merely adopting the common beliefs of their society. Most individuals believing in witchcraft in 1600 were neither stupid nor mad, though their society may have been both.

In Essex, Alan Macfarlane found no correlation between the incidence of illness and witch accusations. 'Concurrently with the years of fiercest prosecution, many people died sudden deaths which were not blamed on witches.' This was true even of a plague of infant mortality. No specific diseases were blamed on witchcraft, though lingering illnesses were more likely to be attributed to witchcraft than sudden attacks. Macfarlane argued that the nature of the illness itself was not important, but rather the victim's perception of the meaning of misfortune. 'The social relationship of the victim, rather than the ... nature of the illness ... determined a person's reaction to misfortune.' To explain the rise and decline of the witch-craze, therefore, we need to look less at the troubles society faces, whether illness, famine, and war, than at 'the social relationships which determine the way in which people react to misfortune.'[1] Thus efforts to tie witchcraft to the enclosure movement in England or the Thirty Years War in Germany may lead to little more than a vague generalization that people are more prone to make negative psychological projections when times are bad.

Midelfort observed, however, that the incidence of witch trials could increase significantly after a natural disaster. At Balingen, for example, the destruction of a large part of the town by fire was followed by the arrest of three women for witchcraft. The prime suspect was tortured, released after the evidence against her was found to be insufficient, but then attacked on the street by a mob, which stoned her to death. Fires and other disasters raise people's fears and increase the likelihood of their seeking scapegoats. But fires often occur without being followed by witch accusations, and witch accusations often occur in the absence of any disaster. Disaster is a contributing element, but disaster produces witch accusations only when certain world beliefs predominate, and the presence of such beliefs depends in turn upon certain social and intellectual conditions.

Correlations between witchcraft and social class are inconclusive. In southwestern Germany both rich and poor were accused, and there was a fairly even distribution of wealth among those convicted. In England, witches were on the whole marginally poorer than their victims, the witches coming mainly from the labouring classes and the victims mainly from the yeoman class. The Caroline Code in Germany forbade the indiscriminate use of confiscation. Despite some gross exceptions, the desire to confiscate property was not among the important motives of the witch-craze. Nor did declining economic conditions necessarily correlate with witchcraft. Macfarlane observed that in Essex prosecutions were at their height in the 1580s and 1590s, a period of relative prosperity.

The firmest generalization coming out of the study of southwestern Germany was that the two groups most susceptible to accusation were people of unusually bad reputation and people of unusually good reputation. Thieves, sex offenders, brawlers, midwives (unfortunately but inevitably these had a bad reputation), and quarrellers were likely to be accused. On the other hand, magistrates, merchants, and teachers were also likely to be accused, though the nobility, physicians (oddly), lawyers, and students were not. People who in any way stood out from the crowd were more vulnerable. In a large witch panic the pattern would be something like this: individuals would lodge accusations against an unpopular person such as a midwife. Once the trial began, the witch would implicate other people under torture, and these would tend to be those they knew personally for good or ill: family, acquaintances, or enemies. Witch trials often involved a whole family for this reason, and sometimes mothers and daughters were executed together. Eight members of one German family were executed for witchcraft between November 1628 and June 1630. Through malice, fear, and threat of torture, accusations would spread, and finally the whole community would be involved.

One hypothetical cause of the witch-craze was the rapidly changing demography of the period between the mid-fourteenth and sixteenth centuries, especially the movement from the countryside into the city. In manorial society, a small, tight community was strictly regulated by tradition and custom and by the authority of the manorial lord and his officials. The opinions and judgments of elders, neighbours, the priest, and the lord's representatives weighed heavily, and there was little sense of isolation. Local courts easily controlled most of the social problems that did arise. When people moved from this settled community life to the city, they experienced a cultural shock similar to that produced in Africa when tribal structure was broken down owing to urbanization. In both continents, traditional patterns of kinship and community shifted, leaving individuals insecure as to their duties towards others and the duties of others towards them. Under such conditions fear of witchcraft increased. There is little evidence, however, to indicate that people new to the urban community were more likely to be accused than the more established inhabitants.

In the countryside, accusations commonly arose among neighbours; ordinarily the alleged witch resented their victim for some real or imagined lack of charity or neighbourliness, such as failure to invite them to a party or to help them when they were in need. In some cases the witch would practise magic in order to retaliate. Or those who had injured them, feeling guilty, would project their guilt and anger on to the alleged witch and blame them for a subsequent misfortune. At Chelmsford in 1579 Margery Stanton was accused of witchcraft by several neighbours who had refused to give her charity and had subsequently suffered illness, the death of cattle, and other misfortunes. In Lucerne, the child of Dorothea Hindremstein had a fight with another boy. Dorothea told the other boy that he would never forget what he had done, and later that day he developed a swelling and lay ill for weeks. Dorothea was accused of witchcraft. In Todi, Italy, a girl contracted a disease after having an affair with a married man, and the wife was subsequently accused of bewitching her!

This pattern of individual hostility and accusation, typical of most continental witchcraft before the fifteenth century, remained common in England until the eighteenth century. During the height of the witch-craze, the pattern changed on the continent, and witches were perceived as part of a vast plot against Christian society. This was especially true in France, the Low Countries, Germany, and the Alpine regions. The explanation for the intensity of the craze in those areas lies in the strong tradition of heresy, the standardization of interrogations by the inquisition, and the disruption brought about by religious wars.

Witchcraft and women

The most marked social correlation is that between witchcraft and women. Over the entire course of the witch-craze about twice as many women were accused as men. Variations in time and geography occurred: in southwestern Germany, for example, more men were accused after 1620 than before, and children were commonly accused after 1627. But this means only that the predominance of women was somewhat less than it had been. Women dominated witchcraft in every period and in every region. The stereotype of the witch is still so powerful that most people are surprised to learn that male witches exist at all or else suppose that the male counterpart of a witch is a 'warlock'. If someone is called 'an ugly witch', the gender is never in doubt.

What is the reason for this sexism, chauvinism, or – more accurately – misogyny? Midelfort observed that the sixteenth century tended to be unusually misogynistic, possibly because demographic changes produced a larger number of women living alone than usual. Marriages occurred later in life, and a greater proportion of people never married. The Reformation brought the dissolution of convents, and even in Catholic regions the number of women in convents declined. If, as Midelfort estimates, perhaps 20 per cent of women never married, and between 10 and 20 per cent were widows, then something like 40 per cent of women may have lived without the legal and social protection of husbands. Many unmarried women and widows found a home with brothers, sons, or others, but the proportion of single and lonely women seems to have increased. Such persons, isolated, unhappy, impoverished, and grumbling, were easy targets for accusations of witchcraft. Such problems, possibly greatest in the sixteenth century, existed throughout the entire span of the witch-craze.

Women living without the patriarchal family support of father or husband had little influence and little legal and social redress for wrongs. They had to do what they could. Since they were barred from normally effective means, they had recourse to means typically employed by powerless people. Arson, for example, was frequently attributed to old women, since it is a crime that can be perpetrated by a weak person clandestinely. In a society that took magic seriously, spells and curses formed another obvious category of response. Once this kind of crime was associated with lonely women, no lonely woman could be free of suspicion. An angry glare would be interpreted as the evil eye, an irate epithet as a curse, muttering as invocation, and loitering as working a spell. Old men also ran this kind of risk, but widows almost always outnumbered widowers. Women tend to live longer, and did then, providing they survived childbirth. During the plagues women survived much more readily, in some places having a recovery rate at least 600 per cent higher than that of males. Under the stress and fear that accompanied the plagues, it was common to suspect the women of using magic to ensure their survival or even of encompassing the deaths of the men. The very weakness of the social position of women, particularly widows or unmarried women, made it safer to accuse them than to accuse men, whose political, financial, legal, and even physical strength rendered the accuser more liable to reprisals. A physically weak, socially isolated, financially destitute, and legally powerless old woman could offer only the deterrent of her spells.

Childbirth, with its dangers to both mother and infant, was commonly attended by a midwife, and the death, deformity, and other calamities that might occur were often laid at her door, as we have seen. Husbands felt guilt and anger at the death of wife or child and readily projected these feelings upon the midwife, who was charged with negligence or, if no physical reason for the disaster could be found, with sorcery.

The connection of witchcraft with heresy encouraged the emphasis upon women. Historians have long observed that women were more influential in heresy than in other aspects of medieval society. Women, finding themselves prevented from rising to positions of influence in the establishment, turned to heresy instead. The Waldensians, for example, allowed women to preach, and the Catharists admitted them to the ranks of the *perfecti*. The relative importance of women in heresy and in heresy trials transferred readily to witchcraft and witch trials.

The misogyny that appeared in such virulent form during the witch-craze had an age-old tradition behind it. Most societies have placed women in an inferior position, and the misogyny of Western civilization was fed by at least three sources: the classical literary tradition, Hebrew religion, and dualism. In the classical literary tradition women's roles reflected their actual status in

Greek and Roman society: that is, as subservient to men. Women do not usually play an important role in classical literature – Creusas are more common than Didos. When they do, it is often as almost passive catalysts of ruin, such as Helen of Troy. Even when they are active, it is more for ill than for good; witness Circe, Medea, and Clytemnestra. And, as with Circe and Medea again, the evil deeds of women are often perceived as black sorcery.

Hebrew religion, more than the other religions of the ancient Near East, placed women in a distinctly inferior position. Ancient misogyny was reinforced by the dualist belief in a struggle pitting the body and evil against the spirit and good. Theoretically this dualism condemns the carnality of men as much as that of women, but society was dominated by men, who projected their lusts upon women and made them responsible for carnality. Thus Eve became the prototypical sensual seductress.

Christianity affirmed the spiritual equality of men and women, but St Paul and many of the most influential Church Fathers blurred that doctrine. Women became the temptresses of men, men who moved the wheels of state, of religion, and of learning, men whose souls were practically, if not theoretically, more important. In most Christian theology and tradition this misogyny was kept within bounds, but sometimes it burst out crudely. Heinrich Institoris, the author of the *Malleus Maleficarum*, spoke from this position when he explained the predominance of women in witchcraft:

> What else is woman but a foe to friendship, an inescapable punishment, a necessary evil, a natural temptation, a desirable calamity, a domestic danger, a delectable detriment, an evil of nature, painted in fair colours.... The word woman is used to mean the lust of the flesh, as it is said: I have found a woman more bitter than death, and a good woman more subject to carnal lust.... [Women] are more credulous; and since the chief aim of the devil is to corrupt faith, therefore he rather attacks

them [than men].... Women are naturally more impression-
able.... They have slippery tongues, and are unable to conceal
from their fellow-women those things which by evil arts they
know Women are intellectually like children.... She is more
carnal than a man, as is clear from her many carnal abomina-
tions.... She is an imperfect animal, she always deceives....
Therefore a wicked woman is by her nature quicker to waver
in her faith, and consequently quicker to abjure the faith, which
is the root of witchcraft.... Just as through the first defect in
their intelligence they are more prone to abjure the faith; so
through their second defect of inordinate affections and passions they search for, brood over, and inflict various vengeances,
either by witchcraft, or by some other means.... Women also
have weak memories; and it is a natural vice in them not to be
disciplined, but to follow their own impulses without any sense
of what is due.... She is a liar by nature.... Let us also consider
her gait, posture, and habit, in which is vanity of vanities.[2]

We may not wish to hear more, but Institoris' contemporaries
did. The powerful influence of the *Malleus* was due in large part
to its resonance with the dualist and misogynist tradition deeply
inherent in Christianity. Far from bringing any relief, the Protestant Reformation, with its return to the primitive Christianity of
the apostles and fathers, emphasized mistrust of women even
more than did the Catholic Church. Luther's writings writhe with
fear of women.

To blame Christianity and Judaism alone for misogyny would
be to miss the point. The Judaeo-Christian tradition of monotheism expelled the feminine principle from the Deity. Yet in fact the
social position of women was often clearly inferior in polytheistic
religions. And Christianity was much more enlightened than its
contemporary rivals. Mithraism, Christianity's chief competitor
for influence in the early Roman Empire, denied women salvation
and even entry into the temple. The terror of women, the belief

that they work dark and mysterious deeds, is an ancient, almost universal phenomenon in men, and must thus be understood in terms of the history of the male unconscious.

Jung and others who have studied the symbolism of the feminine comment on its powerful ambivalence. Male domination of religion, literature, and law created a special symbolism and mythology about women characterized by a tripartite ambivalence. Woman is the pure virgin; woman is the kindly mother; woman is the vicious and carnal hag. In Greek religion, the goddess Artemis was the virgin sister of Apollo, she was the patroness of childbirth and the guarantor of the fertility of animals, and she was also Hecate, the underworld goddess of witchcraft and spells. Christianity traditionally found it difficult to accept the principle of ambivalence in the deity: the Christian God was wholly good and wholly masculine, excluding both the feminine principle and the principle of evil. Repression of the principle of evil from the godhead led to the development of the concept of the Devil. Repression of the feminine principle produced a new ambivalence of idealization and contempt.

Beginning in the twelfth century, a new idealization of the female began. One manifestation of this idealization was courtly love. Courtly love was in large part a literary device, it applied only to aristocrats, and it had nothing to do with practical equality. But it did elevate the lady of high birth to an idealized position of moral superiority over the male.

The second manifestation was the cult of the Blessed Virgin Mary. Though always venerated in the early church, the Virgin was not at first an unusually important saint. But from the twelfth century onwards the cult of the Virgin flourished all over Europe. It was rejected by the Protestants but still remains powerful in the Catholic and Orthodox Churches today. The cult of the Virgin was a limited and unconscious effort to bring the feminine principle back into the concept of the deity, and its current decline in Christianity may be seen as a step backwards.

But the idealization of women had an opposite effect. Whenever any one principle is exaggerated, it tends to create a shadow, a mirror-image, an opposite principle. The exaggeration of the goodness and purity of the female in courtly love and the cult of the Virgin created the shadow-image of the hag. The Virgin Mother of God incarnated two points of the ancient threefold symbolism of the female: the virgin and the mother. But Christianity repressed the third point, the dark spirit of night and the underworld. This dark side of the feminine principle did not disappear: rather, as the power of the Virgin Mother grew, so did the power of the hag. In ancient religion, the dark side had been integrated with the light side, but now, entirely cut off from the positive side of the female principle and repressed, the hag became totally evil. A further transformation occurred. In ancient religions, the hag was a manifestation of a spiritual being, a goddess or at least a demon. But now, in Christian Europe, the hag image was projected upon human beings. The European witch, then, must be understood not just as a sorceress, but as the incarnation of the hag. She is a totally evil and depraved person under the domination and command of Satan.

The salem trials

These are some of the macrocosmic notions of the social origins of the witch-craze. In microcosm, the Salem trials provide a well-documented example of the social mechanisms of witchcraft at a local level. The careful study of Salem by Boyer and Nissenbaum properly treats the history of witchcraft in Massachusetts in the context of other social movements in the colony. The behaviour of the young girls claiming to be victims was not dissimilar to behaviour noted during the religious revival at colonial Northampton in 1734–5. 'With a slight shift in the mix of social ingredients, [Salem and Boston] could have fostered scenes of religious questing in 1692', instead of scenes of witchcraft.[3] In both the religious revival and in witchcraft, young people were dominant and had broken out of their usual subservient and deferential social role. In both instances too the ministers exploited the bizarre behaviour of the young people in order to bolster their own slipping leadership. What then produced witchcraft in the one instance and revival in the other? Primarily the difference in intellectual preconception, the 'interpretation which the adult leadership of each community placed upon physical and mental states which in themselves were strikingly similar.'[4] In Northampton distraught emotional states were seen as the descent of the Holy Spirit, in Salem as an assault by Satan. This observation by Boyer and Nissenbaum confirms those of Midelfort and Monter in Europe: natural and social disasters cannot in themselves explain the incidence of witchcraft; it was the magical explanations people placed upon the disasters that caused them to blame witches. A sophisticated social history of witchcraft will give full weight to the history of concepts and avoid simplistic correlations between external phenomena and witch beliefs.

Boyer and Nissenbaum point to the importance of local geography in the Salem craze. Most of the accusers lived on the west side of Salem Village; most of the accused and those who supported them lived on the east side. The uncertain legal status of Salem Village (as opposed to Salem Town) had caused political disputes and hard feelings. The most important source of unhappiness was James Bayley, the first minister appointed to Salem Village (1679). Bayley was a controversial individual, and the dispute centring on him broadened until it included the whole question of the governance of the church, especially the question of who had the right to hire and dismiss ministers. What made these disputes over Salem Village Church so destructive was the fact that the constitution of the church was so ill defined that the community had no structured way of dealing with disputes and resorted instead to vituperation. This situation, peculiar to Salem Village at least in degree, may explain why the craze was more powerful there than elsewhere. The constitutional disputes attending the overthrow of King James II in 1688–9 also contributed by weakening the authority of the British and colonial governments as well as provoking political dissension in the village. Further, the political relationship between Salem Village and Salem Town was ill defined. The Village resented both its dependence on the Town and the Town's failure to exercise its authority to maintain tranquillity.

In 1689, at the height of the constitutional crisis in London, a new minister, Samuel Parris, was appointed. The village quickly divided into supporters and opponents of Parris. This struggle was exacerbated by taking on a moral aspect, as was typical of Puritan society. The Puritans could not perceive the conflict as merely personal, or political or economic, or even constitutional. They saw it as a 'mortal conflict involving the very nature of the community'.[5] Boyer and Nissenbaum observe that 'the witchcraft episode did not generate the divisions within the Village, nor did it shift them in any fundamental way, but it laid bare the intensity with which they were experienced and heightened the vindictiveness with which they were expressed.'[6] Thus the witchcraft outbreak was the violent expression of deeply felt moral divisions, the moral divisions were generated by the quarrel over the governance of the church, and the quarrel over the governance of the church was exacerbated by strongly felt neighbourhood and family problems. Hostility would have been expressed one way or another, but the existence of the tradition of witchcraft made it a natural vehicle for these angers.

The problems of the Putnam family illustrate the process. The mother died, and the father remarried. The children of the first marriage felt deep resentment towards their stepmother and her son. They projected their bitterness towards their stepmother upon other persons politically or psychologically less threatening to them, notably vulnerable women of the stepmother's generation. The family supported the ministry of Samuel Parris and identified the resentment they felt towards Parris' enemies with the resentment they felt towards their stepmother. Those whom they identified with their stepmother they also identified as opponents of Parris; opponents of Parris were morally reprehensible; the old women were therefore part of an evil conspiracy against Parris.

Such ideas were encouraged by Parris himself. 'He took the nagging fears and conflicting impulses of his hearers and wove them into a pattern overwhelming in its scope, a universal drama in which Christ and Satan, Heaven and Hell, struggled for supremacy.'[7] Personal enemies had been transformed into enemies of the community and enemies of the community into servants of Satan.

Given the existence of the tradition of witchcraft, the possibility that these tensions would be converted into a witch-craze was strong. Then, in 1690–92, a number of unpredictable circumstances came together as the immediate causes of the outbreak. Samuel Parris had a West Indian slave steeped in magical lore; a number of adolescent girls, related to Parris or connected with his political faction, began to dabble in divination and the occult; the Putnam family dispute came to a head; the political and constitutional weakness of the government severely limited its ability to control the situation in Salem Village. The supporters of the minister took the lurid accusations of the hysterical girls as confirmation of what they already suspected: their opponents were evil; they were the willing servants of Satan. Parris' opponents had been transformed into witches, and could now be tortured and hanged.

As Trevor-Roper observed of the witch-craze in general, once a 'great fear' takes hold of society, 'that society looks naturally to the stereotype of the enemy in its midst; and once the witch had become the stereotype, witchcraft would be the universal accusation.'[8] Fortunately, Salem was the last major witch trial in the English-speaking world, and even on the continent the craze had by 1700 begun to wane.

The Decline of Witchcraft

The witch-craze began to decline by the middle of the seventeenth century, but popular opinion, conservative intellectuals, and obstinate judges prolonged it, sometimes against the will and command of government, which increasingly perceived it as disruptive to social order. The delusion persisted longer in Protestant countries than in Catholic, possibly because of the influence of the conservative pietism typical of popular Protestantism at the time. It also lingered in outlying areas after it had begun to fade in cultural centres. This was true in the larger sense – witchcraft reached its height in America and Scandinavia late in the seventeenth century – and in the smaller sense: witchcraft persisted in the countryside longer than in the cities. Sweden's most spectacular trial occurred in 1669 in the town of Mora (see plate XVI). A number of children of Mora claimed that they had been carried by witches to a place called Blocula, where witches held a sabbat presided over by Satan. Most of the traditional elements of continental witch belief were introduced at the trial, many of the accused were scourged, and eighty-five were burnt.

The notoriety of such trials as Salem and Mora helped turn opinion against witch beliefs. The cultural and political leaders of Europe gradually abandoned their support and exerted their influence to end the craze. The decline was continuous, and the prosecution of witches virtually ceased by the middle of the eighteenth century. The last execution for witchcraft in England occurred in 1684, in America 1692, in Scotland 1727, in France 1745, and in Germany 1775.

The legal decline of witchcraft in Britain was gradual but steady. In 1684 Alice Molland was executed for witchcraft at Exeter. It was almost thirty years before the next conviction, that of Jane Wenham in 1712, and she was pardoned and released. In 1717 Jane Clerk was indicted for witchcraft, but the case was dismissed. In 1736 a statute repealed the statutes of Mary of Scotland (1562), Elizabeth I (1563), and James I and VI (1604), stating that 'no prosecution, suit or proceeding shall be commenced or carried out against any person or persons for witchcraft, sorcery, inchantment [sic], or conjuration.' The statute of 1736 continued to provide for prosecution of those pretending to possess magical powers, but it denied reality to those powers. It remained the law until 1951, when it was replaced by the even more liberal Fraudulent Mediums Act, although in 1963 a demand for the reinstatement of the witchcraft laws was made, owing to the desecration of churches and graveyards, which the supporters of the demand supposed, rightly or wrongly, to have been carried out by witches. The statute of 1736 and comparable laws in other countries marked the end of official prosecution for witchcraft.

The same legal, intellectual, and religious elites that had initiated and fomented the witch-craze now slowly brought it to a halt. Belief in witchcraft and sorcery no longer had their stamp of approval. Only after the governing elites had rejected witch beliefs did popular support wither away. Belief in diabolical Satanic witchcraft declined rapidly in the eighteenth century, virtually disappearing save in legend, literature, and jest. On the other hand, belief in simple sorcery continued right through the eighteenth and nineteenth centuries and on into the present. The union between diabolical witchcraft and sorcery was temporary, and it was artificially engineered by intellectuals rather than rising from folk beliefs. Simple sorcery existed before the witch-craze, during the witch-craze, and after the witch-craze; and it still exists today.

Diabolical witchcraft was invented in the Middle Ages, flourished between 1450 and 1650, and then declined and fell. The collapse of the witch-craze between 1650 and 1750 was brought about by a combination of intellectual, pragmatic, and social changes.

Throughout the witch-craze there had been sceptics to write and speak against it, but their influence was limited by the fear of prosecution and by the powerful intellectual pressures exerted by the prevailing belief-system. To reject witchcraft was to court persecution or mockery. No intellectual framework existed from which to fight witchcraft beliefs. The sceptics based their arguments on common sense, on charity, on mercy, or on references to ancient documents such as the Canon Episcopi. But they were still arguing from within the same traditional Christian framework as the witch-hunters. This is why the Protestant Reformation did nothing at all to ameliorate the craze. So long as it was accepted that the Devil exerts great power in the world for the purpose of thwarting the saving mission of Christ, and that organized groups of heretics are plotting against Christian society, then the transposition of heretics into Devil-worshippers was easy and natural. One could argue that this or that heretic was not really a witch, or that flights through the air did not really occur, or that the measures taken against this or that accused witch were too harsh, but one could not challenge the heart of the belief. In this intellectual framework belief in diabolical witchcraft was not a superstition, and opponents of this belief operating within the framework could not oppose it as such. It was part of a coherent, dominant worldview. Only when a different worldview evolved did the sceptics find firm intellectual ground on which to stand and dismiss witchcraft as superstitious.

The modern, liberal, sceptical historians of witchcraft failed to explain the decline of witchcraft because they insisted on seeing the controversy as a battle between superstition and reason and so were astonished that great and learned minds could have believed in witchcraft. They failed to realize that witchcraft was not a superstition before the new worldview emerged in the mid-seventeenth century, and that all worldviews, including scientism, breed their own superstitions. Witchcraft declined because a new worldview made it a superstition. It declined because it was as intellectually disreputable to defend witchcraft under the new system as it had been to attack it under the old.

The new worldview was a philosophical and religious revolution that changed the whole concept of the cosmos and how it worked. The philosophical revolution was led by Descartes (1596–1650), who dismissed the tradition of medieval philosophy and argued for the existence of universal, observable, mechanical, and describable laws of nature that rendered the operation of demons (and angels) unnecessary and illogical. Later, Hume's scepticism went even further, and later, philosophical physicalism declared that only those phenomena demonstrable by scientific method can reasonably be said to exist. To most people today who are brought up under the assumptions of physicalism, belief in witchcraft has indeed become a superstition.

The religious revolution followed the philosophical revolution. Cartesianism led to the assumption of an orderly universe whose regular operations, ordained by the Deity from the beginning, were unlikely to be disturbed by the intervention of spiritual powers. God would have no wish to upset the laws he himself had established; much less would he give the Devil power to do so. Mysterious events, whether supposed miracles caused by God or supposed *maleficia* brought about by the power of the Devil, were either false reports or could be assigned a material explanation. The 'liberal' religious thought that grew out of the Enlightenment abandoned the ancient struggle between the good Lord and the evil Devil, each of whom intervened in the operations of nature, and postulated instead a dispassionate, just, orderly, rational Deity. Pietism and optimism reinforced the idea of a kindly and reasonable God, and the idea has remained to the present – for better or worse – among most of those who maintain belief in God at all. This bloodless God being superfluous in the mechanical view of the universe, the result of diluted Christianity has been increasing atheism. Liberal religion naturally perceived belief in witchcraft as a stupid superstition, since there was no logical role for it in the mechanical world. After about 1700, few people with any claim to intellectual respectability dared claim a belief in witchcraft. The clergy either modified their views to reflect the new ideas or found themselves unheard.

The difference was enormous. Whereas in the sixteenth century Montaigne's position of 'eternal doubt' was largely ignored, a century later the more advanced scepticism of Malebranche was almost universally accepted, at least among the élite. In 1674, Malebranche argued that witchcraft and demonic possession were a delusion produced by overactive imaginations and the use of soporific drugs. Those who imagine that they go out to sabbats or change their shapes are unable to distinguish between their dreams and physical reality. Jesus Christ has redeemed the world, and Satan no longer has power over those who are reborn in the Lord. Malebranche believed that God might rarely for special reasons give Satan limited power to work harm and that sorcerers might occasionally work charms and incantations, but that these things were very rare.

Malebranche's position was very moderate and transitional; others were going much further. Cyrano de Bergerac's 'Letter against Witches' (1654) ridiculed all belief in witchcraft as arrant nonsense and blamed it (mistakenly) on the ignorance and folly of the common people. In England, as we have seen, Francis Hutchinson's *Historical Essay* in 1718 was the last work of importance that found it necessary to attack witchcraft in a serious vein. Laughter and mockery were taking the place of serious argument, and ridicule kills a belief more quickly than the weightiest logic. It was not until the beginning of the nineteenth century that intellectuals again took witchcraft seriously, and it was in wholly different perspective. Goya's paintings, certainly the most terrifying representations of witchcraft ever made, saw that understanding witch beliefs required a deep psychological grasp of the state of mind of witch and witch-hunter (see plate 1).

The intellectual erosion of witchcraft was accompanied by institutional erosion. The frenzy of witch-hunting destroyed itself when even credulous judges began to perceive that things were out of control. Already in the mid-seventeenth century believing judges were simply finding it difficult to distinguish between the innocent and the guilty. They were troubled that numbers of innocent people were possibly being sent to the stake and appalled at the destruction of whole communities by the witch trials. Fear of witches, fear of being accused of witchcraft, and terror of torture were making life in many regions almost unbearable. A commission at Calw in Germany in 1683, noting the destruction wrought by the witch trials, raised the possibility that the trials were themselves the work of the Devil, who had induced the fear of witchcraft in the Christian community in order to turn it against itself and destroy it. In fact, the spread of the trials and the increasing promiscuity of the accusations led eventually to one of two conclusions: either the Devil was so increasing his power that the end of the world must be near, or else, if Christ still ruled, the witch prosecutions must be a delusion. Opinions varied, but both the change in the intellectual worldview and the lurid excesses of the trials assured the victory of the second opinion.

Like Salem in America and Mora in Sweden, the Loudun incident did much in France to encourage scepticism. Judges, physicians, and theologians debated the Loudun case at length in the Paris of the 1630s and 1640s, and few were able to deny that it was in large part a fraud. The implication of priests in the shameful events at Loudun and Louviers also gave rise to trepidation on the part of the clergy and the professions in general. Accusations of witchcraft were not confined to the poor and ignorant; as they touched the ruling elite more frequently, members of the elite began to fear for their own safety. By the end of the Thirty Years War witch-hunting began to encounter official government opposition in Germany. Punishment of casual and false accusers became more severe, and the complexion of the indictments changed. Charges of simple sorcery – divination, charms, magical treasure-hunting – remained common, but, as had been the case centuries earlier, these were no longer united with charges of diabolism. Poisoning and infanticide were increasingly viewed by the courts as murder by physical rather than by magical means. The concept of *maleficium* lost its vitality, and the theological superstructure of diabolism, weakened by intellectual changes, was ready to collapse when the substructure of *maleficium* was undermined.

Witch beliefs naturally lingered longest in conservative rural areas: witchcraft was begotten in the cities but laid to rest in the countryside. In England, after the statute of 1736 repealed the laws against witchcraft, villagers continued to use informal and illegal means of seeking redress against witches, including lynching. In Hertfordshire in 1751 an elderly couple suspected of witchcraft were attacked by a mob that ransacked the workhouse in which they were living, dragged them two miles to water, stripped them, and threw them in. When they rose to the surface, they were thrust down until they were choked, then dragged out and beaten to death. Such occasional atrocities occurred well into the twentieth century, but they were no longer condoned by society. The leader of the Hertfordshire mob was convicted and hanged as a murderer.

Other social changes helped undermine belief in witchcraft. If lack of charity or kindness to a neighbour were often at the root of witch accusations, change in society's response to poverty and need could alter the pattern. In England, the National Poor Law (1601, amended 1722, 1782, and 1785) converted the support of the poor into a legal obligation of the community, relieving the individual from feeling guilt about the poor (though it did not prevent the Hertfordshire crime). The movement of the seventeenth century towards a 'combination of a less collectivist religion, a market economy, greater social mobility, [and] growing separation of people through the formation of institutional rather than personal ties' weakened witch beliefs.[1] The chief effect of shifting social conditions on witchcraft remained indirect. Witch beliefs shrivelled and disappeared once their intellectual vitality had been sapped. A worldview that insisted upon natural explanations of events meant that one was more likely to blame the death of a cow or the illness of a child on natural causes than upon sorcery and demons.

As witchcraft declined, different kinds of occult phenomena took its place. The Black Mass was never part of the history of witchcraft. It appeared for the first time during the reign of Louis XIV. In 1673 some priests informed the Paris police that penitents were confessing that they had used poison to resolve marital difficulties. On investigation, the police discovered an international ring of poisoners and vast stores of poison. The evidence persuaded the king to create a secret court to investigate the matter. The court, established in 1679, was called the *Chambre ardente* because the room in which it sat was draped in black and lit with candles. Many distinguished people were among those prosecuted, but severe sentences including execution were handed down exclusively to the poor and uninfluential. At first the charges were limited to the use of substances such as poisons, abortants, aphrodisiacs, and other drugs, but in 1680 a number of priests were accused of saying black masses on the bodies of naked girls and sexually abusing them; they allegedly performed ritual copulation, desecrated the sacraments, mixed loathsome substances in the chalice, and sacrificed children. Some of the charges may have been true, but they do not constitute real witchcraft or even real Satanism, but a perverted parody of Christian service, a grotesque refinement introduced by the fevered baroque brain. The charges touched the court and even the king's former mistress

Madame de Montespan, who was accused of plotting to poison the king and his new mistress Mademoiselle de Fontanges. The king, judging that the investigations had got out of hand, ordered them stopped; in 1682 he issued an edict denying the reality of witchcraft and eliminating prosecutions for witchcraft and sorcery. The conservatism of the provinces, however, allowed isolated witch trials and executions to continue in France for another sixty years.

The case of Catherine Cordière at Aix-en-Provence in 1731 is another example of how witchcraft was being replaced by other dark phenomena of the soul. Jean-Baptiste Girard, a Jesuit priest, was accused of using sorcery to seduce Catherine, a beautiful girl of about twenty-one who was obsessed with the idea of becoming a saint. Catherine related her visions and mystical experiences to Father Girard, and the priest seems to have been convinced of her holiness and agreed to aid her in her devotions. Their relationship gradually became excessive and improper. Then, at some point, Father Girard dismissed Catherine's visions as false, and the resentful girl began to manifest convulsions, hallucinations, and other forms of hysteria. She accused the priest of using demonic aid to debauch her. Father Girard was arrested, but after a long trial the charges were dismissed. Witchcraft in the classical sense was virtually absent from the trial, and demonism gave way to explicit and lurid sexuality. In an increasingly secularized world sensations would continue to appear, but they would no longer be linked with demonism.

In such a secularized world where witchcraft beliefs were superstitions, revivals of demonic belief (except in some remote rural areas) were wholly artificial. In England in the eighteenth century, Sir Francis Dashwood presided over the Hellfire Club, which boasted a number of distinguished and liberated spirits, including Benjamin Franklin. The club met in natural caves in Buckinghamshire to enjoy food, drink, gaming, and sex. As in the old tradition, they met underground, at night, secretly, and practised something like orgies. But they did so in jesting parody. They enjoyed their reputations as rakehells, but none of them believed in either hell or the Devil, and their salutations to Satan were wholly jocular (of course the Devil's best wile is to persuade us that he does not exist, and the Church of Satan is likely to be materialistic, hedonistic, anti-spiritual, elitist, and cynical). In the late eighteenth and nineteenth centuries no educated person believed that witchcraft had ever existed or ever could exist; and folk wisdom, always at least half a century behind the intellectuals, followed, proclaiming that 'there is no such thing as a witch'. Simple sorcery continued, and grimoires, popular 'do-it-yourself' books based in part on cabbalistic sources but more on the traditions of simple sorcery, began to be published in the eighteenth century and have remained popular in rural areas into the twentieth and twenty-first. But the diabolical witch returned to the realm of fantasy whence she had sprung.

The Romantic revival

Even as folk wisdom turned at last against belief in witchcraft, however, the hint of a new point of view among the intellectuals was already appearing at the beginning of the nineteenth century. In 1828 Karl Ernst Jarcke argued that witchcraft was a nature religion that had continued through the Middle Ages into the present. It was the ancient religion of the German people, which the Church had falsely condemned as Devil-worship. Such a position stemmed from a romanticism that glorified the past and a nationalism that glorified Germany. The tradition exemplified by Jarcke bore hideous fruit a century later when the Nazis proclaimed their pseudo-revival of the ancient religion of the Teutons. In 1829, the French writer Lamothe-Langon, who also fabricated an alleged collection of the private memoirs of Louis XVIII, published a number of documents relating to witchcraft in the fourteenth century which he claimed to have transcribed from records of the inquisition that had subsequently been destroyed. The effect of the fabrications was to establish what looked something like an organized witch-cult as early as the fourteenth century and thus to lend more credence to the idea that witchcraft might have been an old religion surviving through the Middle Ages.

Romanticism helped the revival of the idea of witchcraft in England as well as in Germany. In 1830 Sir Walter Scott published his *Letters on Demonology and Witchcraft*, which, owing to Scott's popularity and prestige, had a great effect in reviving interest in witchcraft. None of these new writers argued that witchcraft was a diabolical cult or that the witch trials should be reinstated. Quite the contrary, they believed that the alleged witches had been misunderstood and mistreated. But they did take a position markedly different from the rationalists of the eighteenth century who denied that witchcraft had existed at all. In 1839 Franz-Josef Mone argued that witchcraft derived from a pre-Christian clandestine cult of the Greco-Roman world, a cult connected with Dionysos and Hecate and practised in the lower strata of society. Mone's argument had an impact upon a world frightened of revolutionary excesses and afraid of secret societies. In 1862, Jules Michelet took Mone's argument and stood it on its head. Witchcraft did originate in the lowest social levels, Michelet argued, but this was admirable: witchcraft was an early manifestation of the democratic spirit. It arose among the oppressed peasants of the Middle Ages, who adopted the remnants of an ancient fertility cult in protest against the oppression of Church and feudal aristocracy. Michelet's argument that witchcraft was a form of protest was adapted later by the Marxists; his argument that it was based on a fertility cult was adopted by anthropologists at the turn of the century, influencing Sir James Frazer's *Golden Bough*, Jessie Weston's *From Ritual to Romance*, Margaret Murray's *Witch-Cult in Western Europe*, and indirectly T.S. Eliot's *The Waste Land*.

Interest in the occult grew in the jaded world of the late nineteenth century. The Rosicrucians and the Order of the Temple of the Orient (O.T.O.) – secret, semi-elite magical societies – were gaining reputations. In France, the abbé Boullan, Eliphas Lévi, and J.K. Huysmans prompted the revival. In England, where spiritualism had long been prominent, occult movements proliferated. Of these the most influential was the Hermetic Order of the Golden Dawn, which boasted as members noted writers such as William Butler Yeats, Algernon Blackwood, Arthur Machen, Bram Stoker, and Sir Edward Bulwer-Lytton as well as dedicated occultists such as MacGregor Mathers, A.E. Waite, and Aleister Crowley, who styled himself The Great Beast. The Hermetic Order of the Golden Dawn delighted in literary and occult jokes and impostures. Crowley and Mathers engaged in a lurid feud in which they sent out spiritual powers against one another: Mathers sent a vampire to attack Crowley, and Crowley responded by sending Beelzebub and forty-nine subordinate demons to assault Mathers. Crowley wore a special perfume made of ambergris, musk, and civet, which he claimed made him irresistible to women. The Hermetic Order of the Golden Dawn translated cabbalistic books and grimoires and devised creative systems of numerology, spells, curses, and aphrodisiacs of its own. The elements of ceremonial magic that presently appear in modern witchcraft can be traced back to the influence of Crowley upon Gerald Gardner, the founder of modern witchcraft, and Crowley's own devotion, half-serious though it was, to Pan also helped develop Gardner's Neopaganism. Crowley's *Hymn to Pan* is too violent for most Neopagans, but it has a glorious vigour of its own. It concludes:

> With hoofs of steel I race on the rocks
> Through solstice stubborn to equinox.
> And I rave; and I rape and I rip and I rend
> Everlasting, world without end,
> Mannikin, maiden, maenad, man,
> In the might of Pan.

The great god Pan, who, according to legend, had died when Christ was born, seems not to have perished after all. In the twentieth century he and his fellow gods and goddesses have enjoyed a small but growing revival. With the end of the witch-craze, diabolical witchcraft virtually disappeared, but a new kind of witchcraft, based on the worship of the old gods, has appeared.

PART II

MODERN
WITCHCRAFT

Survivals and Revivals

On 23 June 1978 a metropolitan newspaper reported a formal wedding in an article entitled 'Bewitching Wedding':

> Between 70 and 80 witches and guests attended the ceremony that united the couple in the traditional Wiccan handfast. As the ceremony began ... barefooted witches wearing robes of all colours and guests formed an arch of lighted white tapers leading from the house to the circle where the ceremony took place.... The couple was led in front of an altar draped in red velvet, and adorned on each side by candelabra. Witches and guests, still holding lighted tapers, were also anointed and, because of the large number attending, formed two circles, symbolizing no beginning or end. The couple dressed in long white robes with garlands of daisies, myrtle, and laurel on their heads ...[1]

Reports of witches' weddings and witches' sabbats appear more and more frequently in newspapers, on television, and in popular books. A number of journals and magazines are dedicated wholly or in part to witchcraft. The 2021 UK Census lists 74,000 Pagans and there are thought to be over one million in North America, and more around the world. Witches have been murdered in twentieth-century Germany. Cinema and television have produced a turgid flow of lurid portraits of witchcraft. Advertisements appear in newspapers and magazines offering to divulge the secrets of witchcraft and to train new witches (for a fee).

The rationalists of the eighteenth century would have been surprised and doubtless dismayed to learn that the witch beliefs they had struggled to destroy were surviving – and reviving – two centuries later. But what *survived* is quite different from what *revived*. Survivals include simple sorcery, which persists the world over, and the combination of sorcery and Christian heresy known as Satanism or diabolism. Revivals include ceremonial magic (such as that of the Hermetic Order of the Golden Dawn), and the resurrection of ancient paganism. Sorcery, Satanism, and ceremonial magic are peripheral to this book and are treated briefly; our chief concern will be with the increasingly visible and significant Neopagan revival.

Modern sorcery

Sorcery, often tinged with diabolism, is still found all over Europe, particularly among peasants, although a rapid decline in such beliefs has occurred since the Second World War. Its characteristics vary according to region. German, French, English, Celtic, Italian, and Slavic sorcery each has its own distinguishing features. In Germany in the late twentieth century, sorcery became notorious again.

The sociologist Hans Sebald reported that in a German village in 1976 a poor, elderly, and isolated spinster named Elisabeth Hahn was suspected of being a witch and of keeping three familiars in the form of dogs.

> The villagers shunned her, children threw rocks at her, and a hostile neighbor threatened to beat her to death because of hexes he felt she cast on him. One day, this neighbor set fire to her house, killing most of her animals, badly burning her, and totally destroying her home.[2]

In another German village that same year a young girl named Anneliese Michel died as a result of a long and strenuous exorcism performed by two priests of the diocese. Even more lurid was the case of Bernadette Hasler in 1969. Bernadette was a young girl whose parents fell under the influence of a vicious ex-priest and his mistress. Under their power, the girl confessed to worshipping Satan and to having 'married him'; he appeared to her almost nightly as a large man wearing black fur and slept with her. Having elicited this confession, the sadistic cultists endeavoured literally to beat the evil spirit out of the girl, who died the next day as a result of their ministrations.

A German scholar, Johann Kruse of Hamburg, devoted most of his life to combating such beliefs, and he collected a vast treasury of books, articles, letters, pictures, and other materials on German witchcraft, a collection now housed in the Hamburg Museum of Folklore. The personal letters are the most extraordinary. Many came from people who claimed to have lived closely for years with a secret witch. Hating and fearing this witch, who may be spouse, landlord, or neighbour, they turned to Kruse for help. Most of the suspected witches were women, and frequently one woman would accuse another woman who was competing with her for the affections of a man. The motive of sexual jealousy may go a long way towards explaining the preponderance of women among those accused, since the majority of accusers were also women; the professional witch-hunters, the *Hexenbanner*, however, were almost always men.

The effects of witch belief go far beyond mere suspicion. A woman suspected of witchcraft in 1952 wrote Kruse a frightened letter describing how an elderly couple were driven out of their son's home because their daughter-in-law had fetched the *Hexenbanner* in a car and demonstrated to her husband that his parents were witches. Sometimes the writer was so terrified and upset as to be uncertain whether they had been bewitched or whether they had magical powers themself. One letter dated 1974 is a plea for help from a woman who believed herself to have suffered harm from a witch as a child, had later become a member of a religious group that she fled after discovering they used black magic, and then had suffered for years from the evil spells of her mother-in-law, who among other things had bought and used teddy bears representing her son, her daughter-in-law, her granddaughter, and her daughter-in-law's mother. These fears, though they appear to be silly, were no joke to the woman: her letter shows that she is terrified. It concludes:

> By chance I acquired a copy of the Sixth and Seventh Books of Moses [grimoires]. They contain a few things that I can use to protect myself, but they have not helped much. I am afraid that they [the witches] will destroy us all? Is there no help?

Kruse opposed all belief in witchcraft and attempted to end the publication and dissemination of the popular grimoires entitled the 'Sixth and Seventh Books of Moses'. Allegedly lost books of the Bible, these magical handbooks contain a mélange of medieval ideas and modern folk tradition. Written no earlier than the eighteenth century, they had enormous influence among the semi-literate: a new edition appeared as recently as 1977. Most of all Kruse disliked the *Hexenbanner*, the cunning folk who sold remedies and counter-magics. Born in 1889, Kruse at the age of twelve experienced witchcraft in his own village. A farmer with sick cattle summoned the *Hexenbanner*, who fumigated the barn with *Teufelsdreck* (asafoetida) and told the farmer that whatever person came first to his farm the next day would be the witch who was hexing his cattle. Early next morning an old woman arrived and was immediately accused of being a witch. Kruse estimated that thousands of *Hexenbanner* were active as he collected his letters, sometimes harming or killing people with their remedies, sometimes inciting hatred and violence against the supposed witches.

The usual course of events is like this: a child or a farm animal becomes ill. The family cannot find a physical cause. They consult the *Hexenbanner* directly or are referred to a *Hexenbanner* by a friend or by a fortune-teller. The *Hexenbanner* is probably someone in their own village, but sometimes the 'victims' will seek out one who by reason of his fame is in great demand and travels from place to place earning not inconsiderable sums. One well-known *Hexenbanner* named Eberling specialized in divination with bedfeathers to diagnose the hex. *Hexenbanner* use a variety of herbs, some, like the asafoetida, useful in exorcizing because of their powerful fumigating properties, others, folk medicine containing real or imagined curative drugs. Psychological investigations of the *Hexenbanner* reveal that their primary motivation is not venality. Of Eberling the investigators reported that he was fanatically convinced of his own mission and believed the laws against such practices to be unfair and harmful. Arrested, he compared his arraignment and trial with that of Jesus Christ.

Hans Sebald wrote a thorough and perceptive study of witchcraft in modern Germany. Anyone, according to Sebald, is supposed to be able to work witchcraft with access to information such as that contained in the alleged Books of Moses. But some people were identified as witches, usually those who were thought to cast spells habitually, who acted malevolently, or who had unpleasant dispositions. General belief is that such malevolent magic is done with the help of the Devil or demons. Sebald observed ironically that the peasants talked much about the danger that witchcraft posed to their immortal souls, but they almost always lodged accusations relating to physical damage to health, animals, or property. Women were accused of witchcraft approximately ten times more often than men. Sebald reported a typical accusation:

> One afternoon, a peasant boy surprised a number of unfamiliar chickens in the barn, stealing grain from the freshly threshed crop. The ruckus resulting from the boy's chasing the birds from the premises brought the neighbor woman,

the owner of the chickens, to the scene. She was irate and threatened: 'You just wait, you'll pay for this!' When the boy woke up the next morning, he found his body teeming with lice, while his brother with whom he shared the bed was not bothered with one. The agonizing visitation continued in this most exclusive manner for several weeks until, no longer able to stand the discomfort, the boy went for advice to the village shepherd. The man nodded knowingly and suggested that the boy go to the angry neighbor and beg for forgiveness. Without hesitation, the boy followed the advice and the lice vanished as suddenly as they had appeared.[3]

Such occurrences, common in the 1930s and even the 1950s, are rarer today, partly as a result of work such as that of Johann Kruse, and partly as a result of the triumph of the new mythologies spread by television. Sebald observed in the late 1970s that most children were unfamiliar with the old beliefs. But their elders still believe that witches do what they were supposed to do during the witch-craze: they cause nightmares, give the evil eye, raise storms, bring about accidents and diseases, and harm crops, homes, and animals. They dry up a milch cow or steal its milk: an effective way of doing this without attracting attention is to stay at home and milk the corners of a tablecloth or other fabric; bringing the milk from your neighbour's cows into your own home. Witches use secret books and keep familiars such as black cats and dogs. They are particularly dangerous to children. They ride through the air at night and attend orgies. And they make pacts with the Devil, who takes their allegiance and their souls in exchange for the magical powers he gives them. This is the historical synthesis of sorcery and diabolism that was the basis of the witch-craze, and if the long tradition is now coming to an end, it is no pity.

Neopagan Witchcraft:
the Sources

The religion of modern witchcraft is not historically connected to its medieval namesake, but it is connected to the speculations *about* witchcraft that began to emerge once the phenomenon itself had disappeared. In fact, Neopagan witchcraft today consists in large part of concepts, claims, and terminology that originated during the two hundred years between the end of the Enlightenment and the beginning of the twenty-first century.

Witchcraft as paganism:
Jarcke, Mone, and Michelet

Modern religious witchcraft has its deepest roots in the Romantic movement of the early nineteenth century. By the end of the eighteenth century, the Enlightenment had not only banished witchcraft and other 'superstitions' from the realm of credibility, but it had also banished the rich emotional world of light and shadow that accompanied those beliefs. Rationalism, scepticism, and scientism had conspired to demystify the universe, but they could not eradicate irrationality or exile human emotion. Many longed for the return of transcendent fears and consolations.

> Nineteenth-century man found himself high and dry in a materialistic and boring world. In the Middle Ages, devils were a reality that everybody accepted without question. Now the shadows were gone; the common daylight made everything hard and clear. And the romantics looked back nostalgically

to the age of demons and incubi, altogether more stimulating
to the imagination than railways and paddle steamers. The
universal complaint was boredom.[1]

The romantics sensed that rationalism was hostile to human
significance and human concerns; in response, they exalted the
non-rational and the antirational, the primal, the intuitive, and
the ecstatic. That emphasis had the effect of stirring up a renewed
interest in magic and other occult arts – an enthusiasm that also
helped re-open a discussion about witchcraft and the witch-craze,
the memory of which was still fresh enough to haunt the minds of
Europeans. The *philosophes* of the Enlightenment had reflexively
blamed the Catholic Church for the deaths and dislocations of the
witch hysteria, but by the 1800s, a growing reaction by Catholic
intellectuals came to the defence of the Church, claiming that the
Inquisition had been justified in its response to a genuine threat.

Out of that debate came one of the most important concepts
associated with modern witchcraft: the belief that medieval
witchcraft was actually a surviving form of pre-Christian paganism. That idea, more than any other, has been central to modern
witchcraft's sense of its own religious identity, and provides much
of the motive force behind the movement's countercultural stance.
Today that belief has been thoroughly discredited by scholarship
– and the modern witchcraft movement is still coming to terms
with the implications. But for over 150 years, in its capacity as a
kind of 'Charter Myth', the fundamental belief that witchcraft was
really paganism helped to shape the growth and development of
modern religious witchcraft and, more broadly, of the Neopagan
movement as a whole.

Ironically, the idea of witchcraft as a pagan survival was first
put forward to discredit witchcraft, not defend it – and to vin-
dicate the Inquisition. It eventually worked its way into the lore
of modern witchcraft through a process of dialectical argumen-
tation. The research of Ronald Hutton shows how this seminal

idea took shape in the thrust and parry of controversy between Catholic apologists and the Church's secular critics during the early nineteenth century.

In 1828, Karl Jarcke was a young Professor of Criminal Law at the University of Berlin. He also had a reputation as an articulate spokesman on behalf of the Church and a defender of its public image and reputation. That year, Jarcke edited the records of a German witch trial for publication in a professional journal; he added a brief polemical commentary of his own, in which he described witchcraft as a degenerated form of native, pre-Christian paganism. In Jarcke's scenario, the ancient pagan religion

> had lingered among the common people, had been condemned by Christians as Satanism, and in the course of the Middle Ages had responded by adapting to the Christian stereotype, becoming devil-worship in earnest. As a result, proposed Jarcke, even ordinary people began to turn away from it in disgust, and denounce it to the authorities, who proceeded to extirpate it. In this manner, the young academic brilliantly outflanked the liberals; his explanation of the witch-trials equally accepted the non-existence of witchcraft itself, while exonerating the authorities who had persecuted witches as members of an evil and anti-social cult.[2]

That scenario was restated, in modified form, eleven years later by Mone, another clerical advocate, who, in addition, was a recognized and established historian and Director of the Baden Archives. Mone was a staunch Roman Catholic, but he was also influenced by a German Romanticism that sought its national identity in a glorified national history. Thus Mone felt that Jarcke's theory unnecessarily cast aspersions on native German folk-culture. He suggested instead that the paganism that turned into witchcraft was not the local variety, but a Greek import, a corrupted descendant of the classical mystery cults, involving nocturnal orgies, human sacrifice, and black magic. According to Mone, this devolving foreign religion had been brought to Germany by Greek slaves and was spread by them to depraved and marginal elements of society. As this alien transplant transformed into 'witchcraft', it repulsed both the native pagans and later the Christians, who were sufficiently alarmed to suppress the cult completely.

Between them, the two Catholic apologists seeded the public mind with the creative idea that the witches of European history were actually practitioners of a pre-Christian pagan religion – a religion, moreover, that had gone into radical decay. If you accepted their scenario, Jarcke and Mone had effectively let the Catholic Church off the hook for the witch persecutions. But, as ingenious as that strategy was, it had one problem – it was a pure flight of fancy, with nothing whatever to support it. The theories of Jarcke and Mone were not intended to explain any actual evidence (of which they had none) but to explain away someone else's theory. Nevertheless, in the climate of the times, their ideas achieved enough currency to constitute a challenge to the liberal view of the Church's culpability.

Eventually, the anti-Catholic and anti-clerical party responded with its own ingenious rhetorical strategy, put forth by 'one of the nineteenth century's most famous liberal historians, the Frenchman, Jules Michelet'.[3] Michelet was an academic *enfant terrible*, contrarian and polemical. He continually stirred controversy with the public, the politicians, and his own professional colleagues; he was even suspended from his position at the Collège de France in Paris for a perceived lack of objectivity in his professional work. The truth is that Michelet's work varied widely in quality. On the one hand, he could be a patient and thorough archivist, producing a multi-volume history of France that is still a valued historical resource. On the other hand, he invariably coloured his historical arguments with his own political and social attitudes, which were strongly held, strongly stated, and strongly at odds with the mainstream. He brought a tone of passionate advocacy to every subject he dealt with and what fuelled his passion was his hatred of the medieval Church and all of the miseries he felt Christianity had inflicted on Europe (and especially on France) in the form of the absolute monarchy and the parasitic aristocracy that accompanied it. He was also in the habit of churning out lurid and sensational 'potboilers' to make the most money in the shortest time with the least amount of work, so as to support his more systematic labours.

Michelet's 1862 work on witchcraft, *La Sorcière*, definitely fell into the 'potboiler' category, having been dashed off in a mere two months. The book was, among other things, a sustained attack on his favourite targets – the Catholic Church, the monarchy, and the aristocracy. Michelet argued that witchcraft was a pagan survival that became a widespread protest movement when peasants used their traditional folk-fertility beliefs to mock and defy their oppressors.

Michelet's approach to his subject was the essence of Romanticism. The Romantic temperament regarded passion itself as a badge of truth and a basis for insight and wisdom. In Romanticism, the purest vision springs from the purest passion, and the purest passion of all is the fire of Promethean rebellion. Michelet projected his personal sense of rebellious, Romantic virtue onto the witches with a blissful indifference to facts. His research for the part of his book that dealt with medieval history was

> more or less non-existent, and it represents an extended poetic reverie, being at times actually composed in blank verse. The seventeenth-century chapters were based on a small number of pamphlets, which Michelet reinterpreted to suit his own hatred of Catholicism. As the book went on sale, he noted in his journal: 'I have assumed a new position which my best friends have not as yet clearly adopted, that of proclaiming the provisional death of Christianity.'[4]

No one was surprised that Michelet used the book as an opportunity to indict his usual suspects. That much was familiar from his other work. The real novelty in Michelet's treatment was his radical rhetorical strategy: he accepted the *picture* of witchcraft drawn by Jarcke and Mone, but reversed the *values* attached to it. Michelet argued witchcraft *was* a surviving pagan religion of fertility and nature-worship, but far from being an anti-social cult, it alone had succeeded in nurturing the spirit of freedom through all the 'thousand long, dreary, terrible years' of the Dark and Middle Ages. In that way, Michelet transformed the Catholic apologists' defence of the Church into his attack on it, in effect turning their shield into his sword. The hidden irony in this rhetorical duel is that neither side had any factual or evidential basis for their claims, and the entire controversy arose on a foundation of thin air.

La Sorcière became a best-seller right away (thus fulfilling Michelet's immediate aim in writing the work) and has continued to stimulate the interest of readers right up to the present day. Michelet's own academic peers, however, virtually ignored the book – 'apparently', as Hutton says, 'because they recognized that it was not really history.'[5]

For obvious reasons, Michelet's work on witchcraft has no credibility among historians today, but it has exercised an extraordinary influence in other ways, as we have already seen (see p. 130). Michelet first propounded what eventually became a fundamental theme of the modern Witchcraft movement – the notion that medieval witchcraft was a surviving pagan religion, persecuted by Christianity and standing for life and liberty against the cultural tyranny of the Catholic Church. That idea was then adopted, adapted, and applied by a succession of writers and thinkers over the next hundred years, all of whom modified or elaborated details of the original theory in accord with their own points of view. And all of them made their own unique contributions to the shape and substance of modern witchcraft.

The forerunners: Leland, Murray, and Graves

One of the first and most colourful members of that group was Charles Godfrey Leland (1824–1903), an American folklorist, occultist, writer, adventurer, and all-around soldier of fortune. He grew to maturity during the high tide of Romanticism, and took an active part in the French Revolution of 1848 while he was a student at the Sorbonne in Paris. It was also while in Paris that Leland was first drawn to the historical theories of Michelet, who was then at the peak of his career, and he applied Michelet's ideas in his studies and writings throughout the rest of his life. After returning to America, he was swept up in the Civil War (1861–5), and served with the Union army at the battle of Gettysburg. In later life, Leland moved to England, travelled widely throughout Europe, and became an authority on Gypsy lore. He wrote fifty-five books on a variety of subjects, but his contribution to modern witchcraft comes through his most famous and influential book, *Aradia, or the Gospel of the Witches* (1899).

The story behind the writing of *Aradia* is as intriguing as the book itself. In 1886, when he was sixty-two, Leland moved to Italy to study Italian folk traditions, Italian witchcraft in particular. One of his chief informants was a peasant woman named Maddalena, an enigmatic figure about whom relatively little is known. She apparently worked as a fortune teller, plying her skills in the streets of Florence. Leland believed she was a hereditary witch and hired her as a research assistant to find folklore materials for him. Leland had heard rumours of a manuscript containing the ancient secrets of Italian witchcraft, and he pressed Maddalena to obtain a copy for him. Leland never saw an actual manuscript, but after ten years of prompting, Maddalena gave him some material in her own handwriting that was either copied from another text, or transcribed from oral sources, or both. It claimed to be the book of a secret religion of the witches that was widespread among the peasantry and thrived beneath

the Catholic surface of Italian society. That document, together
with Leland's commentary on it, became *Aradia*.

Aradia presents the picture of an organized cult of goddess-
worship centred around the figure of Diana, the ancient Roman
goddess of the moon, forests, and child-birth. According to Leland,
this 'old religion' was still strong enough among the peasants of
the Romagna district to dominate whole villages. The 'witch' belief-
system as Leland described it was both ancient and elaborate.
Doreen Valiente summarizes its salient features:

> The basic belief of this religion was that the first and most
> powerful deity was feminine – the goddess Diana. 'Diana was
> the first created before all creation; in her were all things; out
> of herself, the first darkness, she divided herself; into dark-
> ness and light she was divided. Lucifer, her brother and son,
> herself and her other half, was the light' ... The legend goes
> on to say that Diana had by her brother Lucifer, 'who had
> fallen', a daughter whom she named Aradia. Pitying the poor
> and oppressed at the hands of their masters, she sent Aradia
> upon earth to be the first witch and to teach witchcraft to
> those who would learn, thus setting up a secret cult in opposi-
> tion to Christianity.[6]

Aradia created no great stir when it was first published. The
occult world was preoccupied with the exoticisms of Theosophy,
and the academic world paid scant regard to Leland's alleged
discovery. Today, scholars generally take the book as a hybrid
creation at best – a blending of Leland's own beliefs with some
genuine folk/occult survivals that he had managed to uncover.
Historian Elliot Rose says that:

> The whole work reads... as if one of its authors was consciously
> seeking to establish that the witch-cult was a cult of this

particular nature, and grafted material calculated to prove
it onto an existing straightforward book of incantations.[7]

Leland's 'research' methods were woefully deficient by modern standards (though normal enough for his own times) and he willingly let himself be led by his informant. Knowledgeable in folklore, and full of Michelet's ideas, Leland read into Maddalena's material what he already knew – or thought he knew – about witchcraft. Maddalena, for her part, readily discerned what Leland was looking for and began to tailor her information to his expectations. She was, after all, not a dedicated archivist, but a professional fortune-teller, skilled at 'reading' her clients. In the preface to *Aradia*, Leland went so far as to acknowledge that 'this woman, by long practice, has perfectly learned what few understand, or just what I want, and how to extract it from those of her kind.'[8]

Even Valiente's sympathetic description of *Aradia* suggests a scholarly invention. The book draws on a knowledge of gnosticism, paganism, and mythology for much of its content. To that mixture it adds an awkward parody of the biblical creation story and a literate attack on Christianity. That particular combination is quite likely to occur in the mind of a nineteenth-century man of letters, but it is not at all likely to occur as a historical artefact.

Nevertheless, the ideas expressed in *Aradia* have had a real and continuing influence. Leland's work has been appropriated – some of it word for word – by the modern witchcraft movement. Leland was the first to use the term 'the Old Religion' (*la vecchia religione*); some of the spells and rituals used by contemporary witches are simply passages lifted from *Aradia* virtually unchanged. *Aradia* also appeals to modern witches for another reason: while the 'feminist' focus of Leland's construction was an oddity in his own time, it is more compatible with ours, which seeks a religion to support its cultural enthusiasms and endorse its social agendas. Yet Leland's book would probably not have had the influence it did if not for the credibility allegedly bestowed on it by the work of Margaret Murray (already noted briefly on pp. 41–2).

In 1921, Murray startled academics and historians with a sensational new theory of witchcraft in her book *The Witch Cult in Western Europe*. Murray (1863–1963) was an anthropologist and an Egyptologist, not a medieval historian, but she developed a fascination with witchcraft alongside her personal interest in British folklore. By Murray's account she was staying at Glastonbury, the legendary site of King Arthur's burial, when someone (whom she never identified) suggested to her that what the Church called 'witchcraft' was really a leftover, pre-Christian fertility religion that had once pervaded Europe. Murray was apparently unacquainted with the theories of Michelet and Leland; to her, the concept was a revelation that led her to begin an intensive study of the Inquisition's trial records.

Although Murray seemed unaware of its nineteenth-century roots, she eagerly related the idea of witchcraft as paganism to another framework she was already familiar with – the theme of the death and rebirth of Nature in Sir James George Frazer's *The Golden Bough* (1890), including Frazer's emphasis on the regular sacrificial murder of sacred kings. After much investigation, Murray argued that 'witchcraft' was the Inquisition's term for an older religion that worshipped nature's fertility and abundance. At least initially, the religion had nothing to do with opposing Christianity, but became an underground pagan resistance movement because of the Church's attempts to stamp it out. As Murray described the cult, it was based on ancient notions of sexual polarity as the driving force behind all of nature – the male–female, positive–negative interaction at all levels provides the energetic tension that makes nature function. Natural religion acts out that relationship in its seasonal rituals. The 'witch-cult' therefore acted out the endless sexual cycle of birth, growth, death, and rebirth, which is the rhythm of Life and Nature.

Murray believed that the original deity behind natural religion was a bipolar, 'bi-sexual' figure that showed up as either male or female, depending on the demands of circumstance.

> After reexamining the trial documents of the Inquisition, she argued that witchcraft could be traced to 'pre-Christian times and appears to be the ancient religion of Western Europe' centered on a deity which was incarnate in a man, a woman or an animal. One of its forms was the two-faced, horned god known to the Romans as Janus or Dianus. Murray wrote that the feminine form of the name – Diana – was found throughout Western Europe as the leader of witches. Because of this, Murray called the religion the Dianic Cult, although she wrote that the god rarely appeared in female form and a male deity had apparently superseded a female one.[9]

In an eerie echo of Michelet's rhetorical strategy, Murray accepted the factual findings of the medieval and Renaissance witch-trials, but reinterpreted their meaning. The inquisitors recorded that the Devil would appear at the witch rituals in the form of a goat or other animal. Murray wrote that this 'Devil' was really just a human high-priest in ritual costume. His adornment included the horns and shaggy animal skins that represent carnal potency. That was 'one of the pointers given to Dr. Murray by her unknown informant at Glastonbury. It proved to be the key that unlocked the door of the whole mystery. The Christians called him the Devil and the witches seem eventually to have accepted this term also.'[10]

Murray believed that she had discovered the secret meaning behind the religious history of Europe. And so did others; her theories created an enormous stir when they first appeared – chiefly because of her credentials and her reputation. Eventually, her ideas became the generally accepted view of witchcraft; in fact, she wrote the article on 'Witchcraft' that appeared in the *Encyclopaedia Britannica* from 1929 until 1968. Today, scholars are agreed that Murray was more than just wrong – she was completely and embarrassingly wrong on nearly all of her basic premises. In two later books (*The God of the Witches* [1931] and *The Divine King in England* [1954]) she extended her thesis even further, claiming that the witch religion of the god who dies and is reborn not only survived, but actually dominated British royalty to the point that many English kings were ritually murdered according to the rites of the cult. Murray's increasingly extreme opinions were matched by her increasingly sloppy scholarship. Elliot Rose, an unsympathetic Anglican scholar, characterized Murray's work as 'vapid balderdash'. Mircea Eliade, a kinder, gentler critic, said that 'neither the documents with which she chose to illustrate her hypothesis nor the method of her interpretation are convincing.'[11] A serious critique of Murray's work reads like a litany of scholarly blunders. She took witch practices that were peculiar to certain times and places, such as the coven (a late development peculiar to Scotland) and the sabbat (which she makes the centre of her fertility cult although it is not mentioned in any sources before the fifteenth century) and read them back into the whole history of witchcraft, as though they had been a central part of the witch-cult from the beginning.

Indeed, Murray's use of sources in general is appalling. Not only did she force evidence to fit her theory, but she ignored vast bodies of materials, particularly for the Middle Ages, that were readily available to her and that, ironically, in some cases would even have strengthened her position. Murray's work was subjected to criticism during the latter stages of her career, and subjected to outright rejection after her death in 1963. By the 1970s, the demolition of her scholarship, her thesis, and her reputation was complete. Yet Murray's theories did have enormous influence, and continued to do so long after the theories themselves had been rejected by scholars. Hutton remarks that for many years they 'had the curious status of an orthodoxy which was believed by everybody except for those who happened to be experts on the subject.'[12]

Despite its serious shortcomings, Murray's work captured the public's imagination because it seized on one historical reality that was being otherwise ignored – namely that paganism had been suppressed but not eradicated by Christianity; that pagan folk beliefs did not die out with the introduction of Christianity but rather remained and constituted a basic substratum of witchcraft. An honest investigation reveals that some – indeed many – pagan customs, beliefs, and symbols survived throughout the Middle Ages and on into the present day. The question is not *whether* pagan survivals existed, but how many, of what kind, and to what extent they had any coherence as a body of belief or practice.

Despite its distortions of fact (or arguably because of them), Murray's work was an important preparation for the later rise of modern witchcraft. Her theories set off a wave of enthusiasm for things ancient, native, and pagan that is still with us and still gathering strength. Murray's constructions, like Michelet's and Leland's, have been blended into Neopagan lore in generous measure. She has contributed ideas and terminology, as well as actual practices, to the modern witchcraft movement. Her scholarship may have been bogus, but its results have been very real. Murray did not single-handedly start the witchcraft revival, but she almost single-handedly set the stage for its arrival.

The influence of Robert Graves (1895–1985) differs from the others discussed here, in that his work was not a source for the creation of modern witchcraft directly but was introduced later, through one of its early proselytes (see Chapter 10). But once introduced, Graves's ideas took hold quickly and had a powerful effect on how modern witchcraft developed and the form it took.

Graves was an English poet, essayist, and novelist. He is the author of *Good-bye to All That*; *I, Claudius*; and *King Jesus*, as well as a large number of lesser-known works. His impact on the formation of modern witchcraft comes from his 1948 book *The White Goddess*, subtitled *A Historical Grammar of Poetic Myth*.

The White Goddess is a strange book – rambling and diffuse, both erudite and naive, both brilliant and muddleheaded. But if the book itself is strange, the way it was written is even stranger. In 1944, Graves was living in Devonshire when he was seized by

> 'a sudden overwhelming obsession' which compelled him to suspend work on the historical novel he had set out to write, in favor of discovering the inner meaning of a mysterious old Welsh poem called *The Battle of the Trees*. In three weeks, he tells us, he had written a 70,000 word book, called at first *The Roebuck in the Thicket*, but which eventually became *The White Goddess*. His mind worked so furiously, he says, under the influence of this inspiration, that his pen could scarcely keep pace with it.[13]

As Graves's subtitle indicates, his book is basically about the sources of myth and poetic inspiration. It is not a work of history or of anthropology, but a self-conscious literary *tour de force*. Nevertheless, Graves did rely on his considerable (if eccentric) learning to piece together a picture of an ancient, pre-Christian Goddess religion that gave birth to the original language of poetic myth. Thus, for Graves, the quest for the muse of poetic inspiration led directly to the primal fertility goddesses of pagan Europe, and the often orgiastic fertility religion(s) that grew up around them. As Graves depicts that religion, it resembles a variation of the version described by Murray. Graves believed that poetry was originally created to mythologize the cycles of Nature by casting them in the form of a dramatic story of the god-king who is born and flourishes with the waxing Summer sun, who struggles with Autumn's waning sun, who dies in the dark and chill of Winter, only to be reborn in the renewal of Springtime.

The Goddess was both worshipped and desired by the god-king. She was Nature, she was Abundance and Fertility, she was the Earth. She was the mother, the wife, and the one who received him in death, all at the same time. Thus Graves portrayed her in 'triple form' – a sequence of three developmental phases that paralleled the three phases of the waxing, full, and waning moon (which was also her symbol). 'She was the young maiden of the new moon, the glorious lady of the full moon, and the wise old crone of the waning moon.'[14] According to Graves, the original, universal, goddess religion was overthrown and suppressed by an emerging patriarchal culture that was violent, warlike, and hostile to Nature. The last 4,000 years of human history, therefore, represent a steady spiritual decline from that original, pre-patriarchal golden age.

In his concluding chapter, entitled 'The Return of the Goddess', Graves pronounced the failure and irrelevance of what he called 'Father-god worship'.[15] He earnestly believed that the time was coming when humanity would be ripe for the Goddess's return. But until then, the outlook was grim; Graves was not an optimist in the short term.

> I see no change for the better until everything gets far worse. Only after a period of complete political and religious disorganization can the suppressed desire of the Western races, which is for some practical form of Goddess-worship, with her love not limited to maternal benevolence ... find satisfaction at last.

> But the longer her hour is postponed, and therefore the more exhausted by man's irreligious improvidence the natural resources of the soil and sea become, the less merciful will her fivefold mask be, and the narrower the scope of action that she grants to whichever demi-god she chooses to take as her temporary consort in godhood. Let us placate her in advance.[16]

In that connection, Graves articulated another idea that has achieved wide currency among modern witches. It is the idea that the gods – all of them, from Jehovah to Jupiter, as well as 'the Goddess' herself – derive their substance, vitality, and power from the faith placed in them by their believers. The more believers a deity has and the stronger their belief, the stronger, more powerful, and more 'real' the deity itself becomes. 'One of the central arguments of *The White Goddess* is that once people start to believe in her in large numbers again, her reign will commence in earnest.'[17]

Graves's version of history and anthropology is not taken seriously by historians or anthropologists. His theories are a fanciful rearrangement of his own eccentric erudition, and they express his own spiritual inclinations far more than they describe any historical realities. And yet those theories have had a remarkable impact. Like Michelet, Leland, and Murray before him, Graves combined literary invention, historical speculation, defective (even appalling) scholarship, and ideological conviction to produce a work that has made major and detailed contributions to modern witchcraft. Together, the four of them have created a school of historical revisionism that has taken hold at a grass-roots level, despite repeated official refutation; collectively, they are a primary source for the ideas that define Neopagan witchcraft.

Michelet took the speculations of his rhetorical adversaries and turned them into a counter-speculation of his own, depicting witchcraft as a pagan survival that became a bastion of light and freedom against the darkness and repression of the Roman Catholic Church.

Leland built on Michelet in portraying witchcraft as a surviving form of goddess-worship that was preserved and transmitted in detail. He contributed the 'Old Religion' terminology, a feminist emphasis, and further opposition to Christianity, as well as specific ritual content in the spells that he described.

Murray emphasized the idea that the 'Old Religion' was really an ancient fertility religion. She denied that witchcraft arose in opposition to Christianity, saying instead that it was a pagan survival that Christianity challenged. Murray also established the terminology of the 'Sabbat', and the 'Esbat'. She contributed the concept that the witch-cult was organized into 'covens' of thirteen people, consisting of twelve witches and their leader, or priest.

Graves added an even more powerful feminine focus (or 'gyno-centrism') to the theories of the other three. In addition to a generalized anti-patriarchal bias, Graves contributed the specific concept of a 'pre-patriarchal golden age', a time of peace, harmony, and goddess-worship. His emphasis on the lunar connection led him to speculate that the number thirteen had special significance, since there are thirteen lunar months in a solar year, with one day left over. Graves also provided the 'triple form' imagery of the goddess that is widely used by modern witches; he stressed the spiritual power of the feminine, and proposed that the medieval witch covens were led by women. Finally, he suggested that the gods and goddesses of religion are made real and powerful by the faith of their believers.

Gerald Gardner: father of modern witchcraft

However, the man who pulled all of the pieces together and founded the religion of modern witchcraft was Gerald B. Gardner (1884–1964), an Englishman with an unconventional outlook and idiosyncratic interests. Drawing both from literary sources and personal experiences, he assembled a version of witchcraft that has dominated the modern movement. Gardner was widely travelled and spent much of his adult life in the Far East. He worked on a tea plantation in Ceylon (now Sri Lanka) as a young man; later, he moved to Borneo, and finally to Malaya (now Malaysia) where he prospered as a rubber planter. Gardner did original research on early Malay culture and even received academie recognition for his work, some of his articles being published by the Royal Asiatic Society. Later he became a British customs officer and lived for a time in India, where he studied tantric Hinduism, among other things. Gardner remained a British civil servant until he retired and returned to England in 1936. Gardner's sojourn in Asia gave him ample opportunity to indulge his fascination with the exotic, the eccentric, and the esoteric. He apparently became a nudist early in life, and plunged with relish into the off-beat and occultic aspects of whatever culture he found himself living in.

> Prior to his involvement with Wicca, he had become a member of the Sufi order as well as a Co-Mason. He was also familiar with Hinduism (particularly Kali worship) as a result of his residence in India and Malaysia with the British civil service. In addition, he corresponded with Charles Godfrey Leland, author of *Aradia: The Gospel of the Witches*.[18]

Gardner (see plate XIX) was also familiar with the work of Murray and knew her personally – she even wrote an introduction to his *Witchcraft Today* (1954). He was an initiate of the Order of the Temple of the Orient (O.T.O.) and an acquaintance of the notorious English magician Aleister Crowley, who called himself 'the Great Beast 666'. In general, it is evident that Gardner had an in-depth familiarity with many systems of occultism and many religions. It is hardly surprising under the circumstances that his story of how he 'rediscovered' witchcraft should be subject to challenge and outright denial, even by some modern witches.

By Gardner's account, he came across a surviving coven of the 'Old Religion' almost by accident. After returning to England, he continued his occult interests and associations, becoming involved with the Fellowship of Crotona, founded by the daughter of Theosophical luminary Annie Besant. Among the circle of occultists and eccentrics that revolved around the Fellowship, Gardner encountered some people he found to be different from the others and more interesting. Among them was 'Old Dorothy' Clutterbuck, who, according to Gardner, turned out to be the leader of a secretive, surviving coven of the 'Old Religion', and in 1939, she initiated him into what she called 'wica'. Gardner could not write openly about the Craft because the 'witchcraft laws' then in effect would have subjected him to legal penalties. Consequently, he disguised his work as fiction and published a 'novel' in 1949, entitled *High Magic's Aid*, under the pen-name 'Scire'. It was presented as 'a historical novel about the Craft and contained two initiation rituals, but there was no reference to the Goddess.'[19]

The witchcraft laws were finally repealed in 1951, due primarily to the political efforts of the Spiritualist societies. Free at last to acknowledge his real affiliations, Gardner published two books under his own name that are generally considered to be the founding texts of modern religious witchcraft: *Witchcraft Today* (1954) and *The Meaning of Witchcraft* (1959). In *Witchcraft Today*, Gardner spun the tale of himself as a folkloric Indiana Jones – an intrepid explorer who had stumbled onto one of the last remaining enclaves of a surviving pagan religion, had been initiated into their secret ways, and was now bringing news of their existence and beliefs to the outside world. Gardner was already familiar with the work of Murray and presented his 'discovery' as a validation of her premise that some paganism had survived as witchcraft. Unfortunately, the witchcraft he described was so different from her version that it could not possibly be the same phenomenon – a fact she conveniently overlooked in her supportive introduction to Gardner's book.

> Gardner's version of the Craft was very different from that described by Murray. To him, Witchcraft was a peaceful, happy nature religion. Witches met in covens, led by a priestess. They worshipped two principal deities, the god of forests and what lies beyond, and the great Triple Goddess of fertility and rebirth. They met in the nude in a nine-foot circle and raised power from their bodies through dancing and chanting and meditative techniques. They focused primarily on the

Goddess; they celebrated the eight ancient Pagan festivals of
Europe and sought to attune themselves to nature.[20]

Gardner's style of witchcraft has dominated the subsequent
growth of the witchcraft movement. The spread and evolution of
'Gardnerian Wicca' happened rapidly – a brief but complex story
we will examine in more detail in Chapter 10. Suffice it to say at
this point that Gardner was charismatically effective in recruiting
converts to his point of view, and that some of them helped to
spread his version of the Craft beyond the British Isles, to both
Europe and America. The rest, as they say, is history.

But is the *beginning* history? Is Gardner's story of his own
initiation credible? Or is it a work of imagination, based on personal experience and erudition? And a second issue is inseparable
from the first: was there, in 1939 in England, an existing coven of
'witches' that was actually a survival of an older teaching? Or did
Gardner encounter something else, which he then embroidered?
Or did he encounter nothing at all, and concoct the tale from
whole cloth? The issue is an important one for modern witches.
Even though many of them have relinquished the claim to be
heirs of an ancient pagan tradition, they do have a unique history
of their own, which is also the basis for their own tradition-in-
progress. Unfortunately, the earliest parts of that history have
proved frustratingly difficult to pin down. Gardner's demonstrated
tendency to exaggerate, embellish, and misdirect adds a further
layer of uncertainty to his story.

Some have tried to show that there was a pre-existing group
of surviving pagan 'witches' in the New Forest area that could have
initiated Gardner as he claimed, but the proposals range from
the improbable to the simply unprovable. It seems more likely
(though equally difficult to prove) that Gardner encountered a
group in the New Forest that was trying to re-create some form
of 'paganism' based on their reading of modern literature. 'It is
possible that by the late 1930s and early 1940s, members of the

Crotona Fellowship were already performing rituals based on Co-Masonry ... and inspired by the writings of Margaret Murray, and that this was the group Gardner referred to as the New Forest Coven.'[21] In this scenario, Gardner took his inspiration, as well as his initiation, from the New Forest group, and then went on finally to succeed at what they were only attempting.

In general, it is clear that Gardner's Wicca is an assemblage that draws on a variety of resources, some of them personal and subjective. It remains unclear to what extent Gardner's system is based on (or includes) anything genuinely ancient. Doreen Valiente, an early associate of Gardner and a long-time member of his coven, traced the sources of Gardner's Wicca to 'the works of Margaret Murray, Charles Godfrey Leland, Rudyard Kipling, Aleister Crowley, the Key of Solomon and the rituals of Freemasonry.' Nevertheless, she continues to believe there was a real coven for Gardner to build on, primarily because she discerns a basic, underlying structure 'which was not from Crowley or Margaret Murray or any of the other sources mentioned.'[22]

Another development in that discussion has been the work of Aidan Kelly, who has oscillated between Catholicism and witchcraft. Kelly was raised Catholic, but acquired a fascination with witchcraft and paganism during his school years. It was an interest he pursued with increasing seriousness at school and college; by 1971, he had become a practising and self-identified 'witch'. From 1974 to 1980, he studied 'Christian Origins' at college in Berkeley, California; in 1977, he returned to Catholicism, the religion of his youth. Ten years later, he left the Catholic Church for the second time and became active in the Craft again. Using the tools of textual criticism he had acquired in college, Kelly attempted to unravel Gardner's version of Wicca. He began by analysing a leather-bound manuscript written in Gardner's own hand, which Gardner called 'Ye Bok of ye Art Magical'. It had been discovered behind a filing cabinet in Gardner's study and turned out to be the very first version of what Gardner eventually called his 'Book of Shadows'; it contained various spells and rituals, and Gardner's commentaries on them. It is generally taken as a basic resource in the study of Gardnerian witchcraft. Kelly's investigation, entitled *Crafting the Art of Magic* (1991), correlates the various components of 'Ye Bok' with what he considers to be their likely sources.

At the end of his textual analysis, Kelly's primary conclusion is that no 'traditional Wicca' survived and no pre-1939 coven existed – in other words, that Wicca was essentially invented by Gardner. Beyond his assessment of Wiccan history, however, Kelly makes a larger point about the significance of history itself. He says that the recent origin of Wicca, and its status as an invention, are irrelevant and beside the point. In Kelly's view, many of the world's great religions were essentially 'invented' by their founders, who were typically reluctant to admit that fact. Instead, they tried to portray their religious innovations as developments within established traditions. In that context, Kelly depicts Gardner as a creative genius who succeeded in framing the worldview for a religion of the future.

Kelly's revisionism sparked a heated debate in the witchcraft community. Traditional Gardnerians came to Gardner's defence, claiming that his story is not only plausible, but supported by credible evidence at key points. They also questioned Kelly's research and the thesis based upon it. An extensive critique of Kelly's sources, methods, and conclusions by D. Hudson Frew and Anna Korn appeared as a review in *Gnosis* magazine.[23] Frew 'enthusiastically' endorsed Kelly's idea that historicity does not matter, but he defends the historicity of Gardner's claims in any case, because he believes the evidence is there to support them. Frew summarizes the state of Gardnerian historical studies:

> When many people talk about the history of the Craft, their attitude is: 'Why do all this speculating, when we have so little to work with?' But with Gardnerian Craft, that's just not

true. Between the different versions of the Book of Shadows, Gardner's personal magical notebooks and the correspondence between the people involved in the middle of the century, we've got thousands of pages of documents ... If anything, there's so much that it's hard to wade through. People have this idea that the craft is just about speculating in the wind. But it's exactly the opposite.[24]

Describing modern witchcraft

However Gardner's vision of witchcraft came together, the movement that sprang from it began to grow and change almost immediately. Witches today look back on more than half a century of evolution and innovation; having made the principle of creative invention a part of their religion, they believe that their ability to 'make it up as they go along' is one of the strengths of their community. Because of that ongoing self-transformation, modern witchcraft is difficult to define. But there is another reason outsiders find it hard to pin down. Witchcraft is individualistic to the point of being anarchic, with no centralized authority or even any agreed upon definition of what a 'witch' is.

After struggling with the issue, one of the leading Witchcraft groups in America (the Covenant of the Goddess [CoG]) decided that they simply could not define the term at all. In their 1975 statement, CoG's organizers said:

> We could not define what a Witch is in words. Because there are too many differenees. Our reality is intuitive. We know when we encounter someone who we feel is worshipping in the same way, who follows the same religion we do, and that's our reality, and that has to be understood, somehow, in anything we do.[25]

Thus, the religious identity of witches is to be sensed rather than specified – an approach that (needless to say) accommodates great variety in the forms of belief and practice. Under those circumstances, it is obviously difficult to speak in general terms and say that 'witches' believe this or that, or that 'they' do such and such in practising their religion. Any statement along those lines should come with a disclaimer attached, warning that the formula is riddled with exceptions. Nevertheless, if we keep that disclaimer in mind, it *is* possible to discern a religious attitude – if not a full-blown religious ideology – behind the differences of detail in modern witchcraft. There are some unmistakable commonalities that unite the movement and bond together those who make it up.

The common threads of witchcraft today are less in the details of belief and practice than they are in a sense of agreement on attitude, outlook, and perspective. Witchcraft's religious attitude begins with distinction and opposition; witchcraft asserts itself (as the sociologists say) 'against the rejected background' of the predominant culture. Its identity is proclaimed in terms of its *difference* from, and its *opposition* to, the Christian-based culture and religion(s) of the West. In fact, much of the motive force behind the growth of modern witchcraft lies in this vital sense of 'standing against' the powers that be in contemporary culture. The contagious excitement of cultural insurrection is modern witchcraft's functional substitute for missionary zeal.

Wiccan priestess Margot Adler described witchcraft's religious attitude in four major points (one of which explicitly repudiates a cardinal doctrine of Christianity). The four points can be summarized as (1) animism/polytheism/pantheism, (2) feminism, (3) 'there's no such thing as sin' (her formula) and (4) spiritual reciprocity (i.e., the idea that you get back what you mete out to others). All four points are facets of witchcraft's 'oppositional identity'. Witchcraft breaks at every point with the prevailing (Christian) religious attitude, and in particular with its monotheism and its transcendence. Witchcraft's outlook sees the divine not only as multiple, but also as immanent, and therefore as accessible – both for enlightenment and for occult empowerment. Witchcraft's viewpoint is female centred and goddess oriented, earth-based and environmentally sensitive. Witchcraft strongly repudiates the concept of sin. Finally, witchcraft's attitude fundamentally rejects the idea that we are accountable for our behaviour to a higher moral authority and a revealed moral standard. Instead, consistent with its pantheism, witchcraft believes that ethical behaviour arises naturally out of the workings of 'spiritual reciprocity'. In effect, witchcraft asserts an ethic of self-will, tempered with a self-restraint bolstered by a fear of 'reciprocal' consequences.

Neopagan Witchcraft:
the Movement

Whether Gerald Gardner discovered the religion of witchcraft or invented it, there can be no doubt that he publicized and promoted it – and that he did so with alacrity. By 1949 (the year he published his 'novel', *High Magic's Aid*), Gardner had already accumulated a body of ritual scripts and commentaries that was to be the nucleus of the emerging witch religion. By 1950, Gardner was spreading information about it to – and through – his occult acquaintances in London. By 1951 (the year the Witchcraft Laws were repealed) Gardner was putting witchcraft – and himself – into the public eye by contributing to a series of high-profile articles on the subject for a popular weekly magazine. In Hutton's words, 'Wicca was a tradition that hit the ground running.'[1]

Gardner was convinced from the outset that publicity was the key to Wicca's survival. He was also aware that publicity was a two-edged sword (given the infamous reputation of witchcraft), with a real potential for ugly sensation and backlash. But since Gardner was independently wealthy, he believed he could be a high-profile spokesman and ride out the backlash, thereby allowing others to remain in the closet.

He seriously underestimated the fallout that would ensue. Journalistic interest in Gardner's witchcraft, initially curious and respectful, quickly turned lurid and hysterical, with headlines declaring (among other things) 'Witches Devil-Worship in London'! Some members of his coven were sufficiently frightened by the furore to withdraw from further participation; many of those who remained acquired an enduring aversion to media attention. But by continuing to press for publicity, Gardner polarized opposition within the group, thus sowing seeds of the first major schism that would occur later in the movement he was building.

But Gardner had pursued the spotlight for a reason – to spread the news about his religion and attract new adherents – and his campaign succeeded in doing so. Among those drawn by the publicity was a young woman who would come to play a prominent role in the development of modern witchcraft: Doreen Valiente. Ms Valiente was possessed of a keen mind, a probing intellectual curiosity, a strong personality, and a creative streak that amounted to a poetic gift. She read the magazine articles about witchcraft and wrote to request more information; her letter was eventually passed on to Gardner, who first met with her, and later initiated her into Wicca at Midsummer of 1953.

The re-visioning of Wicca: Doreen Valiente to Alex Sanders

Gardner and Valiente's relationship turned out to be pivotal, not only for the two of them, but also for the future direction of the witchcraft movement. Valiente joined Gardner's own coven and soon became its High Priestess. When Gardner met Valiente, he was in the process of writing *Witchcraft Today*, and he began to make use of her poetic gifts right away by having her compose an invocation for a Winter Solstice celebration. Her composition, the poem 'Queen of the Moon, Queen of the Stars', made its way into Gardner's book (and Wiccan practice) as a 'traditional' witches' ritual.

In this, and other ways, Valiente supported Gardner's efforts to claim antiquity for his religion (though she seemed to have doubts about such claims herself); she also went along with the game when Gardner later presented her to journalists as a member of one of the traditional witch families he had written about in his book.[2] But she was less accepting of Gardner's deceptions when they impinged on her personal knowledge. She was familiar enough with other occult teachings to recognize that some of the supposedly 'traditional' Wiccan material in Gardner's 'Book of Shadows' had been borrowed from sources she could identify – in particular, from the works of Aleister Crowley. Valiente was fearful that Crowley's sordid and sinister reputation would spill over and contaminate anything associated with him; in a bold act of confrontation, Valiente the disciple challenged Gardner the teacher over his use of the Crowley material. Gardner rationalized that the 'tradition' he had discovered was fragmentary and he had been forced to fill in the missing parts as best he could, adding '... if you think you can do any better, go ahead.'[3]

Valiente accepted the challenge with enthusiasm. She took Gardner's 'Book of Shadows' (which he was still in the process of putting together), systematically expunged Crowley's influence, and reworked the other material into a poetically eloquent system of belief and practice that became the basis for what we know today as 'Gardnerian Wicca'. For that contribution alone, she has been called 'the Grandmother of Witchcraft'. Today, followers of modern witchcraft all over the world recite her prose and poetry as part of their ceremonies, especially the text known as the 'Charge of the Goddess', which contains the famously evocative line, 'Let my worship be in the heart that rejoiceth, for behold, all acts of love and pleasure are my rituals.'

Valiente also opened the door to Robert Graves's ideas and established a link to Celtic literature and history – thereby helping to fashion the spiritual 'personality' that has come to characterize Gardnerian Wicca (and, indeed, modern witchcraft generally). Today, Wicca is usually presented as Celtic in origin and content, and it draws heavily from Celtic mythology and symbolism – even though there is little evidence of any Celtic influence on Gardner's own work. But Gardner had connected his 'discovery' of Wicca to Murray's theory of a surviving British paganism, and when Valiente began rewriting Gardner's 'Book of

Shadows', she not only excised the telltale traces of Crowley, but she also replaced them with material that re-fashioned Wicca in the image of that (imagined) ancient British religion. To do so, she reached back to Celtic sources, including the *Carmina Gadelica* (a collection of Celtic-based folklore) for inspiration in re-writing the 'Charge of the Goddess' and some of the other ritual scripts.

Sabina Magliocco suggests that the Celtic theme captured the imagination of early Gardnerians partly for political reasons: Gardner had incorporated Greco-Roman motifs into his Wiccari material, but since Britain had so recently been under threat of Fascist invasion from the continent, it may have seemed more appropriate to emphasize traditions that were indigenous and British-based.[4] Whatever the reason, it became a common assumption (and remains one today) that the paganism from which witchcraft derived was Celtic in origin.

For four years Gardner and Valiente formed an intensely creative alliance that altered both the form and the content of Wicca, and helped set the course of the modern witchcraft movement. But their partnership was not to last. The publication of *Witchcraft Today* in 1954 produced a steady trickle of new initiates into Wicca throughout the mid-1950s, but Gardner's policy of seeking media coverage continued to generate tension and controversy within the group. Valiente and some of the older members, from their own painful brush with media frenzy, believed that the movement should keep a low press profile, emphasizing forms of self-presentation (such as books) over which they had more control. The newer members, having been drawn to Wicca by the very publicity in question, tended to be more supportive of Gardner's media activism.

The final break came in 1957. After Gardner had generated a series of articles that were silly and scurrilous by turns, Valiente and some of the others drew up thirteen 'Proposed Rules for the Craft' to protect their secrecy and promote mutual consultation; in short, the proposed 'Rules' had the effect of putting collectively imposed limits on Gardner's publicity-seeking activities. Gardner responded that their proposals were unnecessary, since a set of 'traditional Craft Laws' – which he thereupon provided – already existed. But Valiente questioned why these supposedly 'traditional' laws were just now being trotted out for the first time; also noting that Gardner's 'Laws' severely limited the power of the High Priestess, she rejected them as a modern creation. She, and the others who felt as she did, simply left the coven and went their separate ways. In her words, 'We had had enough of the Gospel according to St. Gerald; but we still believed that the real traditional witchcraft lived ... The Old Religion meant a great deal to us, and we had not stopped believing in its beauty, its magic or its power. Our parting with Gerald simply meant that the quest went on.'[5] Gardner had made her a believer in witchcraft, and she did not lose her faith in it just because she lost her faith in him. Valiente went on to become a leading exponent of independent witchcraft in Britain until her death in 1999.

Valiente's departure closed the phase of creative development that her partnership with Gardner had made possible. At the same time, it opened a new phase of literary activity for Gardner, who published *The Meaning of Witchcraft* in 1959. It also brought a new phase of growth for the movement, based in part on attracting the very sort of attention Valiente had sought to avoid. Now undeterred in his media outreach and propelled by publicity over his new book, Gardner appeared regularly in the press, and his growing notoriety drew a growing number of people to contact him seeking initiation into Wicca. During the final years of his life (from 1959 to 1964), Gardner initiated and trained people who acted both as propagators and as propagandists, carrying Gardnerian Wicca into all parts of Britain and successfully presenting it to the public as the authentic version of witchcraft.

But the Gardnerians' success was not achieved without a challenge. Gardner's claim that he had stumbled across the remnants of a pre-existing religion in the New Forest meant that there might be other remnants, in other locations. During the 1960s, and especially after Gardner's death in 1964, people came forward claiming to represent exactly such independent 'traditions'. None of those claims could be confirmed (and several turned out to be fraudulent), but some of the people who made them played an important part in shaping the early development of the witchcraft movement. One actually succeeded in establishing a new branch of the movement, based on his own, idiosyncratic form of witchcraft. Alex Sanders, by all accounts, was a psychically gifted, charismatic, and flamboyant man who claimed to be descended from a family of traditional witches. He had sought initiation from one of the leading Gardnerian priestesses, but was turned down – a rebuff he refused to accept and never forgot. He was finally initiated into another coven, by a different high priestess, and somehow managed to get hold of a version of Gardner's 'Book of Shadows', which he edited, embellished, and rearranged, claiming that the resulting composite was actually his family's Book of Shadows, passed down to him by his grandmother. That material in turn became the basis on which he eventually founded a series of his own covens and a 'tradition' of witchcraft ('Alexandrian Witchcraft') that became an active alternative to Gardnerian Wicca, particularly on the European Continent.

Sanders was a natural showman with a flair for publicity, but his first foray into the world of media relations ended disastrously when he became the focus of a newspaper article that was so negative and sensational that he lost his job and gained the lasting enmity of prominent Gardnerian witches. Despite this unfortunate beginning, Sanders persevered with his media strategy, and made his way back into the public eye in 1967, when he married Maxine Morris, a beautiful young woman who was twenty years his junior, in a highly publicized 'Wiccan Wedding'. Sanders also made Maxine his High Priestess and they moved to London, taking the titles 'King and Queen of the Witches'. Sanders was soon engaged in a publicity war with the Gardnerians, whom he disparaged as followers of a modern, made-up cult (despite the fact that he had borrowed much of his own material from Gardner himself); he also presented his version of witchcraft as the genuine article, claiming to have been initiated by his grandmother. With Alex's flamboyance, Maxine's beauty, and their dramatic new titles (plus their willingness to let themselves and their followers be photographed doing their rituals 'skyclad' – i.e., in the nude), the pair soon supplanted the Gardnerians as the media's favourite authorities on the subject of witchcraft during Britain's 'countercultural' years of the late 1960s and early 1970s.

Alex and Maxine continued to 'rule' as 'King and Queen of the Witches' until 1973, when they separated and went their own ways (though both continued to promote and practise witchcraft). Alex retired from public life, but worked to develop 'Alexandrian Witchcraft' further; he also devoted himself to initiating and training new witches, particularly from Continental Europe. By the time he died in 1988, the form of witchcraft he had created had established itself throughout Britain and Ireland, with a strong base on the Continent, and had unquestionably secured its continued existence as a recognized branch of the larger witchcraft movement.

Sanders changed the face of modern witchcraft in important ways. Although he presented his system as an independent, self-contained alternative and competitor to Gardnerian Wicca, many of his innovations were eventually adopted by other witches – including Gardnerians – and integrated into their practice. Sanders's main influence on witchcraft was to expand its definition and its demographic. By the nature of his claims, he expanded the public's perception of witchcraft beyond the boundaries set by Gardner and his followers. He also expanded both the content of witchcraft and the membership of the movement. 'Alex brought into Wicca much of the traditional learned magic of the Cabbala, the Tarot and the Golden Dawn, which other branches of it had deliberately kept out.'[6] Gardnerian Wicca also 'deliberately kept out' homosexuals; Gardner himself had stressed the importance of the male–female polarity in Wicca, which meant that an actively counter-homosexual stance was built into his system. A bisexual himself, Sanders worked during his latter years to develop forms of practice that would make witchcraft more accessible and appealing to gay men – a connection that has paid off for the movement, especially in America.

Burgeoning diversity: witchcraft in America

As Gardnerian Wicca and its variants (such as Alexandrian Witchcraft) began to spread beyond their British origins, they travelled most quickly to other parts of the former British Empire – especially to America and Australia. In Australia, witchcraft found a receptive social environment because of the long-standing presence and familiarity of Aboriginal culture, with its 'pagan' (i.e., 'non-Christian') beliefs and practices. The Aboriginal elements also provided handy fodder for eclectically minded witches, and imported British witchcraft blended readily into an expanding array of home-grown Neopaganism.

It is in America, however, that the witchcraft movement has undergone its greatest growth, achieved its greatest influence, and seen its greatest diversification. The movement has converged uniquely with a series of powerful cultural trends in a tide that has carried modern witchcraft to the verge of mainstream acceptability. And as witchcraft 'goes mainstream', American witches have used that status to link their religion with the international interfaith movement – a connection that has helped witchcraft gain worldwide acceptance as a legitimate religious expression.

American society has exhibited a remarkable openness to religious deviance and innovation ever since the dissenting Pilgrims landed at Plymouth Rock in 1620 as refugees from the

English ecclesiastical establishment. The new land quickly gained a reputation for religious freedom and opportunity, a fact that became a lasting facet of America's national character. In the following centuries, a host of new religions (and new sects of old religions) have arrived or arisen to find a home among the American people, from the Quakers, Shakers, and Mormons to the Muslims and Scientologists of today. Some have succeeded and some have failed. But timing is everything and modern witchcraft came to America just in time to coincide with the countercultural upheaval of the 1960s – and with some of the other trends and movements that came out of that tumultuous decade. Witchcraft's rising fortunes were further enhanced by advances in communications technology and by trends in popular culture and entertainment. The result has been to give American witchcraft a social, cultural, and spiritual presence that is increasingly robust and increasingly global in scope.

Organized American witchcraft began in 1962, when Raymond and Rosemary Buckland brought Wicca from England to Long Island, New York, with an explicit 'charter' from British Gardnerians to transmit the Craft in America. Over the course of the next decade, their work was abetted by the spread of information about Wicca through Gardner's books and eventually through the writings of other British witches as well (such as Stewart Farrar's *What Witches Do* in 1971, see plate XVIII). At the same time, witchcraft was attracting favourable attention in the American counterculture. Denizens of the counterculture found Wicca's 'oppositional identity' to be congenial with their own 'turn on, tune in, and drop out' rejection of mainstream society. But the counterculture was also eclectically creative, anarchically individualistic, and anti-hierarchical – all qualities that were an ill fit with the Gardnerians' traditionalism, structure and initiatory elitism. Before long Americans started to mix Gardner's Wiccan material with ideas drawn from other sources, including personal inspiration, other occult traditions, and even science-fiction literature. The result was a rapidly expanding spectrum of new witch 'traditions'.

> As Gardnerian Craft spread throughout North America, it also inspired a number of individuals to develop their own variants of it. Buckland himself, while he had at first railed against the impostors who established their own brand of Witchcraft, split from his tradition in 1973 to create Seax or Saxon Wicca. Because North American society is multiethnic, many innovators injected bits of their own folkmagical traditions into the brands of Witchcraft they concocted, giving the American Wiccan landscape a decidedly multiethnic flavor.[7]

One ethnically based variant that emerged from that burgeoning diversity made yet another connection – a political one this time – that altered both the composition and the direction of the witchcraft movement. 'Z' (for Zusanna) Budapest was a Hungarian immigrant whose mother had been an artist, a spirit-medium, a practising witch, and a goddess-enthusiast. Budapest arrived in America in 1959, three years before British witchcraft and four years before the publication of Betty Friedan's *The Feminine Mystique* (widely regarded as the ideological basis for the feminist movement). Twelve years later, witchcraft, feminism, and Budapest herself all converged in southern California. After having been radicalized by American-style gender politics, Budapest established the 'Susan B. Anthony Coven Number One' in Los Angeles on Winter Solstice in 1971, blending her paganism with her politics to create what came to be called 'Women's Spirituality'.

There was already a tradition in radical politics (dating back to Michelet) of portraying the witch as a heroic figure in the struggle for human liberation. In the late 1960s, radical feminists shifted the focus of that symbolism, portraying the witch as a heroine of gender liberation specifically. Feminists claimed that original witchcraft had been an instrument of female power and independence, that it was accessible to all women simply by virtue of being female, and that it needed to be recovered by women today in order to (re)gain their power and freedom. But the witch-admiring feminists of the 1960s were strictly political and apparently did not know that there were people who actually claimed to *be* modern witches existing at the time.

Budapest and her fellow coveners, on the other hand, knew very well in 1971 that they were cross-fertilizing modern witchcraft and feminist politics. Budapest blended elements of Gardnerian Wicca (specifically, Wicca's symbols, rituals, and emphasis on magic) with the causes and concerns of radical feminism and of radical politics generally. 'Women's Spirituality' emerged from that mix as a form of religious separatism (no men allowed) with an autonomous female deity ('The Goddess') 'whose devotees were pitted against patriarchy, militarism and ecological destruction'.[8] Budapest called her new 'tradition' 'Dianic Witchcraft' (or 'Dianics')[9] after the male-shunning goddess of Greco-Roman tradition. It is not surprising, given its radical feminist origins, that 'Dianic practice has a very high percentage of lesbian participants.'[10] In effect, Budapest did for homosexual women what Sanders did for homosexual men – i.e., opened the practice of witchcraft to their full participation.

Those developments swelled the ranks of modern witchcraft and raised its public profile, but they were not well received by all witches. Gardnerians especially rejected Budapest's sexual exclusivism and deplored the Dianic tendency towards 'Goddess Monotheism' ('Spare us Jahweh in drag!' pleaded one). And the idea that the power of witchcraft was inherent in all women, simply by virtue of being female, directly opposed the Gardnerian view of witchcraft as a closed, structured system of initiation into progressively revealed mysteries based on the dynamism of sexual polarity. The witchcraft movement took a great step forward when that built-in conflict was

brilliantly resolved in 1979 with the publication of *The Spiral
Dance* by Starhawk, a Californian feminist writer who had
been trained by Gardnerians ... She showed how the coven
could be turned into a training group in which women could
be liberated, men could be re-educated, and alternative
human relationships explored. She reinterpreted magic in
terms of psychology, as a set of techniques for self-fullfillment
and the realization of human potential.[11]

Starhawk (née Miriam Simos) founded the 'Reclaiming Tradition' of witchcraft based on her blending of elements from
Gardner's Wicca (and Victor Andersons 'Faery Tradition'[12]) with
the rawer feminist witchcraft and activist politics of Budapest
and the Dianics. Her purpose was to give modern witchcraft
a greater relevance and a wider appeal – and it worked. Sales
of *The Spiral Dance* soon surpassed all the other books on the
subject and before long, 'it had replaced *Witchcraft Today* as
the model text.'[13]

Beyond its alliance with feminism, witchcraft's emphasis
on nature also resonated with the larger culture's rising anxiety
over the environment. Tim ('Otter') Zell was one of many witches
and pagans of the period who took the notion of Earth as a living
entity (James Lovelock's 'Gaia Hypothesis') and conflated it with
the presumed Goddess(es) of pagan religion. Zell, Starhawk, and
other American witches continued to draw energy from environmental issues during the 1980s, further increasing modern
witchcraft's social momentum and bringing it into even closer
parallel with mainstream concerns.

Z Budapest and 'Women's Spirituality' carried witchcraft
from the occult ghetto into the heart of American activist politics. Starhawk carried it back out again to the wider public by
linking it with compatible strains of social critique and self-
development philosophy – thereby diffusing witchcraft far
beyond its esoteric sources.

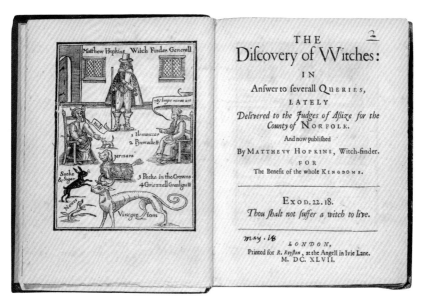

THE
Discovery of Witches:
IN
Answer to severall QUERIES,
LATELY
Delivered to the Judges of Assize for the
County of NORFOLK.
And now published
By MATTHEW HOPKINS, Witch-finder.
FOR
The Benefit of the whole KINGDOME.

EXOD. 22. 18.
Thou shalt not suffer a witch to live.

LONDON,
Printed for R. Royston, at the Angell in Ivie Lane.
M. DC. XLVII.

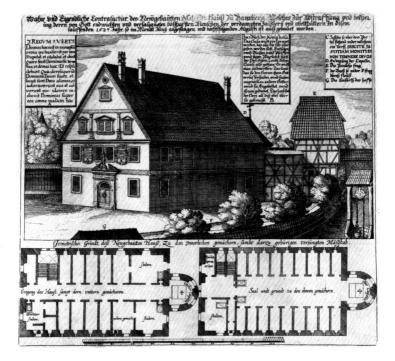

XIV ABOVE The trial of George Jacobs, Salem, 1692, showing the hysterical atmosphere of the courtroom. Jacobs was hanged on the testimony of his granddaughter, Margaret Jacobs, who later admitted her accusations were false.

XV LEFT Frontispiece to Heinrich Institoris' *Malleus Maleficarum*, 'The Hammer of Witches'. First published in 1486, the *Malleus* was frequently reprinted, became enormously popular and helped initiate the witch-craze.

XVI Burning of the witches of Mora in 1670, one of the last manifestations of the witch-craze in Europe. During the trials a number of children claimed that they were carried away by witches to a place called Blocula where they attended a sabbat presided over by Satan.

XVII Collin de Plancy, *The Sabbat*. This nineteenth-century panoramic view illustrates many of the clichés of witchcraft: the flight through the air, the use of sacrificed children in the preparation of the magical salve, the veneration of the Devil, the backward dance and the revel.

xviii Stewart and Janet Farrar dressed as the Horned God and the Moon Goddess, the principal deities of Wicca. The Horned God represents the male aspect of divinity: the Lord of Death, Winter and the hunt. While the Moon Goddess represents the female aspect: the Mother Goddess, Summer, fertility and birth.

xix Gerald Gardner, known as 'the father of modern witchcraft' and founder of Gardnerian Wicca. Gardner's version of witchcraft was drawn both from literary sources and his personal experiences working in Ceylon (now Sri Lanka), Borneo and Malaya (now Malaysia).

THE CRAFT

WELCOME TO THE WITCHING HOUR

xx *The Craft,* released in 1996, follows four teenage girls and their pursuit of witchcraft. As entertainment, the film was strictly run-of-the-mill Hollywood fare, but it was a breakthrough event in the public's perception of modern witchcraft.

Cyber-culture, pop culture, and the rise of the paganoids

The internet is another factor that has taken Witchcraft far beyond its esoteric sources. One of the real surprises of the 1980s was the emergence of a strong connection between witches, high technology, and the computer culture. The relationship came to light in 1986, in the revised edition of Margot Adler's *Drawing Down the Moon*. In surveying witches and Neopagans to bring her research up to date, Adler discovered that 'their job profiles are pretty unusual, with an amazingly high percentage in computer, scientific and technical fields.'[14]

That previously undiscovered link has several implications, one of which is that there have been witchcraft practitioners, enthusiasts, and sympathizers circulating in the high-tech world from the beginning – and those same people were consequently in attendance at the birth of the internet. American witches, therefore, were among the first to stumble upon the power of the net to link scattered individuals together into an entity that is greater than the sum of its parts. The internet has been central to the development of the witchcraft movement for two reasons: it strengthens the hand of culturally marginal types in general by allowing people who would otherwise remain isolated from one another to connect and it does so while maintaining the individual's privacy and anonymity.

Those two characteristics of the internet have also helped to create the homosexual community – a different 'cultural minority', but one that overlaps with witchcraft significantly in its composition. In 'Queer Witches and the World Wide Web: Breaking the Spell of Invisibility', self-described 'Faggot Witch Sparky Rabbit' writes:

> One of the biggest obstacles faced by Queer men and women is the cloak of invisibility put on us by the dominant culture's hetero-sexism ... One of the worst experiences many Queer

people share is the feeling, from childhood on, that 'I am the only one of my kind in the world'... So when the Web became available – *bam!!* – Queers were all over it from the git-go. When I was first learning about computers and the Internet, in the mid-nineties, a friend of mine said, 'The Internet is made up of Pagans and Queers.' I don't believe that statement was statistically correct, but it was definitely an accurate expression of what many Queer Pagans I know were experiencing on the web; there were a Hell of a lot more of us out there than any one of us had ever guessed.[15]

The most important contribution of the internet to political, social, and cultural dissent of every kind – modern witchcraft included – was its 'breaking the spell of invisibility', also known as 'minority empowerment', also known as 'linking otherwise isolated individuals'. It was a development that made everything else possible, as numerous 'alternative cultures' arose, and many of them turned into outright cultural resistance movements. M. Macha Nightmare describes the difference that the net has made to Witches and Neopagans:

Prior to the advent of the Internet and the World Wide Web, Witches and Pagans were isolated from one another ... several covens and traditions could exist in the same city, or even in the same neighborhood and never even know about one another ... most Witches lived their lives in the figurative broom closet. Discretion was the safe and prudent approach when it came to our religion. We kept ourselves, and our groups, to ourselves.

The Net changed all that. On the Web, isolated individuals and groups found one another ... The Web allowed community to be created where none had been. The anonymity of online communications liberated witchen folks to express their thoughts, feelings and experiences in relative safety. So, in a sense, the Web became our church.[16]

The rapid rise and success of the website Witchvox.com, which is no longer active, illustrates the growing presence of witchcraft on the internet during the late 90s and early twenty-first century. Wren Walker and Fitz Jung inaugurated the website in 1997 with 56 pages of content and a brief listing of Neopagan links and contacts.

> By the end of its first year, Witchvox was offering 385 pages which were viewed on personal computers the world over. Within that time, the site had received 1,235,237 hits. It listed several thousand Witches, Wiccans and Pagans on its state and country pages, 385 circles and events, 250 witchen and metaphysical shops (most submitted by customers), 976 Pagan Web sites (with complete contact info), and a site map ... Truly, the Witches' Voice is something for us Witches to crow about.[17]

But even that auspicious beginning was just a trickle in advance of the torrent to come. In the years following its inauguration, Witchvox.com grew as expansively as the community it served. In 2006, the site passed the mark of 200 million hits logged since 1997. Its contact list (entitled 'Witches of the World') contained 4,095 pages of text, with over 99,000 named contacts, including 7,263 groups and organizations and 1,300 shops and stores, as well as individuals, publishers, and booksellers all around the globe. There were extensive listings for all 50 American states, all provinces of Canada, all regions of Britain, and all states of Australia, as well as 40 other countries worldwide. There was also a separate catalogue of electronic contacts ('Witchvox Links') that included 11,628 witchcraft and Neopagan websites.

Today, witchcraft is more visible and accessible on the internet than ever. In fact, without having access to the net, it is almost impossible to get a real impression of how vigorous and expansive the modern witchcraft movement has become. The early close connection between witches and the internet helped to create the movement by bringing its participants together and giving them a way of conversing, as witches used the net mainly to communicate with one another. Later, net-savvy witches took the technology from an inward-looking tool of movement-building to an active tool of cultural outreach, and today they also use it to communicate with the public at large. In the twenty-first century, surfing the web is one of the primary ways that people come into contact with modern witchcraft for the first time.

Another major diffusion of knowledge about modern witchcraft took place in the mid-1990s when there was a sudden proliferation of witchcraft themes in the media that implanted an image and concept of modern witchcraft directly into popular culture (especially teen culture). The results of that mid-1990s pop-culture explosion are still with us today. In 1996, Sony Pictures released *The Craft*, a sensational film about teenage witches, which was a major box office success. Industry trend-watchers instantly took notice and *The Craft* was just the first in a series of film and video productions about witches and witchcraft that came out of Hollywood in quick succession over the next few years. 1996 also saw the inauguration of *Sabrina, the Teenage Witch*, a television series that turned the teen witchcraft connection into a half-hour sitcom. The following year brought *Buffy the Vampire Slayer*, an hour-long teenage/horror/sci-fi/comedy-adventure series that was wildly popular with its target audience and even drew a surprising amount of serious scholarly attention.[18] The media's three-year witchcraft spree climaxed in 1998, with another new television series (*Charmed*) and another new film (*Practical Magic*), both of which featured young actresses at the peak of their careers and the height of their popularity with younger audiences.

But the pace-setting film was unquestionably *The Craft*, with its dramatic tale of four teenage girls who dabble in witchcraft and discover real power in their spellcasting, only to lose control of it – and of themselves. They eventually turn their powers against one another, and the movie ends with a sensational duel of magical powers between good and bad witches. On one level, *The Craft* (see plate xx) is simply a spooky teenage film, of the kind that Hollywood churns out routinely, but on a deeper level, the film has proved to be a break-through event in the public's awareness of modern witchcraft. On a deeper level still, it has even set off changes within the witchcraft movement itself.

The Craft is different from all previous Hollywood films about witchcraft in one important respect: it presents a picture of modern witchcraft that actually resembles the real thing, instead of being based on the standard medieval stereotypes. That is not an accident, of course, nor is it the result of merely casual research. The film's producers sought out a prominent witch from the occult community in Los Angeles to act as a consultant on the script. Pat Devin, who was then Co-National Public Information Officer for the Covenant of the Goddess (CoG), worked with Sony for two years to bring the film version of modern witchcraft substantially into line with the real-life version. The result is that, although modern Witchcraft was sensationalized for the sake of the film, it is still identifiably modern witchcraft. Despite Adler's horrified reaction (she called it 'the worst movie ever made!'[19]), *The Craft* turned out to be a magnet for modern witchcraft for two reasons. The first is a matter of simple psychology: the lesson of the film's 'cautionary tale' (i.e., that the lust for control leads to the loss of control) is largely lost on teenagers, but its dangled lure of occult power definitely is not. A sense of attraction to the dream of control (especially the dream of controlling others) is what the film lastingly conveys. The second reason is more concrete: because the witchcraft in the film resembles the real thing, its lure of occult power is linked to a collection of ideas, rituals, and objects in the real world that teenagers will actually encounter when they investigate further. Thus, curious teenagers have a pre-existing framework of information and involvement waiting for them to plug their curiosity into. And there were *a lot* of curious teenagers coming out of the cinemas in 1996. Pat Devin calculates the numbers:

> *The Craft* was seen by approximately one million people in its first weekend. If one in ten of those people are intrigued enough to look into the subject further, maybe read a book (and now there are shelves full of books!) that's 100,000 people who will at least be more educated about our reality. If one in ten of *those* people chose to pursue the subject further, that's 10,000 people out of the first weekend.

> I began calling myself a Witch at 16 because Donovan wrote a song called 'Season of the Witch.' I do not underestimate the impact of the media on teenagers, and this movie was brewed up for the teenage audience.[20]

The effect was explosive and virtually instantaneous. Within days of the film's opening, inquiries began to pour into the various witchcraft groups. They were all caught off-guard; even those that had some advance knowledge of the film were stunned by the scale and suddenness of the response.

That unexpected surge of teenage interest in witchcraft posed a problem for the movement in more ways than one. In the first place, it was a wave of fascination they were largely unprepared to deal with. Modern witchcraft was not a young person's movement; few witches had any experience of dealing with teenage inquirers and no group had any kind of organized teenage outreach. In the second place, the prospect of having teenagers 'convert' to witchcraft while still under their parents' roof was a hot potato, to say the least – not just emotionally, but legally as well. Any witchcraft organization that deliberately drew a child away from its parents' religion stood a very good chance of being sued into oblivion. With that danger in mind, the witch-craft groups generally took a hands-off approach in dealing with minors. The combined result of their unreadiness and their wariness is that the organized witchcraft movement lost control of the witchcraft phenomenon in popular culture. Teenagers drawn to witchcraft were forced to rely chiefly on one another, as Adler notes:

> The fact is that most Pagan groups won't take teenagers – they're afraid of repercussions from unsympathetic parents. So in fact most teenagers just find like-minded friends, because there are very few groups that teens can enter until they're 18.[21]

As a consequence, the young witch-wannabes had no choice but to build their concept of witchcraft based on what they saw in films, on television, on the internet, or simply from talking with friends. It was an information gap just waiting to be filled and the market responded with a rash of simplified do-it-yourself books on witchcraft for teenagers, explicitly aimed at exploiting the interest *The Craft* had created. The first of these was Silver Ravenwolf's pointedly named *Teen Witch: Wicca for a New Generation* (1998) – which turned out to be the bellwether for a whole new genre of teen literature. That new, teen-specific literature then began to shape both the image and the content of witchcraft in teen culture. Thus, as teenagers embraced witchcraft, witchcraft itself became part of the self-contained, self-referential world of teen culture, disconnected even from its roots in adult Neopaganism. It became a subculture unto itself.

It became, in fact, a whole new branch of modern witchcraft among young people that quickly took on a life of its own. Before 1996, the movement consisted mostly of religious witches, who saw themselves connected by their common separation from the 'mundane' world and all of its (Christian-based) values, institutions, and activities, but *The Craft* created an instant crop of new 'witches' who adopted the identity glibly and had no part in the psychological universe that traditional witches shared. Pop-culture witches, generally speaking, had no initiation, or any kind of occult training; they had no connection to any teaching or tradition; they either could not or did not join existing organizations; they took their impression of witchcraft from sources that traditional witches disdain, such as popular entertainment; and they were fully part of the mundane world, with little sense of separation from it (apart from having a teenager's rebellious attitude towards adult society in general).

For their part, pop-culture witches were inclined to see traditional witches as stodgy and hide-bound, un-hip and out of touch. It is one of the ironies of the movement that even as modern witches are striving to establish their tradition of less than a century *as* a tradition, they are already faced with a cadre of younger, self-proclaimed 'witches' who are out of touch with that tradition and largely indifferent to it. Websites such as Witchvox.com made an effort to serve both cultures and thereby act as a bridge between them. Nevertheless, the incompatibilities remain, and have not been resolved in the years since *The Craft* was released.

Witchcraft and the interfaith interface

One of the incompatibilities between traditional witchcraft and pop-culture witchcraft has been in their approach to the mainstream. Pop-culture witchcraft is sufficiently vague in structure and content to qualify more as a 'lifestyle' than a 'religion'. It moves towards mainstream acceptability through repeated exposure of the public to (often shallow and sensationalized) media versions of itself. Traditional witches, on the other hand, are committed to mainstreaming themselves as 'a religion among religions', with a formal identity, status, and legal protection. The emergence of pop-culture's 'witchcraft-as-lifestyle' confuses the picture that traditional witches want to draw of themselves on that issue.

In that context, some traditional witches have sought recognition *as* a religion *from* other religions, by involving themselves in the Interfaiths Movement. The pioneer in this kind of activism has been the Covenant of the Goddess (CoG), established in Berkeley, California, in 1975. One of the first things CoG did as an organization was to join the local Interfaith Council, but CoG's interfaith work began in earnest in 1985, when Wiccan Elder Don Frew was appointed as Northern California CoG's representative at the Berkeley Area Interfaith Council (B.A.I.C.). Frew walked into his first meeting to find a room uneasily divided between traditional believers on one side (Christians, Jews, Buddhists) and 'alternative' believers on the other (Scientologists, Hare Krishnas, 'New Age' groups). Long-serving council members recognized CoG from years before, and because Frew represented an alternative faith, but had friends among the traditionalists, Frew was able to act as a bridge between the two sides; witches and Neopagans have been an integral part of the B.A.I.C. and its work ever since.

Perhaps only in Berkeley could a witch spontaneously act as a bridge between traditional and 'fringe' religions at an interfaith meeting, but the eventual effects of that connection were not localized at all. In fact, they literally went around the world. What had started on a small scale and at a local level, eventually became organized policy – first for CoG, and later for other witchcraft and Neopagan groups in America.[22]

Nevertheless, for several years after Frew became an interfaith activist, his work was pursued on a local and largely personal basis. It was one thing to receive religious respect and recognition in the context of Berkeley's spiritual zoo, where traditional witches sometimes seemed like the 'safe and sane' part of the religious fringe, but it was quite another to get recognition in the larger religious community, where witches were viewed with scepticism at best, suspicion at worst, and disrespect in any case. But all of that changed in 1993 – partly out of commemoration and partly out of convergence.

The commemoration in 1993 marked the hundredth anniversary of the 'Parliament of the World's Religions'. The original Parliament in 1893 had been part of the century-ending Columbian Exposition in Chicago, and is widely acknowledged to be the founding event of the modern interfaith movement. A hundred years later, an elaborate celebration was planned, including the holding of a second Parliament in honour of the first. As 1993 approached, word of the second Parliament spread throughout the North American Interfaith Network. CoG representatives learned of the event through their interfaith connections and made plans to attend. CoG was originally going to send three representatives to the Parliament, but their members responded so warmly to the project that they assembled a volunteer group of more than forty, all of whom travelled to the event at their own expense. As the group departed for Chicago, they were uncertain what they would encounter, or what their reception would be; this would be their first major engagement with the world of inter-religious dialogue beyond the rather exotic spiritual environment of Berkeley.

What the group encountered in Chicago was a striking convergence of worries and hopes that placed witches squarely in the international spotlight and placed witchcraft directly within the mainstream of modern religious thought – literally overnight. CoG officer Don Frew tells how the coming together of religious and environmental themes pushed modern witchcraft to centre stage in the international arena.

> In the first plenary session of the 1993 Parliament, Dr. Gerald Barney, the scientist who had prepared the Global 2000 report on the environment for President Jimmy Carter, told the crowd about the imminent environmental collapse of the planet ... Dr. Barney, a Christian, went on to lay much of the blame for this with the major, 'world' religions, especially Christianity. 'What we need', he said, 'are new spiritualities and new ways to re-sacralize nature, if the Earth is to survive.'

And there we were.

From its very first session, the 1993 Parliament was focused on re-sacralizing Nature ... Suddenly, we Witches found ourselves the media darlings of the conference! Our 'What is Wicca?' workshops had to be moved to larger rooms to accommodate the huge numbers wanting to attend. Our Full Moon ceremony in a nearby park, planned for a circle of 50, drew 500! ... By the end of the nine days, the academics attending the Parliament were saying 'In 1893, America was introduced to the Buddhists and Hindus; in 1993, we met the Neopagans.' One media person described the Parliament as 'the coming out party for the Neopagans.'

From that point on, Neopagans would be included in almost every national or global interfaith event. At the 1993 Parliament, we ceased being a bunch of weirdos and became a religious minority. As [CoG officer] Michael Thorn said after returning from Chicago, 'This was the most important event in the history of the Craft since the publication of *Witchcraft Today* in 1954!'[23]

Looking forward: growth, validation, and change

After the signal public relations success of the 1993 Parliament, CoG's membership made interfaith work a priority for the organization. Within two years of the Chicago Parliament, CoG was active in another inter-religious project with global reach – Episcopal Bishop William Swing's United Religions Initiative (U.R.I.). The U.R.I. was conceived in 1995 as a religious counterpart to the United Nations, after Swing was commissioned to write an ecumenical liturgy for the U.N.'s Fiftieth Anniversary. Feeling chagrined by the religious world's failure to match the U.N.'s successful half-century, the Bishop decided it was time to bring the world's religions together on a permanent basis in some kind of oganization. The result was that U.R.I. CoG members were involved in creating the U.R.I, and even helped to write the U.R.I. Charter, which reflects the influence of Neopaganism in its opening words:

> We, people of diverse religions, spiritual expressions and indigenous traditions throughout the world, hereby establish the United Religions Initiative to promote enduring, daily interfaith cooperation, to end religiously motivated violence and to create cultures of peace, justice and healing for the Earth and all living beings.

There are numerous opportunities for interfaith work and CoG has moved into as many areas as their resources permit. The 1993 Parliament generated several subsequent conferences; another Parliament was held in Cape Town in 1999 and yet another in Barcelona in 2004. CoG has been involved in all of them, as well as in the ongoing activities of the U.R.I. The witches of CoG see their interfaith participation both as activism and as religion.

> As a person of faith, called by my gods to care for and protect the Earth, how can I not be involved? Interfaith work is, in my opinion, the best hope for the future of the Earth. Neopagans ... are active at the heart of the global interfaith movement. This is our opportunity to be part of the change we wish to see.[24]

Whatever may come of the change they wish to see, it is clear that their interfaith strategy has been successful in at least one of its aims. CoG's interreligious engagement has moved modern witchcraft far towards religious validation and mainstream acceptance – not just in America, but around the world. Frew describes the effectiveness of CoG's interfaith work:

> Neopagans are now welcome in interfaith events all over the world. And it is paying off in increased understanding. In

both Cape Town [the 1999 Parliament] and half way 'round the world in Rio de Janeiro [the 2002 U.R.I. Summit], I didn't meet a single person who didn't know what Wicca is! 'Oh, yeah, the Goddess. Earth-religion. I've heard of that!' was the usual response we got. *We* didn't teach them this, the interfaith groups did.[25]

Modern witchcraft is a religion in transition. In view of the fact that it has already had more significant events in its short history than many religions record over centuries, it would be rash to speculate on its future from this point onwards. But the current movement harbours one internal tension that will plainly have to be resolved. An approaching crisis is built into the process of changing from social rejection to social accept-ance, from being a closed, secretive, initiatory cult to being an open, recognized, public religion. The issue can be put in the form of a question: when one's religious identity, and much of one's religious motivation, has been derived from opposing the mainstream, what happens when one *joins* the mainstream? In a multitude of ways, that process is already under way, and it is certain to involve major changes.

Don Frew, one of the architects of CoG's interfaith policy, offers a glimpse at what some of those changes might turn out to be.

As we enter the 21st century, there is no question that the Craft is 'mainstreaming.' Determining what this means will be our greatest challenge. How will we integrate our traditions of secrecy and anonymity with the realities of being a modern, public religion? How will we integrate the tribal, shamanistic model of religion that has dominated Paganism for the last 50 years with the realities of a modern technological society? How will we integrate our spiritual roots and identity in the pre-Christian religions of Europe with the realities of a diverse,

muti-ethnic America? And how will we do all of this while
remaining true to our Pagan heritage?

Some of us are looking to late Classical models of Paganism in
the Roman world for examples of how a polytheistic, nature religion
can be compatible with an urban, cosmopolitan world and public
lifestyle. The Craft in the twenty-first century will either find a
successful new path, or we will unconsciously replicate the religious structures that the Craft's founders were rebelling against,
and that drove people to the Craft in the first place.[26]

The Role of Witchcraft

Historically the three types of witch are: the sorcerer who practises the simple magic found worldwide; the heretic who allegedly practised diabolism and was prosecuted during the witch hunts; and the Neopagan. They have little in common other than the name 'witch'.

Of the three types, that of the witch hunts has had the greatest historical effect. Historical European witchcraft was a diabolism (Devil-worship) formed out of ancient sorcery, paganism, folklore, heresy, scholastic theology, and trials at local, state, and ecclesiastical courts. Whether anyone actually ever practised this sort of witchcraft is open to question. A few individuals and groups may have conducted diabolical rites, but they were rare. The chief importance of heretical witchcraft is the concept itself: what these witches may really have done is eclipsed by what they were believed to do. People act on the basis of what they believe to be true, and those who believed in the reality of a diabolical conspiracy of witchcraft brought about the death of about sixty thousand persons, terrorized thousands more, distorted educated minds for centuries, and left a blot on the record of Christendom.

Many reasons have been offered for the origins, spread, and ultimate decline of the witch hunts. But the fundamental importance of the hunts is not their particular and intellectual genesis. Fundamentally, the witch hunts attest a hideous flaw in human nature: the desire to project evil on others, define them as outsiders, and then punish them horribly. The burnings at Bamberg and the hangings at Salem are functionally comparable with the ovens of Dachau, the brutalities of the Gulag, and the genocides in Cambodia and Rwanda. The ideology determines the form that the evil takes, but the evil lurking behind the form is built into humanity. Denial of evil only strengthens its power.

To turn from heretical witchcraft to Neopaganism is something of a relief. Contrary to what many people still suppose, modern witches do not worship the Devil, say black masses, or sacrifice creatures. The few people doing such things stand completely outside what is becoming an increasingly accepted tradition of modern witchcraft, and they are no more relevant to the mainstream of Neopaganism than bizarre Christian sects are relevant to the mainstream of Christianity. The mainstream of modern witchcraft is the creation of a new religion with some similarities to ancient sorcery and paganism. What is the reason for the increasing success of witchcraft, and what is its religious validity?

Its success is partly explainable in terms of the general growth of the occult since the 1960s. In a broad historical view, interest in the occult has surged in periods of rapid social breakdown when establishments cease to provide readily accepted answers and people turn elsewhere for assurance. The third century, when Roman society was weakening, the sixteenth century, when the medieval synthesis was crumbling, and the late twentieth century are periods for which this generalization seems true. The roots of the current occult revival are in the soil of the mid-nineteenth to mid-twentieth centuries, when traditional Christianity was weakening. The conjunction of five planets and the sun within the sign of Aquarius in February 1962 seemed to some to betoken a new 'Age of Aquarius', and 1962 was an important year for the more specific reason that it was then that Gardnerian witchcraft was imported into America, which soon became the centre of 'Wicca'. Interest waned somewhat after a peak in the 1970s, but in the 1980s Wicca revived and even established bridgeheads in Continental Europe. Since the early 1990s it has gained considerable strength, a testament to the rapid fragmentation of Western social and intellectual values. One has only to look at the substantial sections on 'metaphysics' in bookshops to see that the level of interest continues to be high.

It is difficult to define the occult and almost as difficult to define modern witchcraft. The cultural revolution in Western society since the 1960s was essentially anti-establishment, and cultural mores based in conservative social values were derided and attacked. In religion, Christianity was perceived as part of the establishment, so Judaeo-Christian values were deemed pernicious. Anything old had to be destroyed so that humanity could be freed to reveal its true self: its basically good nature. (This goodness of human nature, by the way, is unknown to both historians and biologists.)

The radical views of the counterculture were almost identical to – and largely derived from – the movement of Romanticism in the nineteenth century, which was based on the idea of the perfectibility of human nature freed from the bonds of traditional authority. The mantra of the Romantics was that feelings trumped thoughts and that the creative and original trumped the rational and empirical. The 1960s ushered in a renewed Romanticism based upon feelings. Notable manifestations were environmentalism; feminism; sexual liberation; drugs; electronic entertainment; gay, lesbian, and transsexual liberation; occult fiction and films; crystals and tarots. Among intellectual postmodernists and deconstructionists, the relativizing of the arts and humanities and the growing opposition to the physicalist views dominant in the sciences undermined previous certainties. Orthodoxies of all kinds – especially religious ones – were mocked and reviled. This vast seedbed of cultural change was the perfect environment in which modern, Neopagan witchcraft could flourish.

The cracking of religious and scientific orthodoxies allowed scope for the formation of alternative ways of looking at the world.

Many efforts in this direction are bound to be ignorant, uncritical, and therefore ineffective. Indeed, lack of basic critical standards is characteristic of the occult. Earlier we defined superstition as a belief held by an individual who does not have a coherent system of thought in which that belief appropriately fits. By this definition much occult thought is undeniably superstitious. Occultists often adopt beliefs according to the following pattern: it could be; I want it to be; it is. Such non-thought is ultimately self-destructive. Both dogmatic rigidity and uncritical credulity impede the search for truth.

The term 'occult' is probably too closely associated with this sort of position to be able to acquire – or deserve – more positive connotations. But even 'occult' is old fashioned, residing mostly in musty sections of used bookshops. If we replace the vague term 'occult' with 'Neopagan', the concept of creative, synthetic approaches to reality can be looked at more sympathetically. One of the most patently false ideas cherished in modern society is the idea of progress. This eighteenth-century idea, counter to historical and scientific facts, seized anthropology and sociology at the beginning of the twentieth century and produced the assumption that magic progressed into religion and religion progressed into science; that polytheism progressed into monotheism and monotheism into atheism. Exploitation of nature was supposed to represent progress over concord with nature. Everything was supposed to be improving. Technology was supposed to solve all our problems. The cover of the March 2006 issue of the alumni magazine of a famous university boldly asked, 'Can We Know Everything?' This strange combination of arrogance and naiveté is not atypical of physicalist academics. Once such untenable fantasies are removed, we can perceive values in some alternatives that have been rejected. Perhaps syncretic, intuitive thought is as valuable as analytic thought. Perhaps atheism is not an advance over religion. Perhaps pantheism can help us understand insights that monotheism has lost. It is in this context that modern witchcraft or Neopaganism can be seen as a potentially valuable alternative approach to reality.

Neopaganism must, however, be tempered by critical thought. A persistent danger in witchcraft is that unstable people may be led into destructive or self-destructive acts by tinkering with magic. People tempted to believe that they have secret powers should remain extremely sceptical of such powers in themselves – and even more sceptical of such powers in others, because of the danger of being drawn into psychologically and even physically dangerous cults by deluded and manipulative leaders. But irrational behaviour on the part of some witches does not invalidate witchcraft in general any more than irrational behaviour on the part of some Christians, Hindus, or Marxists invalidates their beliefs. The question rather is whether witchcraft has anything of value to offer.

One need not be a witch to understand witchcraft as one expression of the religious experience. The ancient pagan religions, when deeply understood, are ambivalent, with both destructive and positive elements. Anthropologists, psychologists, and others have shown that they can be rich, beautiful, and insightful. Neopagan witches are attempting to retrieve the positive aspects of pagan religion and to weave them into a new, modern synthesis. The positive values inherent in this attempt include an emphasis on individual creativity and expression in moulding rites and beliefs. Neopagan witchcraft and its rites provide a great deal of room for poetry, dance, music, laughter, and whatever the moment and the tradition inspire. Witchcraft encourages openness to the awe of the natural world and reverence and love of the cosmos. It also offers a grasp of the importance of the unconscious in integrating the whole psyche. It offers a sense of the importance of the feminine principle that has often been obscured in the masculine symbolism of the great monotheistic religions. Its validity has recently been argued in both theology and the law.

Whatever the future of witchcraft as a religious force of its own, its values should be introduced as freshly and as deeply as possible. They should also be advanced as honestly as possible. The persistent assertion of some Neopagans that they continue an unbroken tradition of ancient religions is false. There were no Wicca covens before Gardner set them up in 1939. It is the fresh creativity of many forms of witchcraft that is to be admired, not a non-existent ancient tradition. In this way Neopaganism and witchcraft may offer something new and vital.

We have emphasized the vast diversity of modern witch beliefs and practices but find common threads in most of them: pantheism, feminism, rejection of sin, and 'spiritual reciprocity'. Such views are, in part or in whole, contradictory to other worldviews. Yet no religion (and no other kind of knowledge) can sensibly proclaim to know everything, and all religions can profit from learning about what is good in the others. Sorcery persists; diabolical witchcraft is essentially dead; modern witches create a new religion. Witchcraft is not a coherent concept, but a term covering a variety of phenomena loosely linked.

But magic continues to appeal and witchcraft will not soon vanish from this earth.

CHAPTER 12

Witchcraft Today

> Modern witchcraft is a religion in transition. In view of the
> fact that it has already had more significant events in its short
> history than many religions record over centuries, it would
> be rash to speculate on its future from this point onwards.

The concluding statement from the previous edition of this book
has since proved highly accurate. Nearly two decades since it was
published, modern witchcraft has undergone a series of rapid
changes that have taken the witches themselves by surprise. Owing
chiefly to the influence of the internet, this accelerated pace of
change not only continues but will almost certainly increase.[1] But
to get a grasp on the shifts that have already taken place and those
yet to come, we must first consider modern witchcraft within the
larger context of the Neopagan movement.

Neopaganism as we see it today is a direct result of the
modern witchcraft revival, which began with Gerald Gardner in
early 1950s Britain. During the 1990s the internet emerged and
quickly demonstrated its remarkable ability to create 'communities without location', by establishing connections between
like-minded people who would never have been able to find
each other in real life, simply because they lived hundreds or
even thousands of miles apart.

One early result of the net's connection-creating effect was to
stimulate the rapid growth of the witchcraft movement. Another
delayed outcome has been the proliferation of differing branches
within Neopaganism. As other ancient-religion enthusiasts took
note of the witches' success in reviving their 'Old Religion', they

asked 'Why not ours, too?' Courtesy of the internet, these groups were soon able to collect enough fellow devotees to emerge as active and growing communities in their own right. As a result, we have witnessed the advent of 'Pagan Reconstruction(s)': the attempt to revive or recreate various ancient, pre-Christian religions from history. Some of these groups already existed, but as decidedly niche enthusiasms. The arrival of the internet invigorated many of them, enabling them to become vibrant organizations with a visible presence and public outreach. This emerging diversity has created a wide variety of ancient religious systems from which to choose, including:

1. Celtic Reconstruction: an attempt to revive the pre-Christian religion of Britain and portions of Western Europe, including some branches of Druidism.
2. Heathenism, or Norse Paganism: a community that honours the old Germanic deities. It is currently split between those who emphasize the white racial aspect of Norse religion, and the majority of groups who reject this racial focus and subscribe to 'Inclusive Heathenry'.
3. Kemeticism: a revived Egyptian religion (the name derives from *kmt*, the ancient name for Egypt), which notably includes the recent rise of 'Afro-Centric Kemetics', according to which Egypt's rulers were black.
4. Hellenism, or Hellenismos: a revived Greco-Roman religion, featuring the deities of ancient Greece and Rome.
5. The ancient religions of Eastern Europe: collectively referred to as 'Native Faith' groups, they include Baltic (Romuva), Ukrainian (Rodnovery), and Slavic belief systems.
6. African-diaspora religions: beliefs practised or developed by African slaves in their lands of exile. They include Voodoo, Santería, and Candomble, as well as other variations and belief systems.

This proliferation has swollen the number of Neopagans[2] and boosted the religion's presence in the public sphere and the public consciousness. But another, neglected result of the rise of the internet has surfaced and in fact presents a problem for the coherence of the movement. Few people noticed in the beginning that these new communities were likely to be resistant to mainstream culture or to offer dissenting alternatives to it. The internet has a built-in bias in that it brings people together who share a particular grievance or wish to criticize larger groups: it is thus tailor-made for 'oppositional' factions of every kind.[3]

That tendency initially led to explosive growth in the witchcraft movement, since modern witchcraft defined itself by rejecting and opposing the background of mainstream (Christian) culture. But as it matured, the movement began to move away from oppositional self-presentation towards a more positive assertion of its own identity (and virtues) as a religious system. However, as modern witchcraft grew closer to the mainstream, the internet showed its double-edged quality and encouraged the formation of groups that were against this development. The Wiccan Elder Don Frew explains how this process resulted in the splintering of modern witchcraft into various subgroups:

> My observation is that we are in the midst of another explosion of new Pagan groups, many of which do not want to be called Pagan, that are oppositional to the more dominant modern Witchcraft. In the last 15 years, I have seen many groups go through a golden age of first discovery to defining and describing themselves in an oppositional way, to seeing internal dissention and factionalism resulting in significant tensions, to growth and development of new systems to deal with these tensions and the beginnings of defining themselves as themselves (rather than being 'not Craft').

Several different oppositional approaches to Wicca have developed. It seems to me that each of these is focusing on one of the basic aspects of Craft culture and taking it to an extreme – downplaying or even denying the importance of the rest. Unfortunately, as part of being oppositional, they often criticize Wicca in the process.[4]

In the midst of this turbulent change, with its profuse sprouting of new factions, the concern of witches and other Neopagans is that Neopaganism has become so diversified that it no longer holds together as a movement. It has become a collection of beliefs and practices too sprawling to speak with a single voice on any issue, allowing the winds of historical change to disperse its sometimes quarrelsome components out to distinct categories of their own. Conversely, the Neopagan hope is that those same winds will also blow away the chaff of trendiness, posturing, and opportunism, leaving the heavier kernels of commitment and dedication. In the meantime, if one defines 'movement' strictly as a set of disparate individuals acting in concert to achieve agreed-upon goals, then I think at this point it is fair to describe Neopaganism as more of a 'community' than a 'movement'.

That is the larger picture, which serves as an essential background to the other changes that have shaped and continue to shape modern witchcraft. Not surprisingly, the internet has been a leading factor here as well. One of the most significant has been a generalized move away from social forms of practice (such as covens), which involve face-to-face meetings with other practitioners. However, this trend has not diminished the post-pandemic draw of the various gatherings, festivals, and conventions that Neopagans attend.[5]

While the internet encouraged a dramatic increase in the numbers drawn to witchcraft, it drew people in as autonomous individuals who tended to learn about the craft from the internet rather than from personal teaching and who were likely to practise alone (such witches are often called 'solitaries').[6] The pandemic strongly reinforced that trend. Since covens could no longer meet in person, 'online covens' stepped into the gap, gathering virtually via Zoom and other internet meeting platforms.

Yet this new inclination to isolation among Pagans – their increasing lack of connection with movement-based teaching or tradition – has also opened the door to a 'creeping commodification' of the craft that more established Wiccans find disturbing. Some online covens charge joining fees and conduct a lively business on the side, selling occult tools and supplies, and a number of Pagan social media influencers now ask for payment for tarot readings and other types of divination. Witches are traditionally forbidden to charge for instruction and are directed to gather their own tools and supplies.

Also symptomatic of this individualizing trend is the explosion of witch-based accounts on social media; examples include #WitchTok and #witchesofinstagram.[7] As witchcraft has become a trending topic in popular culture, the way it is presented – especially in comic books, films, and television shows – has influenced how witches see themselves. Many, though not all, witches on social media are younger (Millennials and Generation Z), and tend to look at witchcraft very differently from their older forebears in the movement – and depend on different sources for their self-understanding.[8] This has initiated a generational transformation of witchcraft that will almost certainly prove both fundamental and extensive. These younger, newer witches, shaped by debates that marked their own generations, have brought new concepts into the movement, setting off a vigorous discussion that is redefining witchcraft's basic conception of the relationship between sex, gender, divinity, spirituality, and magic. As that discussion continues, a predictable generational divide has emerged, as younger witches challenge some of Wicca's foundational ideas on sexuality.

Wicca, as originally conceived by Gerald Gardner and his immediate successors, was based on an 'essentialist' view of sex and gender. For them, the binary nature of gender was the highest expression of the positive and negative polarity, and pervades all of reality, from the subatomic to the human level. The tension between these poles, at all levels, is what enables the universe to exist, to behave the way it does, and to make its energies accessible for magical use. For this reason, Gardner and his followers regarded sex and gender to be united as one, stable and fundamental, an integral strand in the fabric of the universe and a critical component of magic.

This way of looking at the world doesn't leave a lot of room for homosexuals or transsexuals in magical working. It is therefore being challenged as younger practitioners bring their broadened views of sex and gender to their personal identities as witches.[9] According to the anthropologist Sabina Magliocco, these 'changes in the gender politics of Wicca and Witchcraft reflect the shifts of third-wave feminism, queer theory, attention to trans and non-binary individuals, and a move away from essentialist constructions of gender'.[10] Witchcraft's ideological centre of gravity has adjusted to take account of more politically inflected issues of sexuality, specifically gay and transgender rights. It remains to be seen to what extent the movement as a whole (as opposed to individual witches) takes a politically active stance on such issues.

In surveying the recent history of the modern witchcraft movement, the most up-to-date statement one can make is, 'It's in flux – stay tuned.' Modern witchcraft is not only a religion that is changing, but also a religion of change. It is not just an exemplar of a culture undergoing transformation: it has embraced change itself as an essential part of its nature. Don Frew explains:

The very good thing about this is that Paganism looks to nature for inspiration about the divine. Nature is diverse. Nature grows and nature changes. Our many Pagan religions and spiritualities can grow, and change, and multiply, as well ... and as needed.[11]

Appendix

THE MEANING OF THE WORD 'WITCH'

The ultimate origin of the English word 'witch' is the Indo-European root *weik²*, which has to do with religion and magic. *Weik²* produced four families of derivatives:

1. *wih-l*, which yielded Old English *wigle*, 'sorcery', and *wiglera*, 'sorcerer', and, through Old and Middle French, modern English 'guile'. Also Old English *wil*, Middle and modern English 'wile'.
2. Old Norse *wih-*, 'craftiness'.
3. *wik-*, 'holy', whence Old High German *wīhen* and German *weihen*, 'to consecrate', Middle High German *wīch*, 'holy', and Latin *victima*, 'sacrifice'.
4. *wikk-*, 'magic, sorcery', whence Middle German *wikken*, 'to predict', and Old English *wicca*, *wicce*, 'witch', and *wiccian*, 'to work sorcery, bewitch'. From *wicca* derives Middle English *witche* and modern 'witch'.

Different from *weik²* and its derivations is *wetk⁴*, 'bending', whence Old English *wican*, 'to bend', from which the modern English 'weak' and 'witchelm'. Related to *wican* are Old Saxon *wikan*, Old High German *wichan*, Old Norse *vikja*, all meaning 'to bend, or turn aside'.

Old English *witan*, 'to know', and all related words including 'wise' are totally unrelated to either of the above.

Notes on the Text

INTRODUCTION

1 Lynn Thorndike, *A History of Magic and Experimental Science*, 8 vols (New York 1923–58).

2 Frances Yates, *Giordano Bruno and the Hermetic Tradition* (London and Chicago 1964).

3 Lucy Mair, *Witchcraft* (New York 1969), p. 211.

4 Paul Boyer and Stephen Nissenbaum, *Salem Possessed* (Cambridge [Mass.] 1974), pp. xi–xii.

CHAPTER 1

1 E.E. Evans-Pritchard, *Witchcraft, Oracles, and Magic among the Azande*, 2nd edn (Oxford 1950), pp. 63–4.

2 Geoffrey Parrinder, *Witchcraft: European and African* (London 1958), p. 133.

3 Parrinder 1958, p. 138; Jeffrey B. Russell, *Witchcraft in the Middle Ages* (Ithaca and London 1972), pp. 13–15.

4 Mair 1969, p. 81.

5 Mair 1969, p. 86.

6 Alfred Métraux, *Voodoo in Haiti*, 2nd edn (New York 1972), p. 4.

7 Métraux 1972, p. 323.

8 Métraux 1972, p. 43.

9 Métraux 1972, p. 49.

10 Georges Contenau, *Everyday Life in Babylonia and Assyria* (London 1959), p. 255.

CHAPTER 2

1 Elliot Rose, *A Razor for a Goat* (Toronto 1962), pp. 64, 79.

2 Preceding four quotations about Anglo-Saxon magic: Godfrid Storms, *Anglo-Saxon Magic* (The Hague 1948), pp. 54, 65, 247 and 261.

3 John R. McNeill and Helena M. Gamer, *Medieval Handbooks of Penance* (New York 1938), pp. 198, 246.

4 Marie-Louise von Franz, *Shadow and Evil in Fairytales* (Zurich 1974), pp. 163–4.

5 Jeffrey B. Russell, *Witchcraft in the Middle Ages* (Ithaca and London 1972), p. 67.

6 Russell 1972, p. 75.

7 Russell 1972, pp. 76–7; 291–3.

CHAPTER 3

1 Grado J. Merlo, *Eretici e Inquisitori* (Turin 1977), pp. 27–36.

2 Walter Wakefield and Austin P. Evans, *Heresies of the High Middle Ages* (New York 1969), p. 254.

3 Merlo 1977, p. 65.

4 William of Malmesbury, *De Gestis Regum Anglorum*, ed. W. Stubbs, 2 vols (London 1887–9); vol. I, pp. 253–5.

CHAPTER 4

1 Carlo Ginzburg, *I benandanti ...* (Turin 1966).

2 Richard Kieckhefer, *European Witch Trials: their Foundation in Popular and Learned Culture 1300–1500* (Berkeley and Los Angeles 1976).

3 Etienne Delcambre, *Le concept de la sorcellerie dans le Duché de Lorraine au XVIème et XVIIème siècle* (Nancy 1948).

4 Rossell Hope Robbins, *Encyclopaedia of Witchcraft*

and Demonology (New York 1959), p. 489.

5   Robbins 1959, pp. 106–7.

6   E. William Monter, *Witchcraft in France and Switzerland* (Ithaca and London 1976), pp. 195–6.

7   E. William Monter, *European Witchcraft* (New York 1969), pp. 75–81.

8   George Lincoln Burr, ed., 'The Witch-Persecution at Bamberg', *Translations and Reprints from Original Sources of European History*, vol. 3 (University of Pennsylvania 1896), pp. 23–8.

9   Robbins 1959, pp. 312–17.

CHAPTER 5

1   A.D.F. Macfarlane, *Witchcraft in Tudor and Stuart England* (London 1970), pp. 82–4.

2   Robbins 1959, p. 359.

3   Robbins 1959, p. 252.

4   Robbins 1959, p. 232.

5   Keith Thomas, *Religion and the Decline of Magic* (London 1971), p. 523.

6   Boyer and Nissenbaum 1974, p. 3.

7   Boyer and Nissenbaum 1974, p. 5.

8   Boyer and Nissenbaum 1974, p. 10.

9   Boyer and Nissenbaum 1974, p. 11.

CHAPTER 6

1   Macfarlane 1970, pp. 178–82.

2   *Malleus Maleficarum*, trans. Montague Summers (London 1928), pp. 43–6.

3   Boyer and Nissenbaum 1974, pp. 26–7.

4   Boyer and Nissenbaum 1974, p. 30.

5   Boyer and Nissenbaum 1974, pp. 103–4.

6   Boyer and Nissenbaum 1974, p. 69.

7   Boyer and Nissenbaum 1974, p. 177.

8   H.R. Trevor-Roper, *The European Witch-Craze of the Sixteenth and Seventeenth Centuries and Other Essays* (London and New York 1969), p. 190.

CHAPTER 7

1   Macfarlane 1970, p. 202.

CHAPTER 8

1   Jean Tyson in *The Atlanta Journal*, 23 June 1978.

2   Hans Sebald, *Witchcraft: the Heritage of a Heresy* (New York 1978), p. 223.

3   Sebald 1978, pp. 100–101.

CHAPTER 9

1   Colin Wilson, *The Occult* (London 1971), p. 329.

2   Ronald Hutton, *The Triumph of the Moon: A History of Modern Pagan Witchcraft* (Oxford 2000), p. 136.

3   Hutton 2000, p. 136.

4   Hutton 2000, p. 138.

5   Hutton 2000, p. 140.

6   Doreen Valiente, *The Rebirth of Witchcraft* (London and Custer, Wash. 1989), p. 22.

7   Elliot Rose 1962, p. 218.

8   Charles Godfrey Leland 1899, p. vii.

9   Margot Adler, *Drawing Down the Moon: Witches, Druids, Goddess-Worshippers, and Other Pagans in America Today* (Boston 1986), p. 47.

10 Valiente 1989, p. 25.

11 Mircea Eliade, *Occultism, Witchcraft, and Cultural Fashions: Essays in Comparative Religions* (London and Chicago 1976), p. 58.

12 Ronald Hutton, *The Pagan Religions of the Ancient British Isles* (Oxford and Cambridge, Mass. 1991), p. 304.

13 Valiente 1989, pp. 28–9.

14 Valiente 1989, p. 28.

15 Robert Graves, *The White Goddess: A Historical Grammar of Poetic Myth* (London and New York 1948), p. 484.

16 Graves 1948, pp. 484–6.

17 Hutton 2000, p. 190.

18 De-Anna Alba, 'The Goddess Emerging', *Gnosis*, Autumn 1989, p. 29.

19 Adler 1986, p. 62.

20 Adler 1986, p. 62.

21 Sabina Magliocco, *Witching Culture: Folklore and Neo-paganism in America* (Philadelphia, Penn. 2004), p. 51.

22 Valiente 1989, p. 63.

23 D. Hudson Frew and Anna Korn, 'Or Was It?', *Gnosis*, Autumn 1991.

24 V. Vale and John Sulak, *Modern Paganism: An Investigation of Contemporary Pagan Practices* (San Francisco 2001), p. 95.

25 Quoted in Adler 1986, p. 104.

CHAPTER 10

1 Hutton 2000, p. 242.

2 Hutton 2000, p. 246.

3 Valiente 1989, p. 61.

4 Magliocco 2004, p. 218.

5 Valiente 1989, p. 72.

6 Ronald Hutton, 'Modern Pagan Witchcraft' in Bengt Ankarloo and Stuart Clark, *Witchcraft and Magic in Europe: The Twentieth Century* (Philadelphia, Penn. 1999), p. 60.

7 Magliocco 2004, p. 70.

8 Hutton 2000, p. 62.

9 The witches aligned with Budapest were not the only 'Dianics', just the most publicity minded. There is also a 'Dianic Tradition' propagated by Morgan MacFarland that welcomed both men and women, focused on the Goddess Diana, and took its inspiration directly from Leland's *Aradia*. They are often called 'MacFarland Dianics' to distinguish them from the other kind.

10 Shelley Rabinovitch and James Lewis, *The Encyclopedia of Modern Witchcraft and Neo-Paganism* (New York 2002), p. 75.

11 Hutton 2000, p. 62.

12 The Faery Tradition is a non-Gardnerian form of Witchcraft founded by an American (Victor Anderson) in the 1950s, based on his personal visions and shamanistic experiences, in combination with elements of folk-magic.

13 *Ibid.*

14 Adler 1986, p. 446.

15 Quoted in M. Macha Nightmare, *Witchcraft and the Web: Weaving Pagan Traditions Online* (Toronto 2001), pp. 174–5.

16 Nightmare 2001, pp. 23–4.

17 Nightmare 2001, p. 118.

18 See, for example, *Slayage: The Online International Journal of Buffy Studies* (http://www.slayage.tv).

19 V. Vale and John Sulak 2001, p. 28.

20 Pat Devin, 1998; 'An Interview with Pat Devin' on *Cyberwitch.com* (http://www.cyberwitch.com/wychwood/library/interviewwithpatdevin.htm).

21 Vale and Sulak 2001, p. 28.

22 While CoG took the lead in interfaith work, it was not the only Neopagan group to pursue that connection. Circle in Wisconsin, The Fellowship of Isis in Chicago and Earthspirit Community in Massachusetts, also attended the 1993 Parliament

of Religions in Chicago (and its subsequent conclaves), though they have not remained as engaged in local, national and global interfaith activities as has CoG.

23 Don Frew 2003; 'The Covenant of the Goddess and the Interfaith Movement: Transforming Our Community, Changing the World' (http://www.cog.org/interfaith/index.html).

24 Don Frew 2003.

25 Don Frew 2003.

26 Interview with author.

CHAPTER 12

1 Don Frew and Anna Korn, 'An Introduction to Contemporary Paganism and Wicca' (notes for a class given at the Chaplaincy Institute, Berkeley, 15 January 2023).

2 The Ontario Consultants on Religious Tolerance group recognized the challenge of determining numbers but estimated there were *c.* 2 million Neopagans in the US in 2015, with most being Neopagan witches. See 'How many Wiccans are there?', at http://www.religioustolerance.org/estimated-number-of-wiccans-in-the-united-states-7.htm. In 2014, the Pew Research Center had estimated that there were 1 million witches in the US: https://www.pewresearch.org/religion/religious-landscape-study/ (accessed 6 July 2023).

3 There are two reasons for this: the internet allows culturally marginal types who would otherwise remain isolated to establish contact with one another; and it does so while maintaining the individual's privacy and anonymity. Isolated individuals remain powerless to

challenge the main culture or build a 'countercultural' alternative to it, but connected individuals can do both. Cultural dissent becomes more feasible and less costly.

4 Frew and Korn, 2023.

5 'Pagan conferences return with more attendees, more magick after pandemic hiatus', *Religion News Service*, 19 April 2023, at https://religionnews.com/2023/04/19/pagan-conferences-return-with-more-attendees-more-magick-after-pandemic-hiatus/ (accessed 6 July 2023).

6 See Helen A. Berger, *Solitary Pagans: Contemporary Witches, Wiccans, and Others Who Practice Alone* (Columbia, SC: University of South Carolina Press, 2019).

7 One advertising survey attempted to determine how many people on Facebook alone identify themselves as 'interested' in witchcraft and came up with a total of 77.7 million: https://adtargeting.io/facebook-ad-targeting/witchcraft (accessed 6 July 2023).

8 See Hannah E. Johnston and Peg Aloi (eds), *The New Generation Witches: Teenage Witchcraft and Contemporary Culture* (Abingdon: Routledge, 2016).

9 See Christine Hoff Kraemer, 'Gender and Sexuality in Contemporary Paganism', *Religion Compass,* vol. 6, no. 8 (2012), pp. 389–401; Cassandra Snow, *Queering Your Craft: Witchcraft from the Margins* (Newburyport, MA: Weiser Books, 2020).

10 Personal correspondence with the author.

11 Frew and Korn, 2023.

Bibliography

This bibliography is a selection of the most influential books in English.

SORCERY AND MAGIC

Abusch, I. Tzvi. *Mesopotamian Witchcraft: Toward a History and Understanding of Babylonian Witchcraft Beliefs and Literature*, Leiden 2002.

Bailey, Michael David. *Historical Dictionary of Witchcraft*, Lanham, Md. 2003.

Bond, George Clement, and Diane M. Ciekawy, eds. *Witchcraft Dialogues: Anthropological and Philosophical Exchanges*, Athens, Ohio 2001.

Bongmba, Elias Kifon. *African Witchcraft and Otherness: A Philosophical and Theological Critique of Intersubjective Relations*, Albany, N.Y. 2001.

Drury, Nevill. *Magic and Witchcraft: From Shamanism to the Technopagans*, London and New York 2003.

Dwyer, Graham. *The Divine and the Demonic: Supernatural Affliction and Its Treatment in North India*, New York 2002 and London 2003.

Eliade, Mircea. *Occultism, Witchcraft, and Cultural Fashions: Essays in Comparative Religions*, London and Chicago 1976.

Evans-Pritchard, Edward E. *Witchcraft, Oracles, and Magic among the Azande*, 2nd edn Oxford 1950 and rev. edn 1976.

Golden, Richard M., ed. *Encyclopedia of Witchcraft: The Western Tradition*, 4 vols, Oxford 2003 and Santa Barbara, Calif. 2006.

Hsu, Francis L.K. *Exorcising the Trouble Makers: Magic, Science and Culture*, London and Westport, Conn. 1983.

Kapferer, Bruce, ed. *Beyond Rationalism: Rethinking Magic, Witchcraft, and Sorcery*, New York 2003.

Khanam, R., ed. *Demonology: Socio-religious Belief of Witchcraft*, Delhi 2003.

Kluckhohn, Clyde. *Navaho Witchcraft*, Cambridge, Mass. 1944 and Boston 1967.

Lea, Henry Charles. *Materials Toward a History of Witchcraft*. 3 vols, New York 1957 and 1986.

Lehmann, Arthur C. and James E. Myers, eds. *Magic, Witchcraft, and Religion: An Anthropological Study of the Supernatural*, London 1985 and Mountain View, Calif. 2001.

Levack, Brian P. *The Witchcraft Sourcebook*, London 2004.

Malinowski, Bronislaw. *Magic, Science, and Religion, and Other Essays*, Glencoe and Boston 1948.

Marwick, Max G., ed. *Witchcraft and Sorcery: Selected Readings*, Harmondsworth and Baltimore 1970.

Maxwell-Stuart, P.G. *Witchcraft: A History*, Stroud, Gloucestershire 2001.

Middleton, John, ed. *Magic, Witchcraft, and Curing*, Garden City, N.Y. 1967.

Mishra, Archana. *Casting the Evil Eye: Witch Trials in Tribal India*, New Delhi 2003.

Moore, Henrietta L., and Todd Sanders, eds. *Magical Interpretations, Material Realities: Modernity, Witchcraft, and the Occult in Postcolonial Africa*, London and New York 2001.

Parrinder, Geoffrey. *Witchcraft: European and African*. 3rd edn London 1970.

Robbins, Rossell H. *The Encyclopedia of Witchcraft and Demonology*, New York 1959 and 1981.

Romberg, Raquel. *Witchcraft and Welfare: Spiritual Capital and the Business of Magic in Modern Puerto Rico*, Austin, Tex. 2003.

Rush, John A. *Witchcraft and Sorcery: An Anthropological Perspective of the Occult*, Springfield, Ill. 1974.

Siegel, Lee. *Net of Magic: Wonders and Deceptions in India*, Chicago 1991.

Stewart, Pamela J. *Witchcraft, Sorcery Rumors, and Gossip*, Cambridge and New York 2004.

Storms, Godfrid. *Anglo-Saxon Magic*, The Hague 1948.

Tambiah, Stanley Jeyaraja. *Magic, Science, Religion, and the Scope of Rationality*, Cambridge and New York 1990.

Thorndike, Lynn. *A History of Magic and Experimental Science*, 8 vols, New York 1923–58.

Webster, Hutton. *Magic: A Sociological Study*, Stanford, Calif. 1948 and New York 1973.

'Witchcraft', *Encyclopaedia Britannica*, 2002, vol. 22, pp. 92–8.

Worobec, Christine. *Possessed: Women, Witches, and Demons in Imperial Russia*, DeKalb, Ill. 2001.

ANCIENT, MEDIEVAL, AND RENAISSANCE WITCHCRAFT

Bailey, Michael David, *Battling Demons: Witchcraft, Heresy, and Reform in the Late Middle Ages*, University Park, Pa. 2003.

Burnett, Charles. *Magic and Divination in the Middle Ages: Texts and Techniques in the Islamic and Christian Worlds*, Aldershot 1996.

Clark, Stuart, ed. *Languages of Witchcraft: Narrative, Ideology and Meaning in Early Modern Culture*, Basingstoke and New York 2001.

Davies, Owen, *Cunning-folk: Popular Magic in English History*, London 2003.

Flint, Valerie I.J. *The Rise of Magic in Early Medieval Europe*, Oxford and Princeton 1991.

Golden, Richard M., ed. *Encyclopedia of Witchcraft: The Western Tradition*, Oxford 2003 and Santa Barbara, Calif. 2006.

Jolly, Karen Louise. *Popular Religion in Late Saxon England: Elf Charms in Context*, London and Chapel Hill, N.C.: 1996.

—, *Witchcraft and Magic in Europe: The Middle Ages*, London 2001 and Philadelphia 2002.

Kieckhefer, Richard. *Magic in the Middle Ages*, Cambridge and New York 1989.

Luck, Georg, trans. and ed. *Arcana Mundi: Magic and the Occult in the Greek and Roman Worlds: A Collection of Ancient Texts*, London and Baltimore 1985.

Meyer, Marvin, and Richard Smith, eds. *Ancient Christian Magic: Coptic Texts of Ritual Power*, San Francisco 1994.

Murray, Margaret. *The Witch Cult in Western Europe: A Study* in Anthropology, Oxford 1921 and 1962. (Note: Fanciful but influential.)

Walker, D.P. Spiritual and Demonic Magic: From Ficino to Campanella, 2nd edn London 1958.

Yates, Frances. Giordano Bruno and the Hermetic Tradition, London and Chicago 1964.

Zika, Charles. Exorcising our Demons: Magic, Witchcraft, and Visual Culture in Early Modern Europe, Leiden and Boston 2003.

WITCH HUNTS

Ankarloo, Bengt, and Stuart Clark, eds. The Period of the Witch Trials, London and Philadelphia 2002.

Apps, Lara, and Andrew Gow. Male Witches in Early Modern Europe, Manchester and New York 2003.

Behringer, Wolfgang. Witches and Witch-hunts: A Global History, Cambridge and Malden, Mass. 2004.

Briggs, Katharine M. Pale Hecate's Team: An Examination of the Beliefs on Witchcraft and Magic among Shakespeare's Contemporaries and his Immediate Successors, London 1962.

Briggs, Robin. Witches and Neighbours: The Social and Cultural Context of European Witchcraft, 2nd edn Oxford 2002.

Broedel, Hans Peter. The Malleus Maleficarum and the Construction of Witchcraft: Theology and Popular Belief, Manchester and New York 2003.

Burns, William E. Witch Hunts in Europe and America: An Encyclopedia, London and Westport, Conn. 2003.

Clark, Stuart. Thinking with Demons: The Idea of Witchcraft in Early

Modern Europe, Oxford and New York 1997.

Cohn, Norman. Europe's Inner Demons: An Enquiry Inspired by the Great Witch-Hunt, St Albans 1976 and New York 1977.

Davies, Owen, and Willem de Blécourt, eds. Beyond the Witch Trials: Witchcraft and Magic in Enlightenment Europe, Manchester and New York 2004.

Fischer, Klaus. White, Black, and Gray: A History of the Stormy 1960s, New York 2006.

Goodare, Julian, ed. The Scottish Witch-hunt in Context, Manchester and New York 2002.

Kelly, Henry Ansgar. The Devil, Demonology, and Witchcraft: The Development of Christian Beliefs in Evil Spirits, 2nd edn Garden City, N.Y. 1974.

Kieckhefer, Richard. European Witch Trials: Their Foundations in Popular and Learned Culture, 1300–1500, London and Berkeley 1976.

Kors, Alan C. and Edward Peters, eds. Witchcraft in Europe, 400–1700: A Documentary History, 2nd edn Philadelphia 2001.

Larner, Christina. Enemies of God: The Witch-Hunt in Scotland, London and Baltimore, Md. 1981.

Levack, Brian P. New Perspectives on Witchcraft, Magic, and Demonology, New York 2001.

—, The Witch-Hunt in Early Modern Europe, 2nd edn London and New York 1995.

Macfarlane, Alan D.J. Witchcraft in Tudor and Stuart England: A Regional and Comparative Study, London and New York 1970.

Martin, Ruth. Witchcraft and the Inquisition in Venice, 1550–1650,

Oxford and New York 1989.

Maxwell-Stuart, P. G. *Witchcraft: A History*, Stroud, Gloucestershire 2001.

—, *Witchcraft in Europe and the New World, 1400–1800*, Basingstoke and New York 2001.

—, *Witch Hunters: Professional Prikkers, Unwitchers and Witch-Finders of the Renaissance*, Stroud, Gloucestershire 2003.

Midelfort, H.C. Erik. *Witch-Hunting in Southwestern Germany, 1562–1684: The Social and Intellectual Foundations*, Stanford, Calif. 1972.

Monter, E. William, ed. *European Witchcraft*, New York 1969.

—, *Witchcraft in France and Switzerland: The Borderlands during the Reformation*, London and Ithaca, N.Y. 1976.

Peters, Edward. *Inquisition*, London and New York 1988.

—, *The Magician, the Witch, and the Law*, Hassocks and Philadelphia 1978.

Roper, Lyndal. *Witch Craze: Terror and Fantasy in Baroque Germany*, London and New Haven 2004.

Rose, Elliot. *A Razor for a Goat: A Discussion of Certain Problems in the History of Witchcraft and Diabolism*, Toronto 1962.

Rowlands, Alison. *Witchcraft Narratives in Germany: Rothenburg, 1561–1652*, Manchester and New York 2003.

Scarre, Geoffrey. *Witchcraft and Magic in Sixteenth- and Seventeenth-century Europe*, Basingstoke 2001.

Sebald, Hans. *Witchcraft: The Heritage of a Heresy*, Oxford and New York 1978.

Sharpe, James. *Witchcraft in Early Modern England*, Harlow and New York 2001.

Stark, Rodney. *For the Glory of God: How Monotheism Led to Reformations, Science, Witch-hunts, and the End of Slavery*, Princeton, N.J. 2003.

Thomas, Keith. *Religion and the Decline of Magic: Studies in Popular Beliefs in Sixteenth and Seventeenth Century England*, London and New York 1971.

Trevor-Roper, Hugh. *The European Witch-Craze of the Sixteenth and Seventeenth Centuries and Other Essays*, London and New York 1956 and 1969.

Waite, Gary K. *Heresy, Magic, and Witchcraft in Early Modern Europe*, Basingstoke and New York 2003.

Walker, Timothy Dale. *Doctors, Folk Medicine and the Inquisition: The Repression of Magical Healing in Portugal during the Enlightenment*, Leiden and Boston 2005.

WITCHCRAFT IN AMERICA

Boyer, Paul, and Stephen Nissenbaum. *Salem Possessed: The Social Origins of Witchcraft*, London and Cambridge, Mass. 1974.

Breslaw, Elaine G. *Tituba: Reluctant Witch of Salem: Devilish Indians and Puritan Fantasies*, London and New York 1996.

Cervantes, Fernando. *The Devil in the New World: The Impact of Diabolism in New Spain*, London and New Haven 1994.

Demos, John Putnam. *Entertaining Satan: Witchcraft and the Culture of Early New England*, Oxford and New York 2004.

Gibson, Marion, ed. *Witchcraft and Society in England and America, 1550–1750*, London and Ithaca, N.Y. 2003.

Godbeer, Richard. *Escaping Salem: the Other Witch Hunt of 1692*, Oxford and New York 2005.

Hansen, Chadwick. *Witchcraft at Salem*, New York 1969 and London 1970.

Kittredge, George. *Witchcraft in Old and New England*, Cambridge, Mass. 1929.

Norton, Mary Beth. *In the Devil's Snare: The Salem Witchcraft Crisis of 1692*, New York 2002.

Roach, Marilynne K. *The Salem Witch Trials: A Day-by-day Chronicle of a Community under Siege*, New York 2002.

Robinson, Enders A. *The Devil Discovered: Salem Witchcraft 1692*, Prospect Heights, Ill. 2001.

Starkey, Marion L. *The Devil in Massachusetts: A Modern Inquiry into the Salem Witch Trials*, New York 1949 and 1989.

MODERN WITCHCRAFT

Adler, Margot. *Drawing Down the Moon: Witches, Druids, Goddess-Worshippers, and Other Pagans in America Today*, 2nd edn Boston 1986.

Alexander, Brooks. *Witchcraft Goes Mainstream*, Eugene, Ore. 2004.

Berger, Helen A. *A Community of Witches: Contemporary Neo-paganism and Witchcraft in the United States*, Columbia, S.C. 1999.

—, *Voices from the Pagan Census: A National Survey of Witches and Neo-pagans in the United States*, Columbia, S.C. 2003.

Blécourt, Willem de, and Owen Davies, eds. *Witchcraft Continued: Popular Magic in Modern Europe*, Manchester and New York 2004.

Bonewits, Isaac. *Witchcraft: A Concise Guide*. Earth Religions Press 2001.

Eller, Cynthia. *Living in the Lap of the Goddess: The Feminist Spirituality Movement in America*, Boston 1993.

Farrar, Stewart. *What Witches Do: The Modern Coven Revealed*. London and St Paul, Minn. 1971.

Gardner, Gerald B. *Witchcraft Today*, London 1954.

Graves, Robert. *The White Goddess: A Historical Grammar of Poetic Myth*, London and New York 1948. (Note: a fanciful but influential book.)

Hawkins, Craig S. *Witchcraft: Exploring the World of Wicca*, Grand Rapids, Mich. 1996.

Herrick, James A. *The Making of the New Spirituality: The Eclipse of the Western Religious Tradition*, Downers Grove, Ill. 2003.

Heselton, Philip. *Wiccan Roots: Gerald Gardner and the Modern Witchcraft Revival*. Milverton, Somerset 2000.

Hutton, Ronald. *The Triumph of the Moon: A History of Modern Pagan Witchcraft*, Oxford 2000.

Johns, June. *King of the Witches: The World of Alex Sanders*, London and New York 1969.

Kelly, Aidan A. *A History of Modern Witchcraft, 1939–1964*, St. Paul, Minn. 1991.

Leland, Charles Godfrey. *Aradia, or the Gospel of the Witches*, London and New York 1899. (Note: a fanciful but influential book.)

Lewis, James R. *Witchcraft Today: An Encyclopedia of Wiccan and Neopagan Traditions*. Oxford and Santa Barbara, Calif. 1999

Luhrmann, T. M. *Persuasions of the Witch's Craft: Ritual Magic in Contemporary England*, Oxford and Cambridge, Mass. 1989.

Magliocco, Sabina. *Witching Culture: Folklore and Neo-paganism in America*, Philadelphia 2004.

Martello, Leo Louis. *Witchcraft: The Old Religion*, Secaucus, N.J. 1973.

Nightmare, M. Macha. *Witchcraft and the Web: Weaving Pagan Traditions Online*, Toronto 2001.

Pike, Sarah M. *Earthly Bodies, Magical Selves: Contemporary Pagans and the Search for Community*, London and Berkeley 2001.

Rabinovitch, Shelley, and James Lewis, eds. *The Encyclopedia of Modern Witchcraft and Neo-Paganism*, New York 2002.

Symonds, John. *The Great Beast: The Life of Aleister Crowley*, London 1951 and New York 1952.

—, *The Magic of Aleister Crowley*, London 1958.

Vale, V., and John Sulak, *Modern Pagans: An Investigation of Contemporary Pagan Practices*, San Francisco 2001.

Valiente, Doreen. *The Rebirth of Witchcraft*, London and Custer, Wash. 1989.

—, *Witchcraft for Tomorrow*, London and New York 1978.

Illustration Credits

Index

A

Aboriginal culture 172
Ad Extirpanda 68
Adler, Margot 18, 163, 177, 181, 183
Africa 8, 106, 109; II, III
    sorcery in 15, 26–9, 69, 91
    witch beliefs 22–4
    witch-doctors 95
age, witches and 26, 106, 111–12
Aix-en-Provence 86–8, 128
Alan of Lille 61
Alexander IV, Pope 68
Alfred the Great 52
America, witchcraft in 120, 121, 146,
    162, 172–6, 185, 192
    in the American colonies 99–104
Anderson, Victor 176
Anglo-Saxons 44–5, 49
Apocalyptic Judaism 35–6
Aquinas, Thomas 67
Ardat Lili 30
Aristotelianism 71
arson 99, 111
Artemis 115
atheism 194
Augustine of Hippo, Saint 40, 67; V

B

Babylonians 30, 33
Bacchanalia 33
bagbuduma 22
Bakweri tribe 27
Balingen 108
Bamberg, witch-house of 78–9, 84,
    192; XIII
Bantu tribe 24
Bar 78
Barbato, St 52
Barney, Dr. Gerald 186
Basuto 24
Bayley, James 117

Bechuana tribe 23
Behringer, Wolfgang 17
benandanti 72
Benevento 52
Bergerac, Cyrano de 124
Berkeley, witch of 62–3
Berta 48–9
Berwick 93–4, 95
Besant, Annie 157
Bilson Boy 106
Binsfeld, Peter 82
Bishop, Bridget 103
black mass 9–10, 127–8, 192
Blackwood, Algernon 131
Blocula 120
Bodin, Jean 83
Bogomils 58, 59
Boguet, Henri 83–4
Boleyn, Anne 105
bonae mulieres 51–2
Boniface VIII, Pope 73
Boyer, Paul 17, 18, 26, 102, 105, 116, 117
Briggs, Robin 17
British Isles, witchcraft in 89–99
    see also England
Bronze Age 44
Buckland, Raymond 173, 174
Buckland, Rosemary 173
Budapest, Z. 174–5, 176
Buffy the Vampire Slayer 180
Bulwer-Lytton, Edward 131
burning 67, 80, 82, 192
Burroughs, George 102, 103
Burton Boy 106
Bury St Edmunds 98
'Butterfly Effect' 13

C

Caesarius of Heisterbach 64
Calvin and Calvinism 80, 94
Calw 125

Candlemas 50
cannibalism 16, 24, 33, 55, 58, 60
Canon Episcopi 52–3, 71, 72, 122
canon law 66, 67
Carcassonne, witch trials at 74
Caroline Code 80, 81, 108
Cartesianism 123
Catharism 59–61, 64, 72, 74, 112; VI
Catholic Church 29, 59, 60, 74, 77,
    80, 81, 114, 115, 120, 141, 142, 143,
    144–5, 155, 160
Catiline 33
cats 39, 64, 90, 92, 96, 139
    black cats as shape of witches 29
    sexual relations with 23, 26
Celtic religions 40, 41, 48, 167–8; IX
Chambre ardente affair 127–8
characteristics of witchcraft 24–5
Charlemagne 51, 55
Charmed 180
charms 44
Chelmsford, Essex 91, 96, 110
childbirth 112
children: infanticide 29, 32, 38–9, 55,
    58, 60, 83, 126
    Salem Village 100, 101
    in witch accusations 81, 106–7, 119
    witches as danger to 139
Christianity 8, 15–16, 20, 28, 97, 106,
    142–5, 148, 192, 193, 195, 199
    demonology 34
    festivals 49–50
    function of the Devil 36–7
    images of witches 32
    influence of Mazdaism on 35
    and paganism 38–41, 42, 142, 143,
        149, 152, 155–6
    penitentials 45–6
    renunciation of 38, 55, 56, 58, 65
    as a semi-dualist religion 58–9
    spiritual entities 50
    witchcraft as plot against the
        Church 71, 80
    women and 113–14, 115, 116
    see also heresy

Circe 32, 113
Clark, Stuart 18
Clarke, Ursula 98–9
Clement V, Pope 74
Clerk, Jane 121
Clutterbuck, 'Old Dorothy' 157
Colmar 79
commodification 202
confiscation 81, 108
Connecticut 99
Cordière, Catherine 128
Cory, Martha 101
Counterculture 173
Covenant of the Goddess (CoG) 162,
    181, 185, 186, 187–8
covens 72–3, 90, 98, 151, 156,
    159–60, 202
The Craft 180–4; XX
critical incidents 21
Crowley, Aleister 131, 157, 160,
    167, 168
crucifix, desecration of 38, 55, 58
cunning-folk 95
curanderos 27
Cybele 33
cyber-culture 177–80, 198–9, 202

D
daimones 32
Dashwood, Sir Francis 128
day-sorcerers 23
Dee, John 91
Delcambre, Etienne 77–8
demography, correlation with
    witchcraft 108–9
demonology 30
demons 30, 32, 51; VII
Descartes, René 123
Devil 35–6, 53
    Catharist Devil 59–60
    Christian Devil 16, 36–7
    Devil's mark 78, 79, 84, 93, 103
    Hellfire Club 129
    heretics' worship of 58
    Malleus Maleficarum 77

meaning and origin of the word 34, 35

nuns of Louviers and Loudun 70

pacts with the 55, 56, 70, 73, 83, 98, 139

and pagan magic 40

power of 64–5, 122

as responsible for human sins and vices 80

sacrifices to the 39

Salem witches 101

sexual activity of 65

Devin, Pat 181, 182

diabolism 16, 17, 30, 34, 42, 46, 64, 69, 73, 86, 98, 121–2, 126, 129, 132, 135, 139, 191, 196

Diana 40, 48–9, 52–3, 72, 115, 147, 150, 175

Dianic Witchcraft 175, 176

Dianus 41, 42

Dionysos 32, 33, 130; IV

divination 20, 95, 100

dogs 39, 90, 95, 135, 139

Dominicans 70, 76–7, 81

dreams 21

dualism 34–5

dualist heresies 57–62

Duncan, Gilly 93

E

Eberling 138

Edda 46

Edward I, King 73

Edward II, King 74

Egbert 46

Egypt, ancient 31

Eliade, Mircea 151

Eliot, T.S. 130

Elizabeth I, Queen 91, 121

Elymas (Barjesus) 37

England 72, 80, 108, 120–1, 135, 159–60

death penalty in 66

see also British Isles

Enlightenment 123, 140, 141

Essex 91, 96, 107, 108

Ethelstan 52

ethical behaviour 164

Europe 193

colonialism and witchcraft 28–30

interpretations of European witchcraft 41–3

laws against heresy 66

origins of sorcery 20

roots of witchcraft in 38–54, 55

sorcery, folklore, and religion in pagan Europe 26, 44–51

witch beliefs and motifs 24, 25

witch-craze in 69–88

Evans-Pritchard, E.E. 22, 23

evil 35

executions 52, 66, 68, 75, 77, 78, 91, 106, 109

burning 67, 80, 82, 192

hanging 99, 101, 102, 192

last 120–1

Exodus, book of 52

F

Faggot Witch Sparky Rabbit 177–8

familiars 24, 50–1, 90, 91, 96, 135, 139

see also cats; dogs

Faust 55

Fellowship of Crotona 157, 160

feminism 163, 174–5, 176, 196, 203

films 180–4

Flade, Dietrich 82

Flint, Valerie 18

flying 24, 79

folklore 44–51, 55, 62, 64, 191

Fontanges, Mademoiselle 128

France 74–5, 80, 81, 110, 121, 135

Francis, Elizabeth 92

Franklin, Benjamin 128

Fraudulent Mediums Act (1951) 121

Frazer, Sir James 41, 130, 149

Frew, Don Hudson 161–2, 185, 186–7, 188–9, 199–200, 204

Friedan, Betty 174

Friuli 72

G

Gardner, Gerald 131, 156–62, 165–70, 171, 172, 173–4, 175, 192, 196, 197, 203; XIX
gender 111, 174–5, 203
Germany 66, 75, 80, 84, 91, 108, 110, 121, 125, 129, 134, 135–6, 138, 143
Gervaise of Tilbury 63–4
Gilles de Rais 75
Ginzburg, Carlo 72
Girard, Jean-Baptiste 128
Glanvill, Joseph 97, 98
Gloucester, Duchess of 89
Gnosticism 35, 58, 59, 60
the Goddess 53, 153–5, 175
goëtes 31
Goethe, Johann Wolfgang von 56
Goode, Sarah 100, 102
Goodwin Children 106
Gould, Stephen Jay 9
Gowdie, Isobel 98
Goya, Francisco de 8, 124–5; I
Grandier, Father Urbain 86–7
Graves, Robert 152–5, 156, 167
Greco-Roman sorcery 30, 31–3, 44, 130
Greece, ancient 31–3, 35, 48, 112–13
Gregory IX, Pope 68
grimoires 129, 131, 137
Gui, Bernard 73
Guichard, Bishop of Troyes 73

H

Haan, Doctor Georg 84
hags 8, 24, 106, 115, 116
Hahn, Elisabeth 135
Hallowe'en 50
hanging 99, 101, 102, 192
Hansen, Josef 70
Harpies 32–3
Hasler, Bernadette 136
Hausmannin, Walpurga 82–3
Hebrew sorcery 31, 33–4, 35, 44
Hecate 48, 115, 130
Hellfire Club 128–9
Henry I, King 62

Henry VI, King 89
Henry VIII, King 91, 105
heresy 20, 42, 43, 55, 91, 106, 110, 122, 191
    in 14th century Ireland 89–90
    Christian 20, 25–6, 42, 43, 55
    dualist heresies 57–62
    in England 72
    laws against and punishment for 66
    and Satanism 135
    Templars condemned as 74
    witchcraft defined as 70, 74, 112
    witchcraft, heresy, and Inquisition 55–69
Hermetic Order of the Golden Dawn 131, 135
Herne the Hunter 49; VIII
Herrick, James A. 18
Hertfordshire 126, 127
Hexenbanner 95, 136, 137–8
hexes 46–7
High Priest and Priestess in modern witchcraft 166, 169, 170
Hilda (Holda/Hille/Hulda) 44, 48, 54, 72
Hincmarl Archbishop of Reims 56
Hindremstein, Dorothea 110
Hinduism 35
holidays 49–50
Homer 32
homosexuality 65, 172, 175, 177–8, 203
Hopkins, Matthew 96–7; XII
Horace 32
Hume, David 14, 123
Hutchinson, Francis 97, 124
Hutton, Ronald 18, 141–2, 145, 151, 165
Huysmans, J.K. 131

I

illness 107, 110
infanticide 29, 32, 38–9, 55, 58, 60, 83, 126
Innocent III, Pope 67
Innocent IV, Pope 68

Innocent VIII, Pope 77, 80
inquisition 10, 70, 72–5, 105, 129–30,
141, 149, 150
    witchcraft, heresy, and Inquisition
    55–69
Institoris, Heinrich 76–7, 113–14
Interfaiths Movement 184–7
the Internet 177–80, 198–9, 202
Iran 31, 34–5, 58
Ireland 89
Italy 60, 72, 73, 110, 146

J

James I, King (James VI of Scotland)
34, 76, 93, 94–5, 96, 98, 121
James II, King 118
Jarcke, Karl-Ernst 129, 142, 143, 145
Jesuits 81
Jews 72, 107
Joan of Arc 75
Johann Georg II, Bishop 84
John XXII, Pope 73
Judaism 114
Jung, Carl 115
Jung, Fitz 179
Jungians 25
Junius, Johannes 84–6
Jura Mountains 81
Justinian, code of 66

K

kashaph 33, 34
Kelly, Aidan 18, 160–1
Kieckhefer, Richard 18, 75
King James Bible 34
Kipling, Rudyard 160
kisses, obscene 38
Korn, Anna 161
kosmos 13, 16
Kruse, Johann 136–7, 139
Kyteler, Dame Alice 89–90

L

Labartu 30
lamias 30, 32, 48

Lamothe-Langon Etienne de 129–30
Lancashire witches 95
law: canon law 66, 67
    church councils 40
    cruelty of legal practice 70–1
    English law torture 103
    inquisitional courts 74
    legal sanctions against
        witchcraft 70
    legal status of sorcery 51–4
    Roman law 66, 67
    and tests for witchcraft 79, 84, 91
Ledrede, Bishop Richard 90
Lehmann, Arthur C. 18
Leland, Charles Godfrey 43, 146–9,
152, 154, 157, 160
Leptinnes, Council of 51
Levack, Brian P. 18
Lévi, Eliphas 131
Leviticus, book of 52
Lilith (Lilitu) 30
loa (Voodoo gods) 29
Locke, John 14
Lombards 52
Lombardy 74–5
Lorraine 78
Loudun 70, 86–8, 123
Louis XIV, King 10, 88, 127–8
Louviers 70, 86–8, 123
Lovelock, James 176
Lowes, John 96
Lucerne 110
Luciferans 72
Lugbara tribe 21
Luther 80, 114
lynching 126

M

Macbeth 76
Macfarlane, Alan 105, 107, 108
Macha Nightmare, M. 178
Machen, Arthur 131
Macumba 22
Maddalena 146, 148
magic: in Greece 31

high magic 12, 13–15
low magic 15, 16
and science 13, 14
magicians 11–12
Magliocco, Sabina 168, 203
Magna Mater 33
magoi 31
Malebranche, Nicolas de 124
malefica/maleficia/maleficus 33, 34, 51,
    52, 55, 72, 73, 74, 81, 83, 85, 92,
    96, 101, 126
Malleus Maleficarum 64–5, 71, 77, 80,
    91, 113–14; XV
mangu 23
Manicheans 58
Map, Walter 61
Marlowe, Christopher 55–6
Mary of Scotland 121
Mather, Cotton 99, 101–2, 104
Mather, Increase 103–4
Mathers, MacGregor 131
May Day (Beltane) 50
Mazdaism 34
mbandwa 27
Medea 32, 113
meetings 29, 55
    via the Internet 178–9
    worldwide motif 29
    see also covens; sabbats;
        synagogues
mental illness 107, 117
Metcalfe, William 98
Meyer, Anton 41
Michael, St 72
Michel, Anneliese 135
Michelet, Jules 130, 143–5, 146, 148,
    149, 150, 152, 155, 174
Middle Ages 69, 79, 89, 122, 129, 130,
    140, 142, 145, 151, 152
Midelfort, H. C. Erik 18, 105, 108,
    111, 117
Midsummer's Eve 50
midwives 82–3, 109, 112
minority empowerment 178
Mithraism 114–15

modern witchcraft 131, 133–204
Molland, Alice 121
Mone, Franz-Josef 130, 142–3, 145
monotheism 114, 163, 175, 194, 195
Montaigne, Michel de 71, 124
Monter, E. William 18, 81, 105, 117, 118
Montespan, Madame de 128
Mora 120, 123; XVI
Morris, Maxine 170–1
Moses, 'Sixth and Seventh Books
    of Moses' 137, 138
motifs of witchcraft 24–5
mountains, as origin of witchcraft 70
Murray, Margaret 41–3, 130, 149–52,
    153, 155–6, 157, 158, 160, 167

N
National Poor Law (1601) 126–7
natural disasters 108
ndakó-gboyá dancers 27, 28
neighbours, and witchcraft 109–10
Neopaganism 15, 16, 191–9, 201
    the movement 165–90
    the sources 140–64
Neoplatonism 71
New Forest 159–60, 170
New Testament 36
night-witches 24
Nissenbaum, Stephen 17, 18, 26, 102,
    105, 116, 117, 118
Norse religion 44, 46
Nupe tribe 27
Nyakyusa 26
Nyoro 27

O
occult 9, 127, 130–1, 147, 164, 192–4
Oenothea 32
ointments (salves) 24, 29, 38, 39, 90, 77
Old Testament 59
oppositional identity 163, 173
oracles 27
Order of the Temple of the Orient
    (O.T.O.) 130–31, 157
orgies 24, 33, 39, 55, 58, 60, 65, 75, 90, 92

Orleans heretics 57–8, 59, 64
Osborne, Sarah 100

P
pacts 65, 67, 74, 95
    with the Devil 55, 56, 70, 73, 83,
        98, 139
Pagan Reconstruction(s) 198
paganism 15, 20, 39–43, 55, 134, 135,
    149, 168, 191, 192, 195, 199–201, 204
    and Christianity 38–41, 42, 142,
        143, 149, 152, 155–6
    Classical models of 190
    equated with demonolatry 51, 52
    festivals 49–50
    meaning of term 153
    sorcery, folklore, and religion in
        pagan Europe 44–51
    witchcraft as 140–5
Pan 131–2
Pandemic (Covid) 200, 202
pantheism 163, 164, 194, 196
Paris, synod of (829) 52
'Parliament of the World's Religions'
    186–7, 188
Parris, Samuel 100, 118–19
Paul the Deacon 55
penitentials 45
Peters, Edward 18
Philip IV, King 73, 74
Phips, Sir William 101
Plato 31, 32
polytheism 163, 194, 200
Pondo tribe 26
pop-culture witchcraft 180–4, 202
Practical Magic 180
Prentice, Joan (Jane) 93
pricking, as test of witchcraft 78, 92
Protestantism 81, 94, 114, 120
    Protestant Reformation 79–80, 122
Providence, Rhode Island 99
psychology of witchcraft 70–1
Puritans 118
Putnam family 118–19

Q
Queer Pagans 177–8, 203
Quetzalcoatl 34

R
Ravenwolf, Silver 183
'Reclaiming Tradition' 176
Reformation 69, 111
religion: ancient religions 198
    in pagan Europe 44–51
    and sorcery 34–7
    see also Catholic Church;
        Christianity
Renaissance 69, 71
Robbins, Rossell Hope 81, 96–7
Robin (familiar) 90
Romanticism 129–32, 141, 142, 144,
    146, 193
Rome, ancient 40, 112–13, 192
    Roman law 66, 67
    sorcery 31–3, 48, 51–2
    synod of Rome (826) 52
Rose, Elliot 42, 97, 147–8, 151
Rosicrucians 131
Rudolf II of Austria 81

S
sabbats 38–9, 46, 49, 61, 65, 72, 79, 82,
    84, 120, 124, 134, 151, 156; XVII
Sabrina, the Teenage Witch 180
sacraments, desecration of 38, 77
saints 40, 51
Salem 18, 26, 99–104, 106, 116–19,
    120, 125; XIV
Sampson, Agnes 93–4
Sanders, Alex 170–2, 175
Satan 34, 35, 36, 40
    Diana equated with 53–4
    ritual intercourse between
        witches and 65
    Satanism 9, 10, 56, 135
    witchcraft as plot against the
        Church 71
    witches making pacts with 75
Sathan 92

scholasticism 64–5, 191
Scot, Reginald 94
Scotland 72, 80, 91, 93, 98, 121
Scott, Sir Walter 130
Sebald, Hans 135, 138–9
secrecy 38, 55
    see also covens; sabbats
sexuality 203
    homosexuality 65, 172, 175, 177–8,
        203
Shakespeare, William, *Macbeth* 76
shape-shifting 29–30, 124
sin 163, 196
Smythe, Ellen 92–3
social class, correlation with
    witchcraft 108
social history of witchcraft 43
social media 202
society, witchcraft and 105–19
Socrates 32
Somerset 98
Sony Pictures 180, 181
sorcerers 11, 15, 17, 20, 21, 51, 62
sorcery 15, 18, 20–37, 55, 139, 191, 192
    in ancient times 30–4
    connection to witchcraft 89
    and hanging 99, 101
    legal status of 51–4
    malevolent 16–17
    modern 135–9; XVIII
    in pagan Europe 44–51
    and religion 34–7
    simple 121, 129
    sorcery worldwide 22–30
    spells and charms 44
    transformation to witchcraft
        62–8, 75
Spain 73, 80
spirits 21, 30–1, 36
spiritual reciprocity 164, 196
Sprenger, Jakob 77
Stanton, Margery 93, 110
Starhawk 176
Stark, Rodney 18
statutes: 1542 statute 91

1562 statute 121
1563 statute 91, 95, 121
1604 statute 95, 97, 99, 121
1736 statute 121
Stoker, Bram 131
strappado 79, 84; XI
striga/stria 52
Sumerians 30
Summers, Montague 104
Summis desiderantes affectibus 77
Super Illius Specula 73
supernatural 12–13
superstition 12, 13, 43, 45, 51, 122–3,
    124, 128, 140, 194
Susan B. Anthony Coven Number
    One 174–5
Sweden 120
swimming, test for witchcraft 78; X
Swing, Bishop William 187–8
synagogues 61, 72, 74, 76

T
*Teen Witch: Wicca for a New
    Generation* 183
teenage witchcraft 180–3
Templars 73–4
Teufelsdreck (asafoetida) 137
Teutonic religion 40, 41, 44, 48, 49, 51
Theodore 45–6
Theodosius 40, 66
theology, scholastic 64, 191
Theophilus 55
theurgy 31
Thirty Years War (1618–48) 84, 107, 124
Thorn, Michael 187
Thorndike, Lynn 13
Throgmorton Girls 106
Tituba 100–1, 104
Todi 110
Tolkein, J. R. R. 25
torture 68, 70, 74, 75–6, 81, 84, 87
    to elicit confessions 78–9, 96,
        103, 109
    strappado 79, 84
    witch-hunts 10, 17

Toulouse, witch trials at 74
Trevor-Roper, Hugh 70, 119
Trier 82

U
United Religions Initiative (U.R.I.)
    187–8, 189

V
Valiente, Doreen 147, 148, 160, 166–9
Vallin, Pierre 75–6
Virgin Mary 115, 116
Visigothic laws 47
visions 21
Voodoo 8, 20–1, 22, 28–30, 198

W
Waite, A.E. 131
Waldensians 68, 72, 74, 112
Walker, Wren 179
Walter, bishop of Lichfield and
    Coventry 73
warlocks 11, 111
Waterhouse, Agnes of 92
Waterhouse, Joan 92
Webbe, Susan 92–3
Webster, John 97
weighing, as test of witchcraft 78
Wenham, Jane 99, 121
Weston, Jessie 130
Weyer (Wier), Johann 83, 94
Wicca 15, 157, 159, 160–1, 165, 173, 175,
    176, 192–3, 196, 200–1, 203
        re-visioning of 166–72
Wiccan 52, 134
Wild Hunt 48–9
wild men and women 49
Willard, John 103
William of Malmesbury 62–3
William of Newburgh 62
Williams, Bray 103
Wilson, Angus 41
witch-craze 58, 59, 61

    climax of 57, 81–8
    decline of 120–32
    in Europe 34, 47, 48, 49, 53, 69–88
    start and growth of 55, 67, 73–80
witch detectors 27
witch-doctors 9, 22, 27–8, 95, 106
witch hunts and hunters 10, 14–15, 16,
    17, 67, 81, 82, 125, 191–2
witch trials 74–5, 77, 80, 96–9, 106,
    108, 109, 125, 128, 130, 142
        decline in 97, 99, 119
        first major trial 91–2
        see also individual trials
witches: definition of 8–18, 34
    of folktales 47
witch's mark 78, 96
Witchvox.com 179, 184
wizards 11, 34
wolves 29, 64
women: archetype followers
    of Diana 53
        feminism 163, 174–5, 176, 196, 203
        Malleus Maleficarum 66
        predominance of 65
        and sorcery in Africa 23, 26
        stereotypes 8, 10, 24
        and witchcraft 110–15
        as witches 24, 138–9
Women's Spirituality 174–5, 176
World Wide Web 177–80, 198–9, 202

X
Xenocrates 32

Y
Yates, Frances 13
Yeats, William Butler 131

Z
Zande tribe 22–3
Zandt, Johann 82
Zarathushtra 34, 35
Zell, Tim 'Otter' 176